SUSTAINABLE AFFORDABLE PREFAB

SUSTAINABLE AFFORDABLE PREFAB

UNIVERSITY OF VIRGINIA PRESS   CHARLOTTESVILLE AND LONDON

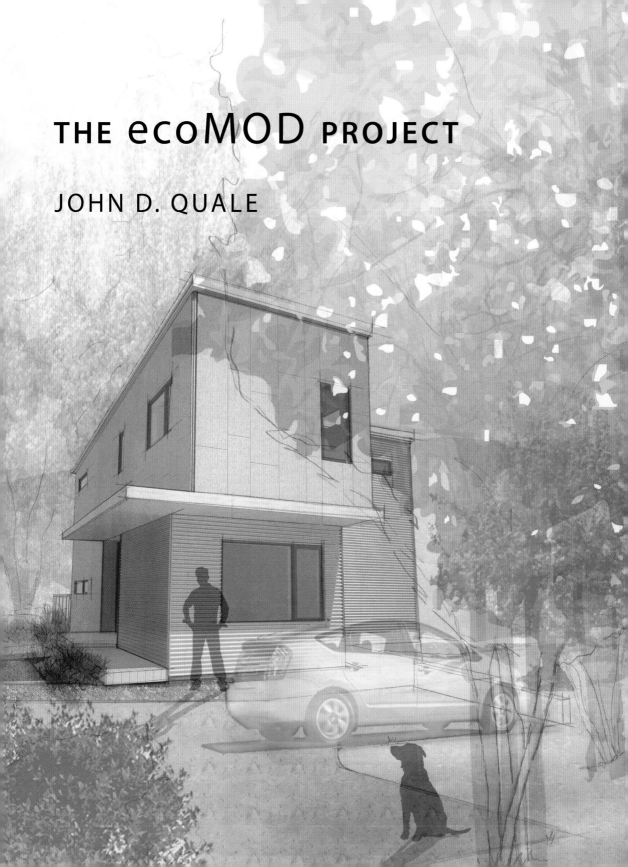

THE ecoMOD PROJECT

JOHN D. QUALE

University of Virginia Press
© 2012 by the Rector and Visitors of the University of Virginia
All rights reserved
Printed in Korea on acid-free paper

First published 2012

9 8 7 6 5 4 3 2 1

LIBRARY OF CONGRESS CATALOGING-IN-PUBLICATION DATA
Quale, John D.
 Sustainable, affordable, prefab : the ecoMOD Project / John D. Quale.
  p. cm.
 Includes bibliographical references.
 ISBN 978-0-8139-3152-4 (cloth : alk. paper) — ISBN 978-0-8139-3233-0
(pbk. : alk. paper)
 1. Architecture, Domestic—Environmental aspects. 2. ecoMOD Project. 3. Eco-
logical houses. 4. Prefabricated houses. 5. Architecture—Study and teaching—
Virginia—Charlottesville. I. Title. II. Title: ecoMOD Project.
 NA7117.5.Q35 2011
 728'.1047—dc22

                                                                2011016850

This book was supported by a grant from Furthermore,
a program of the J. M. Kaplan Fund.

Image credits appear on page 230.

This book is dedicated to Sara, Walker, and Alice
and to my parents

CONTENTS

PREFACE

In an ideal world the income level of a client would have an inverse relationship to the amount of effort put into the design of their housing. In the real world this is seldom the case. Good design is about using creativity to solve a problem, within the context and constraints of a project. The financial constraints of an affordable housing client require an even more creative response than the effort put into high-end residential design—especially when one has to consider the long-term financial and environmental impact of operating the housing unit.

In establishing the ecoMOD project, my intention was to create a design research project and educational initiative that would be grounded in the realities of budgets and materials while striving to address the two most important challenges facing the next generation of designers: the significant environmental impact of buildings, and the growing economic divide between high income and low income individuals. The project, a partnership of the UVA School of Architecture and the UVA School of Engineering and Applied Science, seeks to provide a valuable educational experience while demonstrating the environmental and economic potential of prefabrication, ultimately challenging the affordable housing industry in the United States to explore this potential. While the project stresses design as an iterative process, it has a concrete, and testable, result: UVA students and faculty have, to date, provided nine housing units on six sites through partnerships with organizations such as Piedmont Housing Alliance and Habitat for Humanity.

Good design requires equal parts art and science, and I structured the ecoMOD project to bring together people from a variety of backgrounds to address these challenges. Working with engineers compels architects to synthesize many competing technical, cultural, and aesthetic considerations, and yet resolve buildings so they become coherent, useful objects. The best architecture is both visionary and pragmatic. Buildings must fulfill a perceived need, but they ought to positively influence the lives of the occupants as well—even if that sometimes happens in unexpected ways.

Architects are skilled at sorting through the complex issues associated with any design project and navigating this synthetic process. Yet most Americans are not well informed about architecture. The principles at the core of architectural design are seldom discussed in the public realm or even in our schools. The kinds of discussions that design professionals have among themselves are mostly foreign to those outside the design community. In part this is because architects are not very good at explaining the underpinnings of the discipline to the general public—the standard language of architecture is opaque to many.

Yet the general public feels quite comfortable expressing opinions about buildings. An individual who would never pass judgment on an accountant's balance sheet or a lawyer's brief feels at home discussing the relative merits of the latest local public building or the design of his or her neighbor's McMansion. This is because architecture is a decidedly public profession. Buildings impact our daily lives—even when we don't personally occupy them. I believe Americans should put greater emphasis on design education to help ensure that the general public's opinions are informed by a deeper understanding of architecture—its history and its contemporary theories. In addition, architects should learn to get beyond the usual "archi-babble" and begin to speak with laypeople in ways they can understand. Perhaps most importantly, architects should ensure that their projects are tied to an essential public need—something more than just their design concepts and theoretical explorations.

Embedded in ecoMOD design process is the belief that Americans should reconsider the practice of building oversized houses in gated communities, with strict aesthetic guidelines based on a vague notion of an idealized early twentieth century America. More Americans ought to consider renovating or building smaller homes, in a variety of sizes appropriate for different income levels and household types. These homes can be built following strict guidelines for sustainability. They can be sited in economically, ethnically, and racially diverse communities, using energy- and water-efficient strategies. This new American dream involves mixed-income neighborhoods of mostly attached dwellings (town homes, condominiums, apartment-style complexes) in pedestrian friendly neighborhoods with direct access to shared amenities, outdoor spaces, and convenient public transportation. The old American dream of a four-bedroom home, three-car garage, and a white picket fence can adapt to the current situation: the fence can be replaced with a regionally appropriate hedge to support bio-diversity; the home (preferably a carefully renovated one) can be super-insulated and independent from the utility grid; and the garage can be replaced with a shared-use electric car parked elsewhere—or a bicycle/garden shed. It is in this alternative American dream that ecoMOD housing units could take root.

The coincidence of the current global climate-change crisis and the recent economic downturn points to the need for the building design professions (architects, engineers, landscape architects, etc.) to relearn what they knew before the last century—about how natural forces work with buildings. Centralized heating and cooling systems are important innovations for society, but they have become a crutch for designers—allowing them to design buildings that are entirely dependent upon them. Designers need to relearn the principles of passive design so buildings can be comfortable in most seasons without mechanical systems. Only then should architects and engineers supplement passive design with technology smart enough not to harm us in the long run. It is the responsibility of architects to ensure the low-energy operation of their buildings, and engineers should be less focused on technological solutions and more focused on working with natural forces. Truly sophisticated, carbon-neutral buildings take a little longer to design and require a commitment from society to operate them properly. However, the best of these "next generation" buildings can make for much healthier living, learning, and working environments—and there is growing evidence to demonstrate they will also save us money in the long run. By collaborating effectively, architects and engineers can come up with elegant solutions that address the concerns and interests of both professions. In fact, the argument could be made that no design is truly successful unless it satisfies a variety of conflicting considerations—aesthetic, technical, financial, social, and ethical.

In the age-old form versus function debate, it is important to remember that the two cannot be separated—especially in this era of global climate change. As architects and the general public are finally waking up to the enormous environmental impact of buildings, society needs designers who are skilled at design *and* performance. Two of the very few living architects in the world whose reputations have spread to the general public are Frank Gehry and Zaha Hadid. These very talented designers have built some of the most visually and formally innovative work of recent years, and are hired by clients looking for a dramatic architectural statement. Yet their work appears hollow when one understands that the exquisite forms don't actually serve any purpose other than pure intellectual and spatial exploration. Given the fluidity of their forms, it is not difficult to imagine a performance-based form-making that blends art and science into an inspiring *and* functional building. Isn't it reasonable to ask Pritzker Prize winners (with their access to wealthy clients, and their teams of talented designers and engineers using the latest digital technology) to go beyond image-making? Shouldn't they be testing the performance of these forms to assess how they can be refined to work better? In fact there are emerging designers influenced by Hadid's and Gehry's work who are trying to do exactly that—justifying their assemblages of both aerodynamic and more normative rectilinear forms as strategies to improve natural ventilation and daylighting.

Obviously there are limits to this critique. We should all be encouraged by the recent evolution of the profession to the point that architects are now starting to be able to address environmental and/or social issues without losing credibility as creative designers. Thom Mayne of Morphosis, Norman Foster, and Stefan Behnisch come to mind. But with the possible exception of Foster, none of them have achieved the same level of recognition with the general public as Gehry or Hadid. So shouldn't the most celebrated architects be leading the way on these issues—responding to real problems, limited by reasonable budgets?

One of my mentors, W. G. Clark, taught me that real creativity thrives within the context of challenging constraints. As architects, we must find a way to apply our visionary ideas in the real world, and we must use our skills and experiences to address challenges that directly impact society. Inconvenient constraints like budgets can be seen as opportunities for a creative design response, or for the creation of a process to clearly identify both first costs and potential long-term savings in operating costs.

We as designers must also take responsibility for our work. We must engage in performance assessments and post-occupancy evaluations to learn what works and what doesn't. We must use this feedback in future design processes. Evaluation should not be left only to engineers, who often assume a narrow responsibility for a building. Post-occupancy evaluation must be supported by those responsible for synthesizing all relevant information—architects. Architectural educators have an important responsibility in this arena. We must create an academic culture where creativity, intellectual rigor, and humility all thrive. Rather than create the next generation

of "starchitects," we should be focused on challenging our students to develop a productive design process that is based in both creative and critical thinking.

To distinguish ecoMOD from other design/build projects, I coined the phrase design / build / evaluate in recognition of our commitment to assessing the occupied homes. Each completed housing unit is being monitored and evaluated carefully, with the results guiding subsequent designs. The project is deeply influenced by UVA's participation in the 2002 Solar Decathlon competition, organized by the U.S. Department of Energy. Engineering professor P. Paxton Marshall and I led the university's team from 2000 to 2002, and the partnership has continued into ecoMOD. The UVA team's design—known as the Trojan Goat—is included in this book as well. The "goat" was our first attempt at combining sustainability and prefabrication, but as a prototypical design built with the intention of winning a competition, it cannot be considered affordable in any way. The process was similar to the ecoMOD projects—an interdisciplinary and collaborative team made up mostly of architecture and engineering students—but the structure of the ecoMOD collaborations has been refined and adjusted with each semester. The students learn not only about the process of design, but also about how to be effective collaborators by ensuring that their most important ideas make their way into the built work. The project is structured to allow students and faculty from diverse fields to come in and out of the process, and to take part in all phases of the project—*design, build,* and *evaluate.*

In order to more accurately represent the project, I have included some of the students' voices here. I have one overriding goal in writing this book. I want to present an open and honest picture of the ecoMOD project. Many architectural books are published simply to promote a designer or a building. The graphic representations and the written narratives of these volumes carefully edit out the awkward moments—in the process, the design, and the impact. As an educator, I feel it is important to present an unvarnished version of the project.

While the ecoMOD teams are proud of what they have accomplished, we all tend to learn more from our mistakes than from our successes—so I've done my best to present some of both. The challenges the project teams are trying to explore—sustainability, social justice, alternative forms of construction, hands-on educational experiences—are too important to gloss over.

John Quale
ecoMOD Project Director and Associate Professor
University of Virginia School of Architecture

ACKNOWLEDGMENTS

It is impossible to acknowledge every person who has supported the eco-MOD project since its conception in 2003 and launch in 2004. The complete list would fill many pages, and it is not even possible for any one person to create such a list. The student participants number more than three hundred and fifty at this point and each of them has worked with professionals or fellow students who have in some way helped the overall effort. All of us involved with the project wish to thank these people, as well as all the friends and family of ecoMOD participants, for their support.

On these pages, I'll limit myself to those that have assisted—directly or indirectly—with the preparation of the manuscript.

Thanks to:
All the ecoMODers—the students and faculty from architecture, engineering, landscape architecture, architectural history, planning, business, economics, environmental science, and other disciplines—who have written something about the project during your involvement. As with the collaborative effort of designing the ecoMOD buildings and their landscapes, I feel the texts we use for the website, the grant proposals, the brochures, the booklets, and elsewhere have always benefited from the multiple voices that have contributed over the years. Don't be surprised if you see a small phrase in this book that you added at some point to some document along the way. Occasionally an unknown writer or editor has helped crystallize an important concept at the core of the project, and I am very much indebted.

The "goats" as well—the students and faculty involved in creating the

Trojan Goat as a part of the 2002 UVA Solar Decathlon team. Your efforts inspired eco-MOD, and I hope you don't mind seeing your work discussed and published again in this volume focused mostly on that later project.

Three faculty leaders who have supported the development of the projects—Judith Kinnard, former chair of the Department of Architecture and now a member of the faculty at Tulane; William Sherman, former chair of the Department of Architecture and Landscape Architecture; and Craig Barton, former chair of the Department of Architecture. Each of them has been a thoughtful, supportive mentor—and essential to integrating this form of teaching into our curriculum.

Engineering professor Paxton Marshall—I have now worked with Paxton for over ten years, since the beginning of the design process for the Trojan Goat in 2000. I appreciate his unflappable calm in the midst of chaos, and his willingness to continue to work with architecture and landscape students who change their minds constantly. His suggestions and ideas about the text are also much appreciated. Other important collaborators include Nancy Takahashi, UVA faculty member and ecoMOD landscape architecture advisor, and Louis Nelson, the ecoMOD historic preservation advisor.

The School of Architecture's Dean Kim Tanzer and former dean Karen Van Lengen—for creating the atmosphere in which these kinds of projects can flourish.

ecoMOD research assistant/architectural history graduate student Sarita Herman, who expertly helped craft some of the prose and fill in the pieces; ecoMOD research assistant/planning graduate student Jeff Herlitz, who brought an experienced eye to the manuscript; and ecoMOD research assistant/architecture graduate student Krissy Iverson, who helped write some portions of the ecoMOD2 section.

The UVA Professors as Writers program—which provided important financial support during the editing phase.

Morgan Myers, project editor at UVA Press, who methodically helped to clarify and tighten up the manuscript, Kenny Marotta, freelance editor, who at a critical stage helped me structure the manuscript and strengthen my voice, and Martha Farlow for her skillful graphic design.

Mark Saunders, assistant director of UVA Press, who patiently led me through the academic publishing process and whose comments and suggestions contributed significantly to the final shape and scope of the book.

And to Sara Osborne—who I'm still convinced will never read beyond this page, but who remains the toughest editor.

Portions of this book have appeared in a different form in my previous book, Trojan Goat: A Self-Sufficient House, *published by the University of Virginia School of Architecture and distributed by the University of Virginia Press.*

1 PRINCIPLES

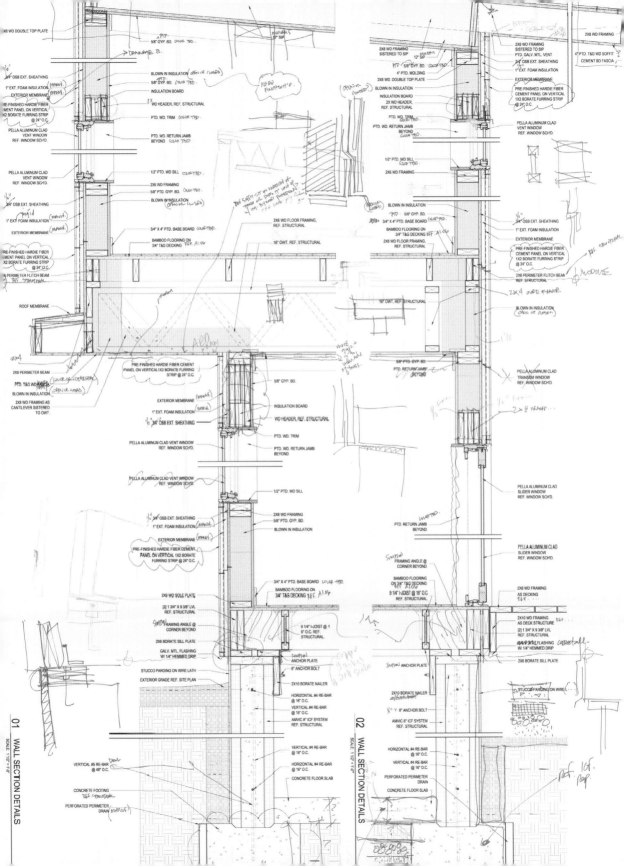

DESIGN, BUILD, EVALUATE

The entire object of true education is to make people not merely do the right things, but to enjoy the right things; not merely industrious, but to love industry; not merely learned, but to love knowledge.—John Ruskin

eco: ecology; economy
MOD: modular; modern

ecoMOD's Process and Guiding Principles

Until now, sustainable residential design has been a luxury reserved for the wealthy. The sustainable homes—even most of the recent prefabricated ones—that grace the pages of shelter magazines are beyond the budgets of most Americans. Yet it is individuals at low and moderate income levels who can truly benefit from the reduced energy, water, and maintenance costs associated with environmentally responsive homes.

The ecoMOD project aims to bridge this divide by creating a series of environmentally sound, modular housing units for affordable housing organizations. In the context of this goal, six ecoMOD projects have been completed to date, creating nine housing units—five single family detached homes, two accessory units, and a two-unit condominium. The size of the nine completed units ranges from 384 square feet to 1,464 square feet. The condominium units and one of the detached homes have been sold to low to moderate income families by Piedmont Housing Alliance in Charlottesville, Virginia, with down payment and financing assistance. Two other single family homes were built in partnership with Habitat for Humanity—one in Charlottesville for an

Afghani refugee couple, and the other in Gautier, Mississippi, for a family displaced by Hurricane Katrina. Rehab and preservation projects, under the name ecoREMOD, have been completed in Charlottesille and Falmouth, Jamaica. By working with affordable housing organizations, ecoMOD has been able to provide these homes for people in need, while also creating prototypes that can be replicated by modular housing manufacturers. The designs have been licensed and efforts are in the works to find manufacturers and other affordable housing organizations to reproduce them.

The ecoMOD project is committed to bringing sustainability to affordable housing by reimagining the idea of *home* through thoughtful, efficient, and responsible design. Each design explores the intersection of sustainable design, affordable housing, and prefabricated construction. The ecoMOD teams, typically made up of architecture, engineering, landscape architecture, historic preservation, planning, business, environmental science, and economics students, participate actively in the design, construction, and evaluation phases of the project. Since ecoMOD started in 2004, it has evolved into many different things for different people. For outside experts it is an opportunity to share their knowledge with creative students. For the students, ecoMOD is a process, a team, a house, or an educational experience . . . some of the more deeply committed student participants might even call it a temporary "lifestyle choice." Together, the teams strive to create well-designed and well-built homes that cost less to live in, minimize dam-

age to the environment, appreciate in value over time, and can be easily replicated within the prefabricated housing industry.

Prefabrication can be a cost-effective method of construction, and highly energy-efficient homes have lower utility costs, making sustainable prefab an ideal combination for affordable housing. Currently, however, prefabricated homes are seldom designed for energy efficiency, and most sustainable homes are expensive to build. The challenge of ecoMOD is to work through the conflicting aspects of these issues and find the best possible overlap.

The ecoMOD teams strive to be both visionary and practical, exploring the potential of prefabricated housing while rethinking certain aspects of it. Embedded in the design process is the belief that some practices within current conventional housing construction can be accepted, while others must be directly challenged. Conventional prefabricated homes are sited without any consideration of solar or wind orientation, or local hydrology. The buildings themselves are aggressively siteless—seemingly adaptable to any environment, yet entirely separate from their surroundings. In contrast, the intent of the ecoMOD designs is to create site-specific homes, using natural lighting and ventilation, nonhazardous materials, renewable energy, and energy-efficient systems to help reduce environmental impact and improve occupant health. The other intention is to structure a process that offers an intensive educational opportunity for the future designers of the built environment.

The ecoMOD projects are broken into

three overlapping and intentionally cyclical phases, allowing the teams to *design, build,* and *evaluate* the housing units.

DESIGN The goal of the design phase is to foster integrated and interdisciplinary collaboration throughout. It is organized around design studios and seminars in the UVA School of Architecture and overlapping technical courses in the School of Engineering and Applied Science. Students from programs outside architecture and engineering either are integrated into one of these classes or participate in one of the interdisciplinary evaluation seminars. The design stage presents students, faculty, and community members with a unique opportunity to learn from previous examples while at the same time outlining and executing proposals for housing units that seek to improve the quality of prefabricated design. The collaborative process is iterative and multifaceted. The participants are required to synthesize complex information and effectively work together to make decisions.

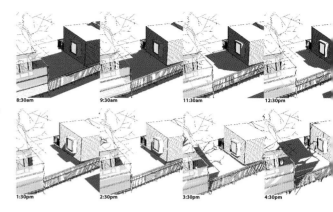

BUILD Each ecoMOD team has the opportunity to build the prototype they design. The goal is not only to provide the affordable housing partners—Piedmont Housing Alliance and Habitat for Humanity—with actual homes, but to expand on that opportunity to test prefabrication as a workable response to the shortage of well-designed affordable housing in the United States. The prototypes are fabricated at a decommissioned airfield hangar owned by the University of Virginia, and shipped as either modules or panels to their final destination. Construction professionals advise the student builders, and they also occasionally coordinate a more complex scope of work such as roofing or HVAC systems—although always with student participation. Based upon extensive research into the prefabricated housing industry and advice from modular homebuilders, the fabrication processes are structured to mimic what a company would expect if the home designs were taken into production.

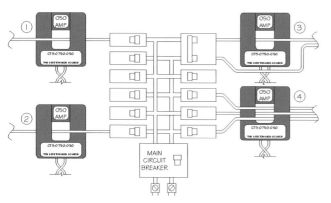

EVALUATE Once the design and construction phases of a conventional house are finished, a project is generally considered complete. One of the goals of ecoMOD is not only to fabricate housing units, but also to evaluate the results. This kind of critical feedback loop is unusual in architecture and engineering education (and the professional world for that matter), and is part of what distinguishes this project from many others. Architects, engineers, and the prefabricated housing industry seldom monitor or evaluate their efforts. The process of evaluating ecoMOD uses emerging strategies and protocols for the analysis of a completed building. Each evaluation process may include analysis of the environmental impact of the systems and materials, energy performance, affordability, human comfort, constructability, and thoughtful placement within a community. Students from various disciplines participate in one of the two overlapping evaluation seminars in the architecture and engineering schools. Each evaluation team formulates hypotheses, determines methodology, and analyzes the relevant data. The evaluation seminars prepare reports,

and as more data becomes available in a later phase, those reports are refined. The objectives are to see how well the housing units live up to sustainable aspirations, to allow the team to fine tune the systems so as to optimize their performance, and to provide feedback to the occupants so they can adjust their energy and water consumption habits.

The ecoMOD project was initially organized as a cyclical process of one academic year for design, a summer of construction, and an academic year of evaluation. However, as the realities of budgets, construction schedules, and the real estate market have impacted the project, the phases have become more fluid. The design and build phases tend to overlap—which is ideal for the integrated design emphasis of the educational experience. By recognizing when a design needs to change or be simplified, the students benefit from the feedback loop inherent in the project. Less ideally, the build and evaluation phases have begun to overlap, due to construction delays—mostly beyond our control. The evaluation team members are new to the project and bring a fresh eye on the design. While it is helpful for them to interview the design/build team as the project nears completion, it is also difficult for them to assess something that is not yet finished. It has become necessary to treat the evaluation reports as incomplete—with further assessment of many issues pushed into later semesters. This is especially true for the engineering teams who are regularly broken into groups—some of which focus on design issues, and some of which focus exclusively on evaluation (especially the monitoring systems). The hope is that as time passes, more useful information will come out of these efforts.

Guiding Principles

Each semester, the ecoMOD teams discuss the goals for the next phase of the project, and the overall intentions of ecoMOD. These conversations have led to the creation of guiding principles for the individual housing projects, which are compiled and expanded upon here. The ecoMOD designs are founded on these principles:

Size
- Keep it small—but design it carefully.
- Make it feel larger than it is.
- Attach dwellings to each other to minimize land usage and reduce costs.

Design
- Design for function, comfort, and beauty.
- Create spaces and elements of the homes that are flexible and have multiple functions.
- Use universal design principles to create spaces for all occupants, including those who are physically impaired.
- Bring in natural light, but diffuse it—and with careful design, encourage a greater awareness of the way the sun participates in our daily lives.
- Design to minimize the need for air conditioning.
- Design details and surfaces to minimize the need for maintenance.

Siting
- Carefully consider topography, urban context, wind, and sun.

- Develop on brownfields rather than on green ones.
- Strive to recharge all stormwater on site.
- Use native, noninvasive, and drought-tolerant planting.

Costs
- Work within the financial constraints of current affordable housing.
- Offer green upgrades, with clear cost/benefit information.

Efficiency
- Design to reduce operating costs.
- Maximize insulation and minimize air infiltration.
- Select equipment and appliances that minimize energy and water usage.
- Use passive heating, ventilation, and day-lighting design strategies to create buildings that can heat up and cool down without mechanical equipment.
- Allow occupants to control systems.
- Provide easy to understand feedback on mechanical and water system performance, so occupants can adjust them accordingly.
- Use equipment that converts solar radiation into electricity (photovoltaics) or allows the sun to collect heat for hot water and space heating.

Materials
- Strive for efficiency in thermal resistance and material use.
- Eliminate off-gassing whenever possible.
- Reuse or reclaim whenever possible.
- Make environmentally and socially responsible material choices.
- Select durable, low-maintenance materials.

Mass Customization

- Offer variations at multiple scales—modules, panels, components.
- Offer modular options so clients can add on to and not replace older homes.
- Design for site- and client-specific responses.
- Offer modules scaled for urban infill.

Evaluation

- Analyze the affordability of the completed projects.

- Monitor the energy and water usage and the thermal comfort of the homes.
- Assess the environmental impact of the materials and methods.
- Thoroughly learn the lessons of the evaluation, and apply them in the subsequent projects.
- Present the information to the public.

ARCHITECTS AND ENGINEERS

The Discipline of Architecture

Americans have a love-hate relationship with architects. On the one hand, the general public respects the profession. Sympathetic portrayals of architects abound in contemporary entertainment, and in major Hollywood films architects are shown to be thoughtful, creative, and knowledgeable. The news media uses the term "architect" for tasks and jobs such as diplomacy that are decidedly nonarchitectural. The phrases "architect of the recent Middle East peace accord" and "architect of the congressional budget compromise" seem to indicate an appreciation for the architect's simultaneous role as a creator and negotiator. So why aren't American architects allowed to lead design processes as they do in many other countries? Why are they often kept at the periphery of major development decisions? Why are they hired for projects with irrational design restrictions forced on them by developers and politicians without any design training? Why are so many strip malls, motels, self-storage facilities, big-box stores, manufactured homes, housing developments, and office complexes built with only minor input from a legitimate architecture firm, if any at all? Why are planning departments and homeowner associations across the country restricting aesthetic choices, rather than focusing on planning issues such as density, public space, and infrastructure? The situation is even worse in the housing industry, where architects are responsible for less than 25 percent of what gets built, and in most of those cases the buildings are simply reworked versions of designs an architect might have touched years ago. Is it even possible to imagine lawyers participating in only 25 percent of legal proceedings, or

participating only indirectly through recycled legal documents for an unrelated situation?

So if architects aren't always in charge, who decides what gets built today? Who decides what buildings will look like and how they will function? Developers and contractors mostly —people trained either to make money or to build designs created by others, who are increasingly being asked to "design" as well, or at least to significantly narrow the design options. In much of the custom residential construction market, clients either design a home for themselves and ask a builder to do the rest, or work with a builder to adapt a design from a selection of uninspired standard models. In commercial and retail construction, the developer is in charge, and decisions are focused on generating the largest return on investment in the shortest amount of time.

Of course, this is as it should be—mostly. Good developers and contractors are an important part of our economy and nothing would get built without them. Many architects have learned more from builders than from fellow architects, and are also inspired by the professionalism of quality developers. Yet it is important to remember that these people are not trained to design and do not necessarily understand all the considerations. Sure, a good builder knows how to keep the rain out (typically much better than any young architect), but do they know how to maximize sunlight without overheating a space or to creatively rethink a building program to provide more functionality in a smaller space? A professional developer might create a very sophisticated pro forma development plan, but can they negotiate the complexities of a structural system with a consultant, while maintaining the design integrity of a project? Do these professionals know how to carefully balance proportion, technology, climate, materials, culture, and spatial organization to make a building that both keeps the rain out and inspires the occupant?

In other cultures and in earlier times in our own history, the issue of what is best for society has been a serious consideration during a building project—and the definition of *best* has not always been interpreted as whatever is the most lucrative strategy for a small group of individuals. A broader interpretation of "the public good" is not understood by some percentage of current developers, so it is no wonder that so much of what has been built in the last thirty years is so cheap, generic, damaging to the environment, energy inefficient, and boring.

So it seems Americans like architects, but don't always trust them to do what they are trained to do. There are several reasons for this. First and foremost, architects' fees add cost to the project budget. For simple projects, some teams decide they can handle the design themselves. While it is easy to see how a bad designer might waste money and time, it is also easy to imagine how a smart designer can help the project team stay focused on the many complex challenges in building. An investment in a good architecture firm is really a question of long-term versus short-term thinking. It is an investment in a building that is thoughtfully designed and thoroughly integrates the client's interests with the site. A more considered design is likely to cost less to maintain and operate, and should also

last longer, as it can be more easily adapted to unforeseen uses over time.

Another reason Americans are suspicious of architecture is that architects have been guilty of bad design. Often this is because architects themselves have not considered that broader definition of the public good, and have been more interested in their own egos. The most significant examples include some of the harsh and brutal housing buildings of the mid-twentieth century, as well as the cheap, surface-oriented commercial and retail buildings of more recent years. Many of these buildings seem to be designed without humans in mind. Sadly, these banal buildings have given modernism a bad name—something good architects have to respond to on a daily basis in boardrooms and living rooms across America. This is one of several reasons that top-notch design firms are not being asked to design major sectors of our built environment. Yet the developers and contractors who control so many projects these days have been guilty of bad design, too— either by forcing questionable design constraints on an architecture firm, or simply by designing badly for themselves. Ironically, many of the bland, generic buildings designed without significant involvement from an architect are either "decorated sheds" (a term borrowed and reinterpreted from Venturi/ Scott-Brown) or simply a watered down version of something designed by an architect. A hint of Frank Lloyd Wright's groundbreaking prairie style homes can still be found (barely) in the brick ranchburgers of today. The red brick neocolonial McMansions sprouting on former farmland around the country are indebted to Stanford White and to America's first architect, Thomas Jefferson. But when translated by nondesigners, without any appreciation for aesthetics, proportion, and spatial ideas, they become cheap knock-offs.

If Jefferson were a practicing architect today, he would not be replicating eighteenth- and nineteenth-century designs in the suburbs. Jefferson's designs were groundbreaking in their day. No one had seen those kinds of buildings in this country at that time. If he had a full-blown practice today, he would more likely be expanding our society's understanding of architectural thought and working in the mode of firms such as Tod Williams and Billie Tsien Architects, SANAA, SHoP Architects, or Behnisch Architects. These are contemporary architects who understand how to work with clients, developers, contractors, and consultants to build extraordinary buildings. They know how to keep the rain out, stay within budget, and, most importantly, educate and inspire those who visit their buildings.

Architects and Engineers

Making the simple complicated is commonplace; making the complicated simple, awesomely simple, that's creativity.—Charles Mingus

Architects and engineers are in a unique position to operate in the interdependent world of buildings, society, and nature. Trained to imagine their problems at multiple scales and to find the connections between those scales, both disciplines are constantly challenged to synthesize complex information and propose solutions. Engineers, grounded in the rigor of scientific inquiry, and architects, driven by an iterative creative process, have the ability to study a problem from more than one perspective.

Despite these similarities, architectural and engineering education are quite distinct. Engineers are taught principles and asked to solve problems with specific and knowable answers. Engineering students can display extraordinary creativity in the methodology for solving a problem, but the answer is still considered to be objectively right or wrong. Architectural education is about exploration—of both questions and answers. Operating within an inherently subjective discipline, architecture students are challenged to reframe assignments for themselves—often ignoring the initial assumptions. Conceptual clarity and critical thinking are as important as visual skills in architectural design. There are no truly right or wrong design solutions. In the best circumstances, these generalizations about the two disciplines can lead to a very productive collaborative design process—especially if each professional (or student, in the case of ecoMOD) is able to learn some of the core values and language of the other discipline.

When it comes to sustainability, there are many reasons for architects and engineers to reengage with each other and with the general public, and especially with developers and contractors. Our society needs professional designers of all kinds who are capable of synthesizing complex information in order to produce truly innovative solutions that are buildable and financially feasible—with the goal of eliminating carbon emissions and reducing environmental impact. Over the years, many architects have gotten sloppy and lazy about designing buildings that respond to their climate. Within a hundred years following the invention of air-conditioning in the early twentieth century, architects in developed nations have forgotten an essential aspect of our collective cultural knowledge that had evolved in the previous several centuries—namely how to make a building thermally comfortable for humans without using electricity or fossil fuels.

Engineers let it happen—they are not innocent in this crime. They gave architects the ammunition, in the form of technology powered with "cheap" energy and sophisticated mechanical systems that have led to an artificially narrow zone of comfort for temperature and humidity in interior spaces. It is something like the conundrum about the chicken and the egg: Which comes first—the overly air-conditioned building with the huge HVAC unit contributing to global warming, or the unshaded glass box without operable windows on the cover of *Architectural Record*?

Americans in particular are noted for their somewhat recent narrowing of the comfort zone. In the last forty years, mechanically driven air-conditioning has become an essential part of almost all buildings from Key West, Florida, to the northern reaches of the upper Midwest. As designers almost universally rejected operable windows in office buildings in the second half of the twentieth century, Americans also began to depend less on their windows at home—choosing to install

increasingly more sophisticated heating and air-conditioning systems with each passing generation. Ironically, all the heat created to heat and cool these buildings raises the temperature of urban areas, with very little of it recovered for useful purposes. On a broader scale, there is a direct correlation between the energy needed to cool buildings and the growing challenge of global warming.

The New York City subway system is the perfect microcosm of this mindset. Enormous amounts of energy are spent to power mechanical systems to heat and cool subway car interiors, sending the waste heat generated into the subway stations and tunnels. No thought has been given to harnessing the waste heat, or the temperature of the ground, or the cooling effect of the trains traveling in the tunnels. The result? When these overworked systems are operating, the cars are decidedly chilly in both summer and winter, and in the summer the station platforms are unbearably hot.

The best solutions are typically simple—even if they don't necessarily look simple, or if they have taken many months or years of hard work to realize. The best architectural and engineering design requires a thorough understanding of the laws of nature, balanced with a respect for the climate, culture, and society from which the design evolves. Yet contrary to conventional wisdom, simple solutions are not typically the traditional or prevalent ones. While good design is always influenced by the normative or vernacular, it doesn't slavishly replicate it. This is well understood in the field of engineering, but it is sometimes challenged in the field of architecture. Segments of the general public remain comfortable with certain forms of traditional architecture—especially domestic buildings—and find it difficult to accept anything else. While there is a lot that BAC (before air-conditioning) domestic buildings can teach contemporary designers, there is also a lot to be challenged. Traditional building materials tend to be more "natural" and therefore have a reduced environmental impact, but some do not perform as well as contemporary substitutions. A rigid use of a traditional compositional strategy (i.e., strict symmetry, legible hierarchy, etc.) is usually at odds with an optimized climate-responsive approach. Design is a form of inquiry, and the best solutions cannot be imagined before the design process begins. Our cultures are constantly evolving, and recent experience tells us that the earth's climate is also slowly—but assuredly—being disrupted, so design must never remain static.

Who Is Responsible for the Performance of Buildings?

It's hard for a man to understand something when his salary depends on his not understanding it.—Upton Sinclair

Al Gore uses the quote above to motivate the public about climate change and to clarify the role of individual responsibility in the effort. Loosely translated to sustainable buildings—a topic that sadly (and surprisingly) was only tangentially referenced in Gore's *An Inconvenient Truth* book and documentary film—the idea becomes something along the lines

of: it's hard for designers to understand the performance of their buildings if their reputation depends on not understanding it.

In an article about the future of architecture published in *Harvard Design Magazine,* architect Zaha Hadid and her partner Patrik Schumacher write that in order to evaluate their provocative and seductive projects "different . . . criteria have to be applied. . . . Originality and innovative potential are *more important than the actuality of its performance*" (emphasis added). In trying to distinguish their work from a conventional practice, they state, "The significance of the avant-garde project cannot be reduced to the contribution it makes to a given concrete life process. Rather it is pointing beyond any concrete problem towards the potential for new generic resources (formal/organizational repertoires) for the future problem solving capacity of the discipline."[1]

All disciplines require trendsetters, and avant-garde architects lead the way both intellectually and artistically. As a profession and a form of artistic expression, architecture should be both practical and inspirational—often with more emphasis on the latter for the leading edge of the discipline. This is also true when it comes to the construction of groundbreaking buildings. Frank Lloyd Wright's houses often leaked, but the adoption of similar forms by others led to the development of more dependable roofing materials and detailing. Frank Gehry's curvilinear forms have broken new ground in digital fabrication and metal cladding assembly. Zaha Hadid is finally able to construct buildings that for many years remained exquisite renderings of formal potential. The architectural avant-garde should take risks, as long as the client understands them.

Yet the comments by Hadid and Schumacher are also disturbing. They have given voice to an opinion that many well-respected contemporary architects (including ones with far less skill or finesse) are not always willing to openly express: for them, form is more important than function. Even in this supposedly golden era of sustainable design, most buildings are still conceived with little consideration for energy performance, let alone the building's impact on its occupants or the resources of the earth.

In Hadid's search for "future problem solving capacity," she limits the scope to "formal/ organizational repertoires." Presumably this means social and environmental issues are fair game for abstract exploration, but is she implying that an actual contribution to resolving social and/or environmental problems is not relevant? Is it more important to Hadid that the "climate-responsive" form of her Madrid Civil Court of Justice project effectively ventilates air, or simply that it gives the impression of doing so?

Comments like Hadid's make clear that a sense of curiosity about the post-occupancy phase of a building is not something easily developed in the world of boutique or large corporate firms with extensive teams of liability and legal consultants. For too many of these firms, the rewards in the professional world are not found in high levels of occupant satisfaction or in a measurable reduction in environmental impact. The fee structure of architectural projects seldom includes a scope of work during the post-occupancy phase— even in this era of greater awareness toward sustainability. If we can't change the structure of the relationship between client, architect, and consultant, at least we can try to change the values of these individuals during their education. This is one of the most important goals of the ecoMOD curriculum.

A well-built building should outlast the trends of architectural design. It should reflect the cultural values of its client, and be designed with a deep understanding of both the short- and long-term impacts of its construction on the local and global environment. A building is not a static object—it is a living, dynamic mechanism. It requires ongoing attention and is deserving of analysis and assessment on many levels—not just as an artistic statement. Designers need to recognize this, and learn how to cultivate the creation of effective, efficient, and comfortable buildings. Enduring values should trump temporary aesthetic preferences. Ultimately, architects and engineers should be held responsible for their building designs, and they should be compensated to perform extensive post-occupancy evaluations of their creations—using the information to educate the building owners, future clients, and themselves.

Note
1. "Stocktaking 2004: Nine Questions about the Present and Future of Design," *Harvard Design Magazine* 20 (Spring/Summer 2004), 19–21.

SUSTAINABILITY

The very act of building is inherently anti-ecological to the degree it induces a displacement of "natural" relationships.—Richard Ingersoll

The Current Situation

In some form or other, the sun is the source of most forms of energy on the earth—from fossil fuels such as natural gas and petroleum, which become depleted over time, to renewable forms of energy such as biomass, wind, and solar power. In fact, each day the sun directly radiates more than 10,000 times the amount of energy required in the world. Efficient and environmentally benign methods of harvesting this direct solar radiation are clearly the wave of the future.

The United States, the world's largest economy, generates and uses more energy than any other nation. Not surprisingly, the U.S. is also the world's single largest generator of greenhouse gas emissions. Buildings alone produce almost one half of these emissions. The average single-family home in the U.S. emits more than 22,000 pounds of carbon dioxide each year (from the electricity generated by utilities to run the home, and oil- or gas-powered equipment and appliances in the home). This is more than twice the amount emitted by the typical American car.[1] The reality is that inefficient McMansions are far more harmful to the environment than gas-guzzling sport-utility vehicles.

The responsibility to address this situation rests on many shoulders— politicians, utility executives, homeowners, building code officials, and builders. As design professionals, architects and engineers bear a special aspect of this responsibility. They must lead the construction industry toward more responsible, intelligent, and efficient buildings. A truly sustainable building—whether residential, commercial, or institutional—is one that meets the needs of the occupants while not encumbering society or future generations with any negative impacts from its construction or operation.

A Passive Resurgence

Buildings and the natural world are inextricably linked. We create shelter to protect ourselves from the elements. In this sense, the very act of building negates nature. Since the invention of air-conditioning systems in the early twentieth century, buildings have increasingly sealed themselves off from weather—even in its mildest form. As Americans have moved to a more narrowly defined interior comfort zone with each generation, mechanical systems have had to continuously improve—requiring more and more energy.

Best building practices now call for a very tightly sealed thermal envelope in order to effectively control interior temperature and humidity. This emphasis on "tight building" has obvious advantages. If done correctly, it can significantly reduce utility costs and the environmental impact of a building. However, while this level of quality construction is becoming more widely used, it is still not the norm in the U.S. The vast majority of new buildings are built to minimum standards, leading to unnecessary energy waste—costing American building owners billions of dollars annually in utility costs. So as American culture has redefined thermal comfort in the

past hundred years, and invented heating and cooling systems to facilitate this change, our building envelopes still lag far behind our thermal preferences and our technology. Ironically—and most importantly—the very act of narrowing the comfort zone in the modern era is a major contributor to the most significant change to our earth's climate in the history of humankind.

At a time when the building industry contributes the most to resource depletion, carbon dioxide emissions, and landfill overuse of any sector of the U.S. economy, and is also responsible for at least some of the recent surge in asthma and indoor air quality–related health problems, architects and engineers responsible for designing buildings can no longer ignore these increasingly urgent ethical issues. Fortunately, a new awareness is emerging. The sustainability of a building is becoming an important consideration for a growing number of designers and their clients. Some designers are once again interested in natural forces—such as solar and wind energies—and are starting to utilize them in new ways. Rather than overpowering the elements with technology, designers are relearning how to temper weather extremes by taking advantage of the best aspects of a local climate while minimizing the worst. Centuries-old strategies for passive design— design that is not dependent on technology for comfort—are being rediscovered and rethought. Shading devices, natural ventilation, daylighting without overheating, selectively used heat gain, and other design strategies are finding their way into buildings. Instead of isolating the occupants from the forces of nature, architects and engineers are starting to imagine buildings that respond to the climate and give occupants selective control over the temperature and humidity of the interior without being limited exclusively to mechanical systems for thermal comfort. In addition, renewable energy technologies—photovoltaics (PVs), solar hot water panels, wind turbines, geothermal systems, and others—that take advantage of the "free" energy of the sun, the wind, or the temperature of the earth, are resurging and becoming more efficient.

Before considering expensive renewable energy technologies, these "free" aspects of good design should be thoroughly explored—especially when designing affordable housing. More designers are revisiting the idea that any rigorous assessment of sustainable design would include a careful analysis of climate conditions. Solar orientation and access, wind rose diagrams, and vegetation should all be assessed early in the design process. Locating and designing a building to maximize the positive and minimize the negative aspects of a climate is the cheapest way to reduce energy usage. Taking advantage of shading to minimize overheating, or breezes for passive cooling, or south facing windows for winter heat gain are "free" technologies—simple strategies that improve indoor comfort for occupants while reducing the amount of energy needed to achieve that comfort.

Our understanding of climate is intuitive—we respond to it daily with our choices for clothing and outdoor activities. Yet in our society's increasing detachment from nature there are common misconceptions of our own local climatic situation. For example, ask

anyone from Charlottesville, Virginia (the home of the ecoMOD Project), about the local climate, and inevitably they'll talk about the hot, humid summers, and the mild "shoulder" seasons in the spring and the fall. Yet surprisingly, locals will seldom reference the most obvious climatic consideration when designing a building in the Charlottesville area—the fact that there are *three times* as many days when buildings require some heat as there are days that require cooling. Measured in "heating degree days" (the cumulative number of degrees by which average day-to-day temperatures fall below 65° in a year), cooler outdoor temperatures are a driving force seven months of the year, and a factor to consider in other months too.

This difference between perception and reality is explained in part by the fact that central Virginia is a mixed-humid climate in the mid-Atlantic region of the United States—a moisture-prone region, with the possibility of temperature extremes in both winter and summer. While the moderate "shoulder" seasons are part of what makes the region an appealing place to live, these seasons also deliver the potential of 50-degree temperature shifts within a few hours. On any given day, Charlottesville can hit temperatures found on the same day in both northern Wisconsin and southern Florida. Unlike in the more consistently moderate hot-dry climate of southern California, which allows for almost year-round indoor-outdoor living, strategic passive design in central Virginia necessitates the ability to be both tightly closed to the elements and easily opened to breezes—often on the same day.

Humidity requires special attention in a mixed climate—particularly when it comes to designing and detailing the skin of a building. Understanding water and water vapor are critical in a region where, depending on the day, warm air could be moving from inside to out (on a cold day) or from outside to in (on a warm one). Moisture moves with air as it passes through a wall, and therefore a wall in a mixed climate must be able to allow condensation to dry either to the inside or to the outside. Incomplete knowledge of these basic principles can lead to inefficient mechanical systems, the development of mold within walls, degradation of materials, and uncomfortable or unhealthy spaces.

A leader in the passive design movement of the 1970s and early '80s, Ed Mazria has recommitted himself to reducing the environmental impact of buildings. His first task was to clarify for everyone the enormity of the actual impact of buildings by carefully studying the information provided by the U.S. Department of Energy and the U.S. Environmental Protection Agency, and reshuffling that information to highlight building-related statistics. He recognized that some percentage of the "industry" and "transportation" sectors of the U.S. economy designated by those agencies is related to the third sector—"buildings." By estimating which industries are creating building materials or equipment, and what percentage of transportation is directly related to construction or demolition, he made it clear that buildings and their operation are doing the most damage to the environment of any sector.[2] As the resulting screaming cover headline for an issue of *Metropolis* magazine

states: "Architects Pollute!"[3] Mazria has since founded an organization to get this message out, and to get the architectural, engineering, and construction industries to do something about it. The group runs a website, Architecture2030.org, which catalogs many of these revised estimates, and is also asking individuals, companies, firms, and other organizations to commit to reducing the carbon emissions associated with the building sector of the economy. The 2030 Challenge, as it is called, has successfully rallied significant support from organizations such as the American Institute of Architects and the U.S. Conference of Mayors, as well as from communities and design firms around the country.

Soon after establishing the 2030 Challenge, Mazria recognized that architectural design education isn't necessarily ready to produce professionals who can make a significant impact on reducing carbon emissions for buildings by 2030. So he established the 2010 Imperative, to encourage design programs to commit to curriculum initiatives that will prepare the next generation of design leadership. Many architectural educators have found the 2010 Imperative to be helpful in channeling curricular discussions and focusing student initiatives. In a related effort, the Society of Building Science Educators established a grant-funded program called the Carbon Neutral Design Project to bring together faculty from around the country to establish standards for carbon neutral design education curricula, and to refine or prepare and distribute educational tools.

The Environmental Impact of Buildings

Today, those involved in the architecture, engineering, construction, landscape architecture, and planning professions cannot avoid the latest information on sustainable design strategies, green materials, and the relative merits of pursuing the U.S. Green Building Council's LEED certification program. It proliferates in the professional literature to a degree that these issues have never before. Firms that once ignored green design are now encouraging their employees to become LEED Accredited Professionals, and bringing in consultants to help their teams address storm-water management, daylighting, and energy efficiency.

It remains unclear whether this transformation has occurred because clients are now talking about environmental impact and therefore professionals associated with the built environment are more focused on it, or the other way around. The truth likely lies somewhere in the middle. Regardless, the fact remains that even well known design firms with no previous background are developing expertise in green design—from large corporate firms such as SOM to smaller, respected "high-design" firms such as Morphosis and Steven Holl Architects.

How long will this emphasis on sustainable design last? It is hard to predict, but there is reason to be optimistic about the future. In the 1970s and early '80s "solar" architecture became closely associated with a specific "style" of form-making. The steep, asymmetrical shed roofs popular then, which were intended for heat gain collection or solar panels, started to be used on buildings purely as an aesthetic choice—sometimes without the actual panels or passive design strategies in place. When the "style" changed, the opportunity for passive design seemed to go with it. (The loss of federal tax credits for renewable energy in the early 1980s also had a significant impact on the integration of passive design or renewable technologies.) Yet today, the aesthetics of sustainable design are open to interpretation. Examples range from the neohistoricism of Quinlan Terry to the radical explorations of emerging firms such as future-cities-lab. Being green doesn't have a "look" today, and in the fickle world of architectural design, this makes it more likely that sustainability could become a permanent part of the profession. The fact that so many people in so many overlapping professions are focused on it is another reason for hope. As these disciplines continue to redefine sustainability in their work, and as research continues to emerge about the real impact that buildings have on our ecosystems

and human health, it seems likely that the insurance industry and the legal profession will start to recognize the relevance of these issues more clearly. Poorly designed buildings that hurt the environment or people will be more clearly seen as a liability. The work of designers and builders directly impacts the lives of people and ecosystems in ways that many are just beginning to comprehend, and slowly a greater recognition of professional responsibility is emerging.

Making the Impact Legible

The building professions, and architects in particular, face another challenge. As noted earlier, the structure of current practice is not set up to continue professional services beyond the first stage of occupancy. The conventional thinking is that design is over when the people move in. More designers are starting to think this mindset needs to change.

Driving the radical transformation of the American building industry over the last thirty or forty years has been the voice of clients saying they want it faster, cheaper, and better—though often with the last objective left out altogether. The rise of fast track projects, where construction starts before the design is finished, and the development of alternative methods of project delivery such as professional design/build companies, have many advantages. However, they do not always lead to more environmentally responsible or energy-efficient buildings. If clients were willing to pay for professional services that include post-occupancy reports on the performance of buildings and the quality of life in them, the profession would drastically change. The needed services include questionnaires for building users and active monitoring of energy usage, thermal comfort, daylighting, and indoor air quality, as well as systems commissioning, whereby engineers and building managers fine-tune the equipment during the first few years of occupation.

Yet the vast majority of building developers and owners don't see the need for these services—especially near the end of the often expensive and stressful process of completing a building project.

It is interesting to compare buildings and automobiles in this regard. An automobile is an investment that depreciates in value over time, yet we have established a car culture that invests considerable time and money in maintaining and repairing our cars. This is perhaps because it is obvious when a car breaks down—the impact is immediate if it keeps you from getting to work. Yet many people also perform high-level preventive maintenance on their cars to protect their investment, to maintain or improve the car's performance, and sometimes simply out of pride. This is laudable, and certainly to be encouraged. Yet the average American car is replaced after ten years.

Americans are not always as committed to maintaining or properly improving their largest appreciable investment—their home. Sure, we'll repair a leaking roof, and paint the exterior regularly, and even invest in gracious interior renovations. But we don't spend as much money on improvements that will actually pay for themselves with reduced energy or water bills. While Americans—especially those in the upper income levels—are spending more each year on home improvements, only 15 percent or so of this money is going toward energy efficient upgrades to insulation, lighting, water heating, mechanical systems, and windows. Part of the problem is the way homes are valued. Typically the quality of insulation and HVAC

systems, or the existence of renewable energy systems such as PVs, solar hot water, and wind turbines, does not directly translate into a higher home value. Unless a comparable home in an area has been clearly shown to sell for more because of these factors, home appraisers do not consider them. Sophisticated homebuyers might choose a home for these reasons, but the intrinsic value of these strategies is not currently embedded in the marketplace.

With recently available tax breaks, there has been a small surge in residential renewable energy systems. Yet a commitment to making those investments does not always come after a rigorous assessment of the best means to reduce energy use. Many Americans don't bother with the smallest yet wisest investment of their home improvement money—upgrades in insulation, and regular renewal of caulking and sealant around windows and other openings. Insulation is a lot cheaper than PVs, and with a super-insulated home the eventual selection of a PV system can be significantly downsized—saving even more money. Admittedly, insulation is something of a financial commitment, but most studies show it pays for itself far more quickly than just about any other home improvement. As for air infiltration, building scientists point out that if you combined all the gaps in a typical American home and put them in one location, there would a hole roughly one foot square in your wall.[4] A few dollars spent at a home improvement store on caulk and sealant, and a few hours spent on a ladder, could eliminate this problem more effectively than a major technological solution.

At the same time, compared to other cultures, Americans seem far more likely than our ancestors to focus on the first cost of a building project, rather than the long term costs including maintenance and operation. The mentality of a speculative developer, who is only interested in selling a new building as soon as possible, seems to have infused many sectors of the economy, and even in this age of sustainability, it is still challenging to get clients to look beyond the costs associated with construction alone. Whether a sustainable building costs more to construct is still debatable (some argue that there is no difference, although with smaller projects the green upgrade costs can be slightly more noticeable), but most upgrades, if properly designed, installed, and maintained, can easily pay for themselves long before the end of their useful lives.

The costs of fuel and water are increasing, and are likely to continue to increase as oil production begins to plateau or decrease and competition for water resources increases exponentially. Perhaps the tendency to ignore ongoing costs would change if we were met on a daily basis by clear information, displayed on screens, about how much energy or water we were using—with real-time updates. Returning to the car analogy, the instantaneous feedback about fuel usage in the dashboard of the Toyota Prius is apparently one of the reasons the cars are so fuel-efficient. If the average American homeowner or office worker could get instantaneous feedback on how many gallons of water they are using as they shower (and how much that is going to cost them) or information about how their daily activities affect the thermal and energy

performance of a building, our society might be far more energy efficient. The ecoMOD monitoring systems strive for this type of feedback—to help both the ecoMOD evaluation teams and the occupants understand how well the homes are performing.

Aldo Leopold, the conservationist and scientist who authored *A Sand County Almanac,* developed his concept of a land ethic in 1949, and it has deeply influenced many environmentalists since. Within his subtle and thoughtful observations on the flora and fauna of an ecosystem in central Wisconsin, Leopold establishes a framework for resolving the conflict between the demands of the economic marketplace and the simultaneously fragile and robust systems of nature. "All ethics so far evolved," he wrote, "rest upon a single premise: that the individual is a member of a community of interdependent parts. His instincts prompt him to compete for his place in the community, but his ethics prompt him also to co-operate. . . . The land ethic simply enlarges the boundaries of the community to include soils, waters, plants and animals, or collectively: the land."[5] For Leopold, it was "inconceivable" that a land ethic could thrive in a modern society in which we are increasingly separated from nature. One can only imagine what he would think if he were alive today—with the rapid suburbanization of the countryside and the incredible technological advances since the mid-twentieth century. He goes so far as to write, "Economic feasibility limits the tether of what can and cannot be done for land. It always has and always will." He argues that as a society we must find value in the "uneconomic aspects" of land use, and makes a case for a "biotic" community whose health is determined by things that preserve its "integrity, stability and beauty."[6] In a sense, he says that if an economic argument for the environment fails, we have to encourage society to value ethics more.

From a pragmatic point of view, there is reason to question why the "tether" of economic feasibility has to remain such a significant problem in today's society. Perhaps this tether could be cut if we had a more thorough and commonly accepted cost-benefit analysis method that rigorously addressed ecological, technical, aesthetic, and social issues and did not sever them from financial ones as they are currently defined. Rather than finding value in the "uneconomic aspects" of nature, this new method might clearly demonstrate nature's economic value and not depend on society to come around to Leopold's land ethic by making a purely ethical choice. Recent research into quantifying the "ecological services" of wetlands, trees, and streams is one step in this direction. If we can make the true economic and health consequences of environmental devastation visible and undeniable to our contemporary society in measurable terms, we might have a chance for real change.

There is some reason to be optimistic. When significant challenges have presented themselves in the past—the perception that our wildlife areas were being destroyed, the serious problems American cities faced with air pollution from the early twentieth century into the 1970s, and the hole in the ozone layer due to the use of CFC compounds— the American government and public have risen to the occasion and made great strides

towards resolving these issues. The creation of our national parks and other protected areas, the air pollution restrictions put in place over the second half of the twentieth century, and the restrictions on CFC compounds in personal and industrial products are examples of the capacity for American society to respond to pressing needs. Surprisingly, we have also made progress on energy usage in buildings since the fuel crisis of 1973. On a per household basis, residential energy use has declined since the late 1970s.[7] This is despite a significant increase in both home size and energy loads from the wider range of electronic equipment found in homes today. We are doing better than we were, largely because energy isn't cheap anymore, but the problems are not as immediate to the general public as the smog of the '60s and '70s—which was quite visible and made so many people sick.

Researchers and designers are developing tools to make the impact visible—or at least understandable—to the general public. The evolving fields of life cycle analysis, ecological footprinting, and valuations of natural resources are the beginnings of an attempt to bridge economics and ecology. Life cycle analysis (LCA) is perhaps the best tool to use in the world of buildings. LCA assesses all environmental impacts of a product or material—from the extraction of the raw materials through the end life or possible recycling of it. This area of research is still emerging, and the metrics are often imprecise. They still require considerable development to be practically implemented widely. One problem is that it's difficult to operate in this realm without making direct comparisons between specific options—forcing designers to determine what is "less bad." Comparisons are difficult to make across scales of operation or between radically different materials.

LCA typically includes energy usage, greenhouse gas emissions from manufacturing and transportation, any damage to human life or an ecosystem, waste generated, and other categories. In its purest form, LCA is an excellent comparative tool to guide in the choice between things like paper, plastic, or reusable canvas bags at the grocery store. Unfortunately, it is often difficult for laypeople to get comprehensive information of this type, since access to the databases is often fee based. In addition, it is common to see LCA information published by the popular press or in marketing material that is essentially comparing apples and oranges. For example, the environmental impact of bamboo flooring can be interpreted as relatively low, given that bamboo is often described as a rapidly renewable resource—meaning that bamboo grows quickly, and harvesting it doesn't harm the plant's ability to regenerate. However, much of the world's bamboo flooring comes from China and southeast Asia, and for a project in the U.S., the energy impact of bringing the material across the ocean could easily tip the scales in favor of an alternate flooring option from America. So when bamboo flooring companies present environmental information about their products, they typically leave out the transportation energy embodied in their materials, making it difficult to compare them to locally based alternatives. In addition, bamboo panels and flooring are often asembled

with urea formaldehyde binding agents, which can negatively impact indoor air quality—although many other commonly used panel products use the same strategy. As more and more companies try to market the "green advantages" of their products, the public needs better ways to assess the accuracy of these claims.

As complex as it is to assess the relative greenness of grocery bag options or cloth versus disposable diapers, the challenges of LCA are exacerbated with a "product" as complex as a building. Depending on its size and scope, a building project could utilize literally thousands of different materials, and, when assembled as a structure, building materials are not simply inert, but components in dynamic systems. For a truly sophisticated assessment of building materials, it is important to prioritize decisions according to how the material or system will actually be used in a specific application. The use of a certain type of petroleum-based material, which could have a significant environmental impact, might be justified in some applications more than others—for example, an exterior waterproofing installation versus an interior wall finish. Sometimes, the material with the least environmental impact is also the least durable—which means it has to be renewed or replaced more often in some applications. Materials also interact with each other, which might lead to galvanic reaction or to the off-gassing of volatile organic compounds (VOCs), significantly harming indoor air quality and possibly damaging human health. Yet used in isolation, the material might be completely inert.

A designer's (or contractor's) head begins to spin when imagining all the possible combinations and impacts of building material assembly. A classic example is the process of considering insulation types. In many climates, the obvious choice when considering only the performance of thermal resistance is foam that expands to entirely fill an insulation cavity. The heat flow resistance (R-value) is higher compared to other options, and because it fills the cavity with a material that doesn't settle, the potential of gaps where moisture can get trapped is significantly reduced. Yet there are legitimate concerns about using a petroleum-based product such as foam when there are other options that utilize natural or recycled materials. The manufacturing process for many highly efficient insulation materials is energy intensive and requires the use of dangerous chemicals. Yet when these materials are used properly, the benefits of increased energy efficiency from insulation can outweigh the negative environmental aspects of the creation of the products. In an assessment by one of the ecoMOD teams performed on a very specific comparison of products in a specific situation, we found the impact of an open cell foam insulation over time was significantly less than the alternatives because of the reduced energy use associated with the superior thermal performance. In fact, it can be generally stated that for materials related to the thermal performance of the building, the impact of the operation phase is more important than the manufacturing phase, assuming there are not problems with off-gassing, the energy intensity of the manufacturing process, the safety of the

workers that produce the material, or the safe disposal or recycling of waste or the material at the end of its useful life.

This ecoMOD team did their best in this and other assessments—gathering LCA information from various sources and trying to make an "apples to apples" comparison. They tracked resources found in the well-respected *Environmental Building News,* as well as LCA information available from the product manufacturers, the Athena Institute, the BEES database, the McDonough Braungart Design Chemistry C2C Certification program, and other resources. Yet there is no guarantee that they properly assessed all aspects of the decision. Inevitably, the scientists and researchers that generated the LCA information made assumptions about the type of energy used to create or transport the materials, or the specific chemical makeup of the materials themselves. These assumptions may or may not correspond to the specific ecoMOD choice. The need for greater standardization of this information and more transparent documentation of the analysis process is clear. Perhaps even more important, there is a need to have these concepts more clearly translated to a nonexpert audience. As designers get deeper into this process, it is important they have confidence that they are actually comparing relevant information. In the ecoMOD project, the teams have the luxury of pursuing this research as far as the schedule allows, but professional architects and engineers are not typically compensated for that type of work, so time constraints can be even more challenging.

This is not to imply that there aren't simple

and commonsense strategies that are likely to reduce the impact of a building. In the last five to ten years we have seen such strategies applied in contemporary buildings more often. These include passive design, increased insulation, natural or fully recyclable building materials, and energy efficient appliances and equipment. Sustainable design on many levels is really just good, commonsense design. Michael Pollan has been quoted distilling the message of his book *In Defense of Food* to this simple aphorism: "Eat food, not too much, mostly vegetables." In the realm of buildings, it could be rephrased: "Renovate before creating new buildings, with an awareness of the local climate and ecosystem, using mostly simple materials."

Notes

1. Environmental Protection Agency, "Climate Change: Individual Emissions," http://www.epa.gov/climatechange/emissions/individual.html.
2. Architecture 2030, www.Architecture2030.org.
3. Christopher Hawthorne, "Turning Down the Global Thermostat: Mazria's Equation," *Metropolis Magazine,* October 2003, 102–7.
4. Oikos, "Advanced Air Sealing: Air Leakage in Homes," http://oikos.com/library/airsealing/air_leakage.html.
5. Aldo Leopold, *A Sand County Almanac, and Sketches Here and There* (Oxford: Oxford University Press, 1949), 203–4.
6. Ibid., 224–25.
7. Energy Information Administration, U.S. Department of Energy, Residential Energy Consumption Survey, http://www.eia.doe.gov/emeu/recs/.

Additional References

Carbon Neutral Design Project, The Society of Building Science Educators. http://www.sbse.org/resources/index.htm and http://www.architecture.uwaterloo.ca/faculty_projects/terri/carbon-aia/.

Energy Information Administration of the U.S. Department of Energy. www.eia.doe.gov.

Environmental Building News. www.buildinggreen.com.

Fitch, James Marston. *American Building: The Environmental Forces That Shape It.* Oxford: Oxford University Press, 1947.

Guy, Simon, and Steven A. Moore. *Sustainable Architectures: Natures and Cultures in Europe and North America.* London: Routledge/Spon, 2005.

Hagan, Susannah. *Taking Shape: A New Contract between Architecture and Nature.* London: Architectural Press, 2001.

Ingersoll, Richard. "Second Nature: On the Social Bond of Ecology and Architecture." In *Reconstructing Architecture: Critical Discourses and Social Practices.* Tom Dutton and Lian Hurst Mann, eds. Minneapolis: University of Minnesota Press, 1996.

McDonough, William, and Michael Braungart. *Cradle to Cradle: Remaking the Way We Make Things.* New York: North Point Press, 2002.

Olgyay, Victor. *Design With Climate: Bioclimatic Approach To Architectural Regionalism.* Princeton: Princeton University Press, 1963.

Roaf, Sue, David Crichton, and Fergus Nicol. *Adapting Buildings and Cities for Climate Change: A 21st Century Survival Guide.* Oxford: Architectural Press, 2005.

Scott, Andrew, ed. *Dimensions of Sustainability.* London: E&FN Spon, 1999.

Steele, James. *Ecological Architecture: A Critical History.* London: Thames & Hudson, 2005.

Van Der Ryn, Sim, and Stuart Cowan. *Ecological Design.* Washington, DC: Island Press, 1996.

AFFORDABILITY

Income Disparity

The economic divide between high income and low income Americans has grown considerably in the last thirty years, to the point that the top 1 percent control almost 34.3 percent of all private wealth—which is more than the total combined wealth for the population in the bottom 90 percent.[1] This is the greatest concentration of wealth since 1928, the year before the stock market crash that led to the Great Depression, and despite an increasingly diverse society, white Americans control the vast majority of this wealth.

In the post–World War II era, low and middle income Americans made real progress toward income parity, and a large middle class emerged. But in the last twenty-five years, the trend has reversed: the rich have gotten much, much richer, and the poor have gotten poorer. According to the economists Emmanuel Saez and Thomas Piketty, the top 5 percent of the U.S. population saw their real income rise 81 percent between 1979 and 2005, while the bottom 20 percent saw their income decline 1 percent. In 1979, the average income of the top 5 percent was 11.4 times higher than that of the lowest 20 percent, but by 2005, that figure had risen to 20.9 times.[2] The period from 1979 to 2005 presents a significant contrast to the years between 1947 and 1979, when the greatest income increases by percentage were among those Americans at the bottom of the economic ladder, and the smallest increase was for those at the top. For the first time since the Great Depression, area median income (AMI) over a ten-year period in the U.S. failed to increase from 1999 to 2008. In fact, in most parts of the country, AMI fell from a little over $52,000 per household to just over $50,000 between 2007 and 2008—a 3.6 percent fall in one year alone. As this information shows, when income numbers are adjusted for inflation, it becomes even more obvious that low income workers are falling behind previous generations.

With the recession that began in 2008, Americans' awareness of this income disparity has expanded in ways it had not in the prior fifteen to twenty years, and many now recognize that this situation has serious impacts on our economy and society as a whole. One example is the ability of low to moderate income Americans to purchase a home—or to hold on to it if they already have one. The U.S. savings rate is one part of this puzzle. Twenty-five years ago, the savings rate in the United States was over 11 percent. Yet during the housing boom in the years leading up to 2008, the U.S. savings rate was expressed in negative numbers—approximately negative 1 percent.[3] With regard to this statistic, the comparison between the Great Depression and the so-called "Great Recession" that has continued into 2011 is telling. Only four years in U.S. history produced negative savings rates: 1932, 1933, 2005, and 2006. Economists believe that during the early 1930s, this was in large part due to unusually high unemployment, but during the housing bubble that burst in 2008—when the cost of borrowing money was unusually cheap—Americans' spending on housing (and just about everything else) often went beyond what they could afford in the long term. Many economists attribute the negative savings rate to this false sense of wealth. As recession overwhelmed

the economy in 2008, the average savings rate began to rise to about 5 percent, but a close look reveals that much of that rate comes from more savings at the top of the income ladder, and very little of it from those below the top 10 percent.[4]

What does this mean for Americans trying to buy a home? For many low to moderate income families and individuals, it is becoming clear that the era of the affordable single-family detached dwelling is drawing to a close. In 2008, the poverty rate in the U.S. reached 13.2 percent overall, and 24.7 percent for African Americans. People who make less than 50 percent of the area median income (AMI) are considered very low income—and identified by most federal agencies as below the poverty line. Those making from 50 to 80 percent of the AMI are considered low income, and those making from 80 to 120 percent of the AMI are moderate income. Across the U.S., especially in urban centers, it is becoming increasingly difficult for individuals and families earning less than 100 percent of the AMI to purchase and own a detached home. The ability to save for a down payment has been severely affected as housing prices across the U.S. doubled between 2000 and 2007 while most household incomes stagnated or dropped.[5] Many who strive for the American dream of a modest single-family home with a yard and a white picket fence are forced to live in distant suburbs or rural areas, but recent research into suburban and rural poverty indicates that the lower housing costs in these areas are not always paired with an overall lower cost of living.[6]

In Charlottesville, home prices doubled

during that same seven-year period, and then leveled off and began to decline with the economic meltdown. Yet home prices remain considerably higher than they were ten years ago. Economically, Charlottesville is a relatively stable community, with the university playing a large role in this stability. In addition, over the last ten years, Charlottesville has been named in several magazine top ten lists of best places to live in the United States. The appeal of the community, and the quality of the health care available for a relatively small city, makes the area a magnet for both young people and retirees. These trends tend to inflate the cost of living in the city—including housing prices—compared to the surrounding counties. The cost of living is about 15 percent higher in Charlottesville than in the counties that make up the metropolitan area for census purposes. It is well known that many people who work in Charlottesville cannot afford to live there, and often find cheaper housing that requires a half-hour or forty-five-minute commute each way. Despite the economic strength of Charlottesville, the city ranks in the top five of Virginia cities with the highest percentage of people living in poverty—approximately 24 percent.[7] The statistics also reveal that a disproportionate number of those below the poverty line in Charlottesville are African Americans. For a city with a reputation for progressive politics and a stable economy, Charlottesville still faces many challenges when it comes to race relations, income equity, and availability of well-paid jobs—and all of these issues contribute to the housing affordability problem.

Making Housing Affordable

The most commonly used definition of affordable housing dictates that costs including rent or mortgage, insurance, utilities, and taxes total less than 30 percent of one's income. According to the Joint Center for Housing Studies, almost one in seven Americans are "severely housing cost-burdened," defined as those that are spending more than 50 percent of their income on housing costs.[8] Perhaps even more surprising is that a family with a single wage-earner receiving minimum wage cannot find an affordable two-bedroom apartment or house anywhere in the U.S. under this definition.

With lower or stagnant incomes, a low savings rate, and high home prices, it is easy to see why low and moderate income families find it increasingly difficult to enter the housing market. Over the years, Americans have tried various solutions to address this problem. The federal government provides assistance to make housing more affordable in two ways: tax benefits for homeownership available to all income levels, and budget outlays for funding affordable housing programs. Since the 1970s the amount for tax benefits has grown significantly, while the amount for housing programs has decreased. According to the National Low Income Housing Coalition, federal housing assistance money decreased 48 percent from 1976 to 2004, but tax benefit spending increased 260 percent in the same period—to the point that tax benefit spending is now four times that of affordable housing program funding.[9]

With the shift from affordable housing

spending to housing tax benefit spending, the availability of affordable housing units—both subsidized and unsubsidized—has been reduced considerably in many parts of the country. As overall federal funding declines, rental units convert to condominiums, and new urban infill homes drive up real estate values, housing affordability—especially in urban areas—decreases. A concerted effort to increase homeownership, combined with low interest rates, resulted in some improvement in the rate of homeownership among low and moderate income Americans in the 1990s, but the subprime mortgage crisis of '00s has exacerbated the affordability problem. The homeownership rate had reached its highest level—69.1 percent—in 2005, but fell to 67.8 percent by 2008, the sharpest decline in twenty years, while the accompanying drop

in renter households has reversed itself and jumped significantly since 2005.[10]

Racial bias played a part in the subprime crisis and the resulting foreclosures, and sadly Charlottesville leads among all metropolitan areas in the nation in this regard. According to the National Community Reinvestment Coalition, African Americans in Charlottesville were far more likely than whites to be offered subprime/high-cost loans. In Charlottesville, for example, African Americans are four times more likely to end up with a high-cost loan than Caucasian borrowers—and apparently this difference is not connected to the borrower's income level or credit rating.[11]

According to Piedmont Housing Alliance, the affordable housing partner for ecoMOD1 and 3, there has been a 175 percent increase in housing affordability problems for low income people in Charlottesville in recent years, and this problem will likely continue across the U.S. for the foreseeable future.

Contemporary affordable housing can be created and financed in a variety of ways. Affordable housing organizations combine federal, state, and local funding with grants and donations to develop housing that is offered for sale or rent with restrictions on the segment of the population who qualifies. Low income individuals and families that purchase housing from these organizations typically face restrictions when it comes to the sale of their homes to ensure the housing units stay in the affordable housing market for as long as possible. Affordable housing organizations sometimes partner with market-rate developers to finance and manage the affordable housing units in a mixed-income development. These relationships often come about when a local government has required a minimum number of affordable housing units—either as a zoning regulation, or as an incentive program allowing developers to create more housing units overall. Local governments also use federal, state, and local funding on housing—typically in the form of public housing projects that sometimes receive partial funding from grants or donations. Most Americans are familiar with multi-family rental public housing projects funded in part by the Housing Choice Voucher Program—commonly known as Section 8. Typically Section 8 funding is used to subsidize rental costs for low income people—covering housing costs that exceed 30 percent of their income. Projects with Section 8 funding often have long waiting lists.

One creative solution that has recently emerged is the National Housing Trust Fund (NHTF), established in 2008 by the federal government. Intended to be similar to the Highway Trust Fund, the NHTF is supposed to be protected from the whims of lawmakers, with the money set aside from the rest of the federal budget for the exclusive purpose of building and rehabilitating affordable housing. The initial funding strategy was dependent on fees from mortgages owned by Freddie Mac and Fannie Mae, before the two organizations were put under conservatorship by the federal government. As of this writing, the fate of NHTF remains unclear, and Congress has not provided adequate funding. Yet one idea that has emerged from the congressional debate is the possibility of linking NHTF financing for specific housing projects to the use of energy-efficient design strategies and technologies. If enacted, this linkage would go a long way toward helping low income people occupy well-designed housing that uses substantially less energy than standard housing. This is especially important because for these individuals and families, a utility bill is a much higher percentage of their monthly income than for wealthier Americans.

In the last decade, as the general public has become more familiar with the ideas behind sustainable design, some affordable housing organizations and public housing authorities have begun to consider these issues in the design of renovated and newly built affordable housing. Grant funding is slowly becoming available to integrate sustainable design strategies and technologies for affordable housing—although it is not widely utilized yet. The linkage of sustainability and afford-ability could benefit both homeowners and the environment.

The Future of Affordable Housing?

The design of affordable housing is an im-portant public responsibility, and as such, it ought to be done with great care and clarity of purpose. Affordable housing in the U.S. today often means poor quality construction, char-acterized by short-term thinking that leads to the selection of cheap materials, which are then put together in such a way as to achieve the absolute minimum standards of comfort. With little thought given to the lifespan of the building or to energy efficiency, the worst of these poorly constructed housing units tend to decrease in value over time. In some urban areas, the land they are constructed on is more valuable than the buildings, making them ripe for gentrification. They also have unnecessar-ily high utility costs and ultimately produce an enormous amount of material waste. Many of these units appear to have been optimized for a ten- or twenty-year lifespan.

However, by the year 2030 (which aligns with Ed Mazria's 2030 Challenge referenced earlier) over half of the buildings that will exist in the U.S. will have been built since 2000—and another large segment will have been significantly renovated. A substantial percentage of these buildings—over 100 billion square feet—will be residential.[12] This means we have the opportunity to rebuild housing in America, and create homes that are sustainable and affordable for all income levels. Current research suggests that with as little as 4 to 5 percent in additional first costs for construction, homeowners can see a sub-stantial reduction in operating cycle costs over time. One study on occupied green affordable housing units documents that with no more than 5 percent more in first costs, it is possible to create buildings that use 30 to 50 percent less energy, and 10 to 20 percent less water—with healthier indoor air and more durable, easier to maintain buildings and landscapes.[13]

The strategies and technologies already exist to create this next generation of hous-ing—we simply need to make sure designers and builders understand them and use them appropriately. In addition, we need to remem-ber that doing a renovation on a building is an even lower impact way of responding to the environmental and social crisis we face.

Notes
1. Emmanuel Saez and Thomas Piketty, "Striking It Richer: The Evolution of Top Incomes in the United States," Pathways, Winter 2008, 6–7.
2. Ibid.
3. "U.S. Savings Rate Sinks to Lowest Rate Since Great Depression," New York Times, February 1, 2007, business section.
4. Andrew Kaplan, "The Savings Rate Has Recov-ered . . . If You Ignore the Bottom 99 percent," Naked Capitalism (blog), August 31, 2009, http://www.nakedcapitalism.com/2009/08/guest-post-the-savings-rate-has-recoveredif-you-ignore-the-bottom-99.html.
5. National Low Income Housing Coalition, "Out of Reach 2009," www.nlihc.org/oor/oor2009/.
6. Alan Berube and Elizabeth Kneebone, "Two Steps Back: City and Suburban Poverty Trends 1999–2005" (Washington DC: Brookings Insti-tute), 2006.
7. U.S. Census Bureau, "State and County Quick-

Facts: Charlottesville, Virginia," quickfacts
.census.gov/qfd/states/51/51540.html.

8. Harvard University Joint Center for Housing
Studies, *The State of the Nation's Housing 2010*,
38, www.jchs.harvard.edu.

9. Cushing N. Dolbeare and Sheila Crowley,
"Changing Priorities: The Federal Budget and
Housing Assistance, 1976–2007" (National Low
Income Housing Coalition).

10. Harvard University Joint Center for Housing
Studies, *The State of the Nation's Housing 2010*,
25, www.jchs.harvard.edu.

11. National Community Reinvestment Coalition,
*Income Is No Shield against Racial Differences in
Lending: A Comparison of High Cost Lending in
America's Metropolitan Areas,* 2007, http://www
.ncrc.org/images/stories/mediaCenter_reports/
ncrc%20metro%20study%20race%20and%20
income%20disparity%20july%2007.pdf.

12. Architecture 2030, http://architecture2030.org/
the_problem/problem_energy.

13. New Ecology Inc., eds., *The Costs and Benefits of
Green Affordable Housing* (Boston: New Ecology
Inc., 2006), 57.

Additional References

Agyeman, Julian. *Sustainable Communities and the
Challenge of Environmental Justice.* New York:
NYU Press, 2005.

Global Green USA, eds. *Blueprint for Greening
Affordable Housing.* Washington, DC: Island
Press, 2007.

Habitat for Humanity of Greater Charlottesville.
http://cvillehabitat.org/.

Habitat for Humanity International. http://www
.habitat.org.

Morrish, William R., Suzanne Schindler, and Katie
Swenson. *Growing Urban Habitats: Seeking a
New Housing Development Model.* San Francisco:
William Stout Books, 2009.

Piedmont Housing Alliance. http://www.piedmont
housingalliance.org/.

U.S. Census Bureau. www.census.gov.

Wright, Gwendolyn. *Building the Dream: A Social
History of Housing in America.* Cambridge: MIT
Press, 1981.

PREFABRICATION

Prefab in History

Prefabricated construction involves the transportation of building parts manufactured in a factory to a site where they can be assembled into a finished building. The strategy can be deployed at various scales—from components or subassemblies such as trusses and roof or wall panels, to larger volumes of occupiable space known as modules. Although many consider the prefabrication of buildings to be a post–World War II and uniquely American phenomenon, it has roots much earlier in American, European, and Asian cultures. Western histories of prefab architecture begin with early European and American examples—notably the panelized fishing sheds sent to the early English settlement in Cape Ann, Massachusetts, in 1624. The next point on the usual timeline is the impact of the industrial revolution on construction, with industrialized materials lending themselves to prefabricated buildings. Indeed the development of cast iron, structural steel, and larger sheets of glass significantly expanded the range of available building materials and required designers to carefully coordinate the dimensions of their buildings. These elements were manufactured off-site, and had to precisely come together on-site during the assembly process. The use of these materials was limited to industrial and institutional buildings until the twentieth century. Many historians also reference the kit homes and temporary structures sent to California during the Gold Rush of the mid-nineteenth century, and by the British military to remote parts of the Commonwealth in the eighteenth and nineteenth centuries. From there, the story jumps to the popular precut kit homes sold by Sears

Roebuck in the early twentieth century. In the period just before and soon after World War II, the U.S. government invested time and money into expanding delivery methods for housing—leading to the precursors of today's panelized and modular housing industry. Similar efforts were happening in European countries—Britain, France, and Germany—and also in Japan.

In fact, the oldest and most sophisticated tradition of prefabrication comes from Japan. As early as the fifteenth century the Japanese produced examples of buildings that used standardized joinery and a proportional system. These innovations were encouraged by the development of new timesaving tools and greater control (regional and sometimes centralized) of master carpenters than in most countries at that time. By the seventeenth century, these innovations had evolved enough to allow carpenters to precut timber framing in their workshops and assemble the pieces on site. These framing systems included precut columns, beams, purlins, and other framing members prepared to be joined without fasteners. The selection of the length and depth of the structural members was dependent upon the number of tatami mats in a space, the social status of the client, and the function of the room. This systemized approach was like a kit of parts with a palette consisting of timber framing members, tatami mats, and screens—both translucent (shoji) and opaque (fusuma)—available for purchase from specialized fabricators. While some regional differences remained, the standards were controlled by the government in an effort to ensure that the orderly development of build-

ings would align with the social cohesiveness of Japanese society. Yet the system was flexible enough that there were endless variations that could be adapted to the site or the preferences of the client. Some of the finest examples of the Sukiya style, such as the Katsura Detached Palace, used these strategies to great effect. Some of the methods may have been prefab, but what is more important is the quality of the experience of inhabiting the space. Katsura is a masterpiece that impressively blends the inside and outside, making for a simultaneously poetic and practical architecture.

Prefabrication in the contemporary Japanese housing industry is well accepted and fully integrated. Methods of prefabrication range widely from subassemblies to full-scale modules, but off-site construction is now commonplace. Japanese housing clients often upgrade and renew their housing units in much the same way one buys a new car. The American attachment to older domestic buildings is far less common in Japan, and many replaced materials are recycled during this "renewal" phase.

It is no coincidence that two of the most important twentieth-century Western architects—both of whom were interested in a systems approach to prefabricated components—spent considerable time in Japan. Walter Gropius and Frank Lloyd Wright are responsible for some of the most innovative architectural thinking related to industrialized and prefabricated housing in the last century. Wright never formally acknowledged the direct influence that Japanese architecture had on his work, but architects and architectural historians often argue that his early prairie style homes, as well as the later work (including his masterpiece Fallingwater), were deeply influenced by traditional Japanese architecture. Wright's interest in systems thinking coalesced in his Usonian house designs, even if the houses themselves were site-built with only selected prefab elements. His vision of affordable homes made from interchangeable components with endless permutations has a direct correspondence to Japanese carpentry and the tatami-based proportional system.

Gropius, on the other hand, was more open about his debt to Japan—going so far as to write the forward to Japanese architect Kenzo Tange's book about Katsura in the early 1960s. Gropius's interest in industrialized housing dates to before his founding of the Bauhaus in 1919, and continued throughout his long career in the United States. He worked individually and collaboratively on component-based, panelized, and modular housing strategies— for both private clients and large corporations. Many of the ideas he developed in his writing and his prototypical buildings, including the Packaged House and the Copper Houses, still influence contemporary designers today.

Buckminster Fuller and Jean Prouvé, contemporaries of Wright and Gropius, were also fascinated with industrialized construction and the opportunities it presented for residential architecture. Fuller's visionary work included a heavy dose of what would be called sustainability today. His Dymaxion prototypes were heated and cooled using passive ventilation, and in concept they were "self-powered." Prouvé created efficient and elegant structural frames, as well as innovative industrialized exterior cladding systems that were carefully proportioned. Prouvé and Fuller both worked closely with industry to test their ideas, and while neither had commercial success with prefab housing, both were able to see some of their other design and engineering ideas come to fruition—Prouvé with furniture and cladding systems, Fuller with innovative structural systems like his geodesic dome. Yet the world of prefabricated home building these innovators imagined is quite different from today's reality.

Prefab Today

The current prefab housing industry is broken into four major categories:

MANUFACTURED HOUSING Commonly referred to as trailers, manufactured homes must comply with a federal building code known as the HUD code, which is less restrictive than normal building codes on several important issues including energy performance. Manufactured homes are inevitably detached, and are the cheapest entry into the housing market. They are also the lowest quality option since they typically have been built with the cheapest materials available. Assembled on a permanent chassis and towed or craned into place, manufactured houses are often difficult to finance since they are considered temporary structures and therefore tend to depreciate in value.

KIT HOMES Like the old Sears Roebuck homes, these are complete kits including precut pieces, necessary fasteners, and other elements that are assembled entirely on-site.

The most common version found today are log homes.

PANELIZED ROOF AND WALL SYSTEMS An increasingly common form of panelized construction is structural insulated panels (SIPs) —a panel of insulation sandwiched between two layers of a sheet good such as plywood or oriented strand board. While more expensive than standard wood stud construction, SIPs save considerable time and money in labor, and offer significant thermal performance benefits. However, the remainder of the construction work still needs to be done on-site.

MODULAR HOUSING Room-sized volumes of space are fabricated in a factory, including most of the interior and exterior finish work. Rather than being transported on an integrated chassis like a manufactured house, modules are transported on a separate trailer and craned onto a permanent foundation. These homes tend to be indistinguishable from conventional site-built homes and

80 to 90 percent of the work is completed off-site.

In contrast with manufactured housing, the other three—kit homes, panelized homes, and modular homes—must comply with the appropriate code of the local jurisdiction. While this requires regional manufacturers to devise creative ways to track the correct code requirements for a given home going down their assembly line, many states and municipalities in the United States have recently adopted or are about to adopt the International Residential Code. In addition, unlike manufactured houses, panelized, modular, and kit homes are considered permanent construction, and do not face financing problems—and therefore appreciate in value in the same way as a site-built house.

Many laypeople do not recognize the difference between manufactured homes and better quality modular or panelized prefab homes. Research funded by HUD reveals that most Americans still consider prefab housing to be lower quality—largely based upon their perception of manufactured housing. Given this prevailing assumption, it's not surprising that modular manufacturers don't market their prefab homes any differently from site-built homes built with wood studs. In fact, most modular homes look very similar to conventional site-built homes. Some of the owners of those models may not even know about the prefab nature of the construction.

Construction costs for prefabricated housing is typically lower than on-site construction, and there has been a trend towards prefab—although the entire housing market is still recovering from the recent recession. Homeowners are typically restricted to placing their prefab house on a suburban site, where land is cheaper. In addition to cost considerations, most manufactured and modular houses are designed for the orientation of wider suburban lots. No major manufactured home company offers models designed for narrower but deeper urban lots with the entry side facing the street. The typical singlewide module for these homes measures 12' to 14' wide by 48' long—a size difficult to transport into many tight urban areas. As a result, families in the affordable housing market are being pushed to the periphery of the city, where they have the added financial burden of being fully dependent on a car.

Modular and panelized construction techniques have the potential to significantly reduce the environmental impact of the housing industry—although much of that promise is unrealized among prefab homebuilders in the United States today. Centralized within a climate-controlled facility, prefabricated residential construction offers material and transportation efficiencies, as well as opportunities for stricter quality control. Although several U.S. companies have developed EnergyStar-rated models (a program organized by the U.S. Environmental Protection Agency to encourage energy efficiency), and some sell quality homes superior to conventional stick-built (that is, wood stud) construction, few are seriously looking at or reconsidering the environmental impact of the methods or materials they employ.

From a design viewpoint, very few manufacturers offer quality contemporary design—despite the popularity of modern prefab homes in *Dwell* and other mainstream media outlets. The vast majority of conventional modular companies offer standardized designs with open interiors, and exterior skins composed of elements borrowed from late nineteenth- and early twentieth-century home styles. Among the most surprising trends in conventional prefab housing is its recent growth in the upper end of the market. While the public perception remains that prefabricated homes are an inferior product and only appropriate for the least affluent, conventional upscale builders (mostly those pursuing neo-traditional design) are also recognizing the financial and logistical advantages of centralized fabrication. Large McMansions often appear in the portfolios of modular manufacturers.

Contemporary designers and practitioners such as Kieran Timberlake Architects, Marmol Radziner, Michelle Kaufmann, Charlie Lazor, and Resolution 4 Architecture, to name a few, are leading an interesting reexamination of contemporary prefabricated residential design. Their designs make for compelling architecture, at a good value when compared to an architect-designed home constructed by a custom homebuilder. Although no one has gone into true mass production with a house design yet, orders for Resolution 4 Architecture's *Dwell* house and Kaufmann's Glidehouse already exceed those for any Buckminster Fuller or Jean Prouvé design in their own day.

Many of these and other contemporary prefab designs make reference to green strategies and features, but few of them take on sustainability with any degree of rigor. The

Kieran Timberlake and Ray Kappe homes offered by Steve Glenn's company Living Homes in Santa Monica, California, and some of Michelle Kaufmann's higher performance options available through MK Designs in Oakland, California, are exceptions to this rule. Unfortunately, the modern prefab designs currently available are financially beyond the reach of low to moderately low income families.

Migration from On-Site to Off-Site Construction

Major homebuilders can increase their profits by reducing waste and keeping their construction processes as consistent and predictable as possible. Prefab offers a more predictable process and product, with the potential of greater control over quality, schedule, and price. Unlike the companies offering modern modular designs, conventional manufacturers seldom emphasize the prefab nature of the construction—they just see their process as good business. Common examples include the use of prefab roof truss systems and pre-framed stud wall panels.

Some major homebuilders, such as Pulte and Toll Brothers, are testing the waters of a more aggressive move into prefab. They are experimenting with fully panelized and component-based homes and even modular construction, imagining a future in which more American homes will be prefabricated. In 2003, Pulte began an experiment with panelized construction with an emphasis on sustainability in their northern Virginia market, opening a prefab plant in Manassas

called Pulte Home Science (PHS), where they fabricated structural insulated wall panels, roof trusses, floor decks, and precast foundation systems. They were able to "dry-in" a home (complete the exterior skin with components brought to the site, so interior work can begin) in a fraction of the time it takes to build one on-site, and their PHS homes briefly accounted for roughly 20 percent of their single family home market in the region. Yet the benefits of these investments were not improving the bottom line. Hit by the housing market downturn in 2006, the facility was operating at a fraction of its potential capacity by 2007, when it closed. Pulte reports homeowners consistently praised the products, but the cost of keeping the plant open would require an increase in the price of the homes—something they did not want to consider. Beyond the housing market, another possible explanation for the closure of PHS is the compatibility difficulties of blending an on-site home building company with an off-site one. The natures of the two businesses are quite distinct—beyond the operational difference, the opportunities for making a profit are also different. Toll Brothers seems to be having better success, perhaps because it has moved more toward modular construction, which is more radically different from on-site wood stud construction and offers more opportunities for controlling the process.

What Is Prefab Anymore?

As more and more prefabricated building elements and assemblies become commercially available—whether by special order or on the shelves of home improvement stores—the definition of prefab is shifting. What was once considered exotic prefabrication has now become standard construction. Today, precut steel frame buildings arrive on-site to be assembled like a Tinkertoy set. When the same technology was used for industrial and institutional buildings in the nineteenth century, or for the mid-twentieth-century Case Study Homes, it was considered the very cutting edge of prefabricated construction. Steel offers many advantages—such as greater capability to span long distances and a thinner profile to reinforce the modern aesthetic of minimal material. What it doesn't offer is flexibility onsite. Structural steel framing is very hard to adapt with common tools, which is one of the main reasons steel is avoided by conventional homebuilders to this day. Yet steel framing is ubiquitous in commercial, institutional, and retail buildings, and no one really thinks of it as prefab anymore—it is just how things get built.

In conventional home building, techniques have continuously evolved to the point that large sections of what we think of as site-built homes arrive at the site preassembled. Only 150 years ago, it was practically unheard of in the U.S. to order pre-milled trim, standard cabinetry, or fabricated windows and doors already set into frames, but now these elements are commonly purchased from suppliers and are only handcrafted on-site for very high-end custom homes. Many homebuilders no longer bother to build their own roof trusses, ordering them instead from the local truss framing shop and having them shipped to the site—saving themselves and the client

time and money. In fact, it's a reasonable assumption that only a very small percentage of new homes in the U.S. today, even expensive custom ones, are built without any major element that has been prefabricated in a factory. It just doesn't make financial sense to individually handcraft every door, window, stair banister, cabinet, and structural member. Fabricators have researched and designed products that comply with building code requirements, and they offer warranties. Most homebuilders don't have the expertise to efficiently fabricate a high-performance custom window—especially when they can have one made to size, and even return it for a replacement or a refund if there's a problem. Why would a builder want to calculate the structural capacity of a roof truss system, when the local fabricator can use their engineering software to calculate it for them, and deliver the prefab trusses within a couple of days? Most custom homebuilders instead choose to limit the truly "handcrafted" elements of their homes to the pieces the client will notice—fine carpentry in an important interior space, or unique interior finishes— and many of these specialty items are completed by subcontractors.

With the exception of very small companies with one or two employees that do one house at a time, most homebuilders have become construction managers—coordinating the efforts of employees and subcontractors to assemble prefab elements and materials on-site. It is an essential skill in our society, but it is not the romantic notion of the individual carpenter with his or her hammer and saw that many Americans imagine. The builder's "factory" is the job site, and the assembly line is the vehicle that delivers the materials and prefab elements. The employees move back and forth between these temporary "factories." In fact good builders will try to carefully organize their various projects so they can move the mason, the framer, the sheetrock hanger, the tile subcontractor, and the painter through their various construction sites in a logical sequence. Some subcontractors will make deals with contractors if they keep them busy all the time: from their point of view, it is much easier to work for one or two good contractors than to try to balance the schedules and personalities of six.

Large homebuilding companies working on substantial new developments operate in a similar way: they simply move their subcontractors or employees in sequence through the development, and keep them busy for months at a time. The proximity of so many homes to each other on one site offers potential efficiencies when it comes to construction material procurement, waste, and recycling. Theoretically there should be less waste for these companies when they can simply use the remaining lumber from the home next door, but in reality this is seldom the case. Without a clearly laid out waste management plan, and a senior person empowered to implement it, multi-unit development sites are typically significant sources of unsorted construction waste that ends up in dumpsters, and ultimately in landfills. Workers take advantage of the anonymity of these job sites with dozens of pick-up trucks driving between homes in various stages of construction. It's easy to toss empty five gallon buckets of joint compound

into a dumpster meant for wood scraps if there's no one around to police it. Yet there is still the inherent efficiency of having employees and subcontractors report to the same site for several months—so they can be directed to the next home in the sequence at any point, without having to drive to the other side of town.

Understood in this way, such building projects can be easily imagined making the leap to off-site construction for the larger elements of a home—including modules. Modular companies work in a similar way to their on-site homebuilding competitors, except they typically don't deal with site related concerns such as foundation, landscaping, and utilities. They coordinate employees (and sometimes subcontractors) and efficiently procure materials—but all under one large roof, in a climate-controlled situation. This offers financial and environmental benefits— although most modular companies do not typically consider the latter. American home building will likely continue to migrate toward prefabrication and eventually the cultural connotations associated with the word *prefab*— both positive and negative—will drop away. Prefab will simply become the way we build most homes and additions.

Where Do We Go from Here?

The full potential of prefabricated construction in the housing industry, whether at the scale of wall panels, room-sized modules or structural components, is still to be discovered. Prefabricated homes, when designed appropriately, can help reduce both construction costs and utility bills. In fact, this has always been presented as the promise of prefab housing. So why have the many compelling and architecturally significant prefab house designs from the last one hundred years not lived up to this potential? Why are the Case Study homes in California now high-end housing? Why did Buckminster Fuller and Jean Prouvé never get beyond a few exquisite prototypes? Why are the many beautifully designed prefab homes that have appeared in *Dwell* beyond the means of those in the bottom half of the income scale? Why aren't we living in neighborhoods of prefab Frank Lloyd Wright Usonian homes, rather than the ranchburgers and McMansions that dominate the suburban landscape today?

The answer is twofold: first, the economic model of these visionary projects typically depended upon the assumption that once the brilliance of the designer's idea was recognized, the project would go into production, and significant savings would result. These projects often depended too much on the potential cost efficiency of the production phase and not enough on controlling hard costs in the prototype. If it costs 200 percent more to build a prototype, it is unlikely the production versions can come in below the cost of a comparable site-built home. The financial efficiencies of modular construction will typically save between 10 and 25 percent in building costs compared to on-site construction.

Second, many prototypical designs are dependent upon the assumption that the industrialized housing industry in the U.S. will radically transform itself. Transformation

is indeed possible, and to some degree it is happening already. In the U.S., 63 percent of new housing sales are already substantially panelized, manufactured housing (trailers), or modular.[1] However, housing in America will not transform overnight, and designs that are dependent upon a complete rethinking of the materials and the standard labor practices used today are more likely to remain marginal. Home building is a conservative industry, based on a clear profit motive. Most on-site builders and prefab manufacturers see little benefit in changing materials or construction methods if it requires them to retrain their employees, or face the challenges of sourcing or using an unfamiliar material. Alternative construction strategies are usually more expensive—even if the new idea takes less time or utilizes fewer or less expensive materials. If a contractor hasn't done it before, you can almost always be assured they will charge more for it to cover themselves—no matter what the actual cost is. This is not to say that changes can't be made, but it does mean that the onus is on the designer to make sure the changes are worth the effort and money.

One such change is the possibility of combining panelized and modular construction, a strategy employed in ecoMOD1 and 3. By balancing the project's social and environmental aspirations with practical knowledge about materials and the nature of prefabrication, ecoMOD is striving to find the best scale of operation. Modular plants are optimized for standard wood frame construction. It is even more difficult for a modular builder to convert to SIPs or other forms of panelized construction than it is for a conventional builder, because modular homes are built from the inside out. By framing the wall and installing the drywall prior to installing the electrical wiring and plumbing, it is possible to "mud" and paint the drywall while the plumbing and electrical infrastructure is installed as the home moves down the assembly line. The drying time required for the joint compound and paint is the one serious schedule interruption modular manufacturers face. Their goal is to move as many homes down the line as possible in a week, and if the installation of plumbing or wiring delays the application of joint compound, it hurts the bottom line. In addition, if panels arrive pre-wired and pre-plumbed, it would certainly save time installing drywall, but the joint compound still needs to dry. The overlap between drying time and the installation of plumbing and electrical is something most manufacturers find convenient.

Several ecoMOD teams chose to break the convention of wood-frame construction because the combination of superinsulated panels and modular construction offered the opportunity for the least environmental impact (during both manufacturing and operation) and the lowest operating costs for the homeowners. Given the modular industry's experience coming up with innovative ways to save time and money, it seems likely that a smart prefab specialist will figure out how to integrate panels into a plant without losing time. One example of the industry's creativity is the relatively recent innovation used by several builders that simplifies the ceiling drywall process. Using a gantry crane to lower a home's roof structure onto a table

with oversize drywall on it, workers attach the drywall to the framing with structural foam rather than conventional fasteners. When the foam has fully cured, the roof assembly is lifted again on to the house. By using oversized sheets and no fasteners from below, the "mud and tape" process is greatly simplified, and workers don't have to install drywall sheets from below while standing on ladders.

For now, panels cost a plant more than the material and labor cost of roof and wall framing—especially if a different manufacturer supplies the panels. This cost would have to be passed on to the homeowner, and not all homeowners would necessarily want to absorb it even though the performance of superinsulated walls would allow the upgrade to quickly pay for itself.

The assumed reduction of environmental impact from combining panelized and modular construction is a theory. There is no way to prove it at this point, since no major manufacturers combine the two. One company that does—a moderate-sized manufacturer in northern California—started using panels for some homes in 2008. With ecoMOD's evaluation process the project's engineering team is testing the theory that operating costs are actually being reduced. They are monitoring the occupied homes and comparing their performance to simulations and standard assumptions. So far, the theory is supported well, but evaluating the reduced environmental impact of the manufacturing process will require more long-term research. One goal of the ecoMOD project is to convince a modular manufacturer or affordable housing organization to allow the team to test four versions of the same ecoMOD design—one wood-frame site-built (stick-built), one panelized site-built, one wood-frame modular, and one that combines panelized and modular. The site-built panelized and the modular panelized would obviously outperform the others in terms of energy efficiency (assuming conventional insulation in the frame homes), but the embodied energy and material waste for the combined modular panelized home may be the lowest—followed by the wood-frame modular. Although modular homes have more lumber in them to ensure they can resist the forces exerted on them during transportation and delivery—driving on highways at high speeds and being craned into place—modular plants do not waste a single piece of lumber. Scraps of all sizes are collected and used until the smallest trimming is left. With centralized, climate-controlled fabrication, workers are going to the same place everyday, and finishing 80 to 90 percent of a home in four to five days instead of four or five months.

In fact, it is this condensed schedule that appears to create the most significant reduction of overall environmental impact. The author is collaborating with life cycle analysis and modular construction experts on a study to compare the environmental impact of on-site and off-site construction. The results are clear in the residential sector of the industry: the overall impact of off-site construction is substantially lower, largely due to the relatively small footprint of factory workers commuting during a single work week versus subcontractors commuting to a building site for several months. The study does not take into account the operational differences associated with various construction assemblies and types of insulation.

Note

1. "About the Industry," *Automated Builder,* http://www.automatedbuilder.com/industry.htm.

Additional References

Bergdoll, Berry, and Peter Christensen. *Home Delivery: Fabricating the Modern Dwelling.* Basel: Birkhauser, 2008.

Birkbeck, David, and Andrew Scoones. *Prefabulous Homes: The New Housebuilding Agenda.* London: The Building Centre Trust, 2005.

Davies, Colin. *The Prefabricated Home.* London: Reaktion Books, 2005.

Engel, Heinrich, *The Japanese House: A Tradition for Contemporary Architecture.* Tokyo: Charles E. Tuttle, 1964.

Inaba, Kazuya, and Shigenobu Nakayama. *Japanese Homes and Lifestyles: An Illustrated Journey through History.* Translated by John Bester. Tokyo: Kodansha International, 1983.

Kieran, Stephen, and James Timberlake. *Refabricating Architecture: How Manufacturing Methodologies Are Poised to Transform Building Construction.* New York: McGraw-Hill, 2003.

Morse, Edward, *Japanese Homes and Their Surroundings.* London: Ticknor and Company, 1885.

HANDS-ON EDUCATION

The function of education is to teach one to think intensively and to think
critically. . . . Intelligence plus character—that is the goal of true education.
—Martin Luther King, Jr.

The Case for Real Buildings with Real Budgets

The history of hands-on university educational initiatives goes back
to the nineteenth century and the creation of the university extension
movement—whereby college students worked closely with their communities to improve the quality of local life. These early efforts began
at land grant institutions, and were mostly focused on instruction about
agriculture. The first federal money for these efforts was issued in 1887
as part of the Hatch Experiment Station Act to support agricultural
education outreach efforts. The concept took on many forms at universities, and in the early twentieth century some universities took the
idea in a different direction—cooperative education programs, giving
students direct employment opportunities within the context of their
education. The co-op movement was not inherently linked to serving a
community, but instead focused on integrating professional experience
into a university education. Many of those early co-op programs were
associated with engineering and architecture programs.

In the late nineteenth and early twentieth century, philosophers and
education reformers William James and John Dewey delineated the intellectual underpinnings of what Dewey called "experiential education"—
the idea that education cannot focus exclusively on universal truths,
but must be based in real world experience. After the Russo-Japanese

War and during the buildup to World War I, James proposed a nonmilitary form of national service—"a conscription of the whole youthful population"—an idea that eventually took shape in the CCC and WPA efforts during the Great Depression, and more recently in the Peace Corps and Americorps programs.[1] At universities, the extension and co-op program concepts evolved during the 1960s. In 1966, the term "service learning" was first used in the context of a Tennessee Valley Authority–funded program to bring faculty and students at universities associated with the Oak Ridge National Laboratory to work directly with local development organizations. The term is now broadly used and accepted at universities across the country, and is typically defined as education activities that include a component of direct engagement with a community with two key desired outcomes: useful service to a community organization and a life-long commitment to civic engagement among participating students.

Architectural educators have not always embraced this concept. On some level, one could argue that an iterative design process is inherently experiential. Yet the direct application of that process to the creation of actual buildings has been controversial at various points in the history of architectural education. There is a lingering and legitimate concern that hands-on projects introduce pragmatic issues before design students have the opportunity to develop abstract thinking —their ability to temporarily distance themselves from literal buildings and imagine forms or ideas that have not yet been created.

While this is a real concern, it seems more of a potential problem for early design students, who sometimes find it difficult to remove themselves from the normative and put themselves into a more open frame of mind.

The architecture discipline's commitment to community service also has an inconsistent history, and service learning in architecture has only reemerged as an important issue in the past ten years. Today, a commitment to outreach projects that directly impact underserved communities is a mainstay of architecture firms and architecture schools alike. Many of the more interesting initiatives from architectural practice and academia have been collected in the books *Design Like You Give a Damn,* edited by Architecture for Humanity, and Bryan Bell's *Good Deeds, Good Design: Community Service Through Architecture* and *Expanding Architecture: Design as Activism,* the latter of which includes the ecoMOD project.

When addressing the increasingly important topics of sustainability and social justice, the case for a real-world project, compared with traditional classroom learning, is a simple one: the next generation of building industry professionals is best served by projects that involve real buildings with real budgets because these are the situations they will face as professionals. By offering our more advanced students an opportunity to test-drive their design ideas and collaborate with other emerging professionals, we can give these students the opportunity to benefit from the nonthreatening feedback loop of academia and to more carefully hone their critical thinking skills. In the abstract world of a normal design studio or a standard engineering course, a professor will emphasize principles and have students try different strategies. Yet as students gain confidence in their newly found skills, it is helpful for them to test design ideas with an actual building site, a client, a deadline, a budget, and most importantly with the shared knowledge of collaborators in related disciplines. By going beyond building design to take on a construction budget and a schedule—and ultimately the assemblage of construction materials into a building—students find the challenges of making difficult decisions more clearly brought to the forefront. The most successful students in these situations are not the ones who simply display their design skills, but the ones who also learn how to reflect on the design process as it is happening and strategize for the success of the design team.

Creative versus Critical Thinking

Most architecture, engineering, and landscape architecture students tend to excel at creative thinking—which is one of the reasons they are drawn to their chosen professions. The ability to imagine new ideas, technologies, and forms is an essential skill in these disciplines. Yet we should not take the alignment of creativity with well-developed critical thinking skills for granted. The important ability to use both intuition and reflective (or critical) thinking in a design is not always emphasized in the design or engineering curriculum.

Critical thinking, in this sense, is best defined by a consensus document on the topic put out by the American Philosophical Association:

> We understand critical thinking to be purposeful, self-regulatory judgment which results in interpretation, analysis, evaluation, and inference, as well as explanation of the evidential, conceptual, methodological, criteriological, or contextual considerations upon which that judgment is based.
>
> CT (critical thinking) is essential as a tool of inquiry. As such, CT is a liberating force in education and a powerful resource in one's personal and civic life. While not synonymous with good thinking, CT is a pervasive and self-rectifying human phenomenon.
>
> The ideal critical thinker is habitually inquisitive, well-informed, trustful of reason, open-minded, flexible, fair-minded in evaluation, honest in facing personal biases, prudent in making judgments, willing to reconsider, clear about issues, orderly in complex matters, diligent in seeking relevant information, reasonable in the selection of criteria, focused in inquiry, and persistent in seeking results which are as precise as the subject and the circumstances of inquiry permit. Thus, educating good critical thinkers means working toward this ideal. It combines developing CT skills with nurturing those dispositions which consistently yield useful insights and which are the basis of a rational and democratic society.[2]

Opportunities to use critical thinking abound in service learning projects, which are particularly well suited to giving students a chance to expand their thought processes and hone their ability to rigorously sort through complex material. One such example for the ecoMOD project is the selection of building materials and products. In this era of constant marketing of the green benefits of various products and services, it is essential for the next generation of building industry professionals to develop the ability to collaborate and analyze a plethora of information critically. Open any architectural magazine or building material website and you'll see dozens of articles and advertisements emphasizing the environmental benefits of products that weren't described as "green" only five years ago. While there are a significant number of new or newly formulated products that have a reduced environmental impact compared to their conventional alternatives, some of these heavily promoted materials haven't changed in the slightest. What has changed is the culture of design. Both inside and outside the profession, the recognition of the importance of sustainability is now widespread. To get beyond the "greenwashing" of sustainable strategies and building materials, the process of sorting out the options must be approached with careful critical thinking.

Extending the Tradition of Design/Build

Real-world design/build projects have long been a part of architectural education, but in the last five years the numbers have expanded significantly. The majority of accredited graduate programs in architecture now offer some form of design/build in their curriculum—ranging from art installations on the campus of their university to small public buildings. Prime examples include the Rural Studio, started by the late Samuel Mockbee

at Auburn University, and Yale's long-standing Building Project, run by a rotating group of design faculty. Both are important in the way they address the concerns of an underserved community while maintaining a design agenda embedded in contemporary architectural explorations. The ecoMOD project has benefited greatly from an understanding of programs at other universities whose projects overlap in some aspects with ecoMOD. These include Steve Badanes at the University of Washington; Steven Moore, Michael Garrison, Elizabeth Alford, and Louise Harpman at the University of Texas at Austin; Andrew Freear, David Hinson, and others at Auburn University; Sergio Palleroni of Portland State University; and Pliny Fisk at Texas A&M. Other terrific examples of design/build are happening at the University of Arkansas, the Catholic University of America, the University of Kansas, and the University of Utah.

In the ways that other design/build projects challenge ecoMOD teams to push further toward specific goals, ecoMOD can also challenge other projects. For example, some of the projects that choose to pursue ecological sustainability are limited to the selection of a couple of alternative materials or an upgrade in insulation. While this may have some positive effect, few programs make any effort to analyze life cycle impacts or to measure energy usage. The ecoMOD evaluation phase is another way the ecoMOD project can influence others. With the exception of hard research from academic engineers and building scientists, and the university teams participating in the Solar Decathlon, it is difficult to find academic work in which

student-designed buildings are monitored for thermal or energy performance or given a post-occupancy evaluation. Even among the schools that have done some form of design/build project for many years, there are none that support an ongoing monitoring or evaluation process. Design/build projects can be great confidence boosters—this is one of their most important advantages. Yet educators need to also build the capacity for humility in their students. An open evaluation of a completed project is the best way to do that, while at the same time building confidence in these future professionals that they have a complete understanding of the real impact of their work.

All university design/build projects share an interest in craft. When challenged to get their hands dirty and figure out the subtleties of materials, connections, and detailing, young designers can very quickly improve their design and construction detailing skills.

Extremely skilled student designers—with the ability to draw up design schemes with great sophistication—commonly discover that their beautiful drawings cannot be easily assembled in the way they intended. Great teaching moments happen when the designer is forced to assess his or her design and resolve the problem. In the best cases, the design really starts to come together at the point where the logic of the design intentions informs the solution. Rather than watering down a design, it can be a moment of late-stage inspiration that actually brings it all together. For students who have worked all the way through the process and have remained open-minded, these moments can be the final synthesis of the earliest design intuition.

The last major advantage of real-world projects is that they require money to make them happen. Inevitably, the budget is a great tempering force on an affordable housing project, forcing design teams to set priorities.

In the ecoMOD project, the money for the buildings comes from the affordable housing partner. The teams use the same budget that the affordable housing partners would normally spend on a similarly sized house. Grants and gifts are pursued only to support student fellowships and project administration, acquire tools or equipment, and add strategically selected sustainable upgrades for individual housing units. The design teams do not seek donations and discounts for baseline materials, unless the organization (such as Habitat for Humanity) already receives them. The idea is to ensure the prototypes can be replicated easily. This requires the teams to collectively assess what is important for the project and to strategize to ensure these goals can be met. By working within the financial limitations of affordable housing organizations, ecoMOD is able to provide homes for those in need, while also creating prototypes that can be built by modular housing manufacturers.

Intra- and Interdisciplinary Collaboration

Many educators now believe that architectural and engineering education should be transitioning to a curriculum structured to emphasize interdisciplinary collaboration. Often, solutions that are obvious for one discipline are not as clear to others. When disciplines are strategically brought together, the end results are typically richer and more thoroughly studied. An ideal architectural curriculum would move through a process of developing basic artistic and technical skills aligned with guiding principles, and conclude with collaborative and multidisciplinary team activities to design and construct small buildings. When advanced students are offered an opportunity to collaborate with other emerging professionals, all can benefit from being intimately exposed to other disciplines.

If academia balanced traditional design education (individual students working independently) with the more complex process of collaboration with future landscape architects, engineers, planners, contractors, and business people, architecture students could mature more quickly as designers, and truly develop a capacity for designing the future. Rather than allowing the current fascination among architecture students with 3-D parametric modeling of natural flows to be limited to their formal potential in design, we can also encourage students to refine these forms to assess their actual performance. By applying themselves to projects that have a real client, site, and budget, by building their own architectural detailing, and by evaluating the built results, they can appreciate the full impact of their design decisions.

Any good designer will tell you that a rigid adherence to a preconceived idea about the design of a building or a place is a dangerous thing. The process of design requires a clearly articulated vision at the outset, but it also requires the recognition that thorough and thoughtful consideration of site, budget, client needs, and overall concept will inform the design process. In the best collaborations, this will inevitably lead to something that no single individual could completely imagine at the outset.

Design, at its core, is about creatively inventing new ideas and forms through a process of decision-making. By guiding students into these processes, letting them make decisions (within commonsense constraints), allowing some mistakes to happen, and asking them many questions along the way, we can empower the next generation of designers as they attempt to rewrite the future. As David Orr states in the epilogue of his 1992 book *Ecological Literacy: Education and the Transition to a Postmodern World,* "Students need opportunities to work together, to create, to take responsibility, and to lead in a community setting without which they are unlikely to comprehend the full meaning of virtue, ecology, or community."[3] Teaching design is about listening to the student's "inner designer," fortifying it with the knowledge it needs to mature, encouraging critical thinking, and pointing the direction in which all the world's citizens should go: toward a more just and environmentally responsible future. Architects and engineers can't solve all these problems, but it is essential that the next generation of these professionals have the appropriate skills and experiences in place to become truly productive global citizens.

Notes

1. William James, "The Moral Equivalent of War," *McClure's Magazine,* August 1910, 290.
2. American Philosophical Association, "Critical Thinking: A Statement of Expert Consensus for Purposes of Educational Assessment and Instruction," *The Delphi Report* (ERIC Doc. No. ED 315 423), 1990.
3. David Orr, *Ecological Literacy: Education and the Transition to a Postmodern World* (Albany, NY: State University of New York Press, 1992), 183.

Additional References

Architecture for Humanity, eds. *Design Like You Give a Damn.* New York: Metropolis Books, 2006.

Bell, Bryan, ed. *Good Deeds, Good Design: Community Service Through Architecture.* New York: Princeton Architectural Press, 2004.

Bell, Bryan, and Katie Wakeford, eds. *Expanding Architecture: Design as Activism.* New York: Metropolis Books, 2008.

Dewey, John. *Democracy and Education: An Introduction to the Philosophy of Education.* New York: The Macmillan Company, 1916.

Facione, Peter A. "Critical Thinking: What It Is and Why It Counts." *Change Magazine.* March-April 2007.

Learn and Serve Clearinghouse. http://www.service learning.org.

2 PRACTICE

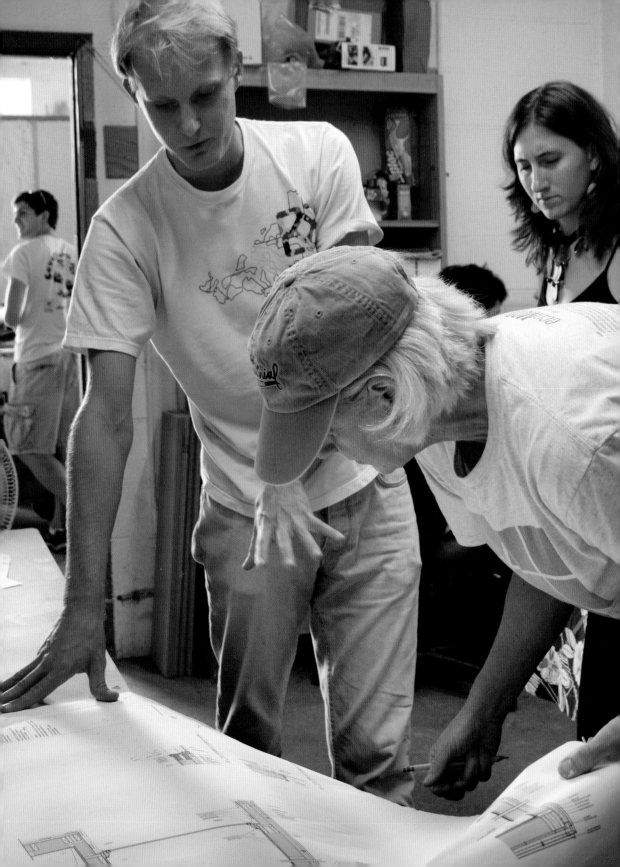

THE PROCESS

Crafting a Collaborative Design Process

In Harvard University's *Report of the Task Force on General Education,* the authors state that the aim of liberal education should be "to unsettle presumptions, to defamiliarize the familiar, to reveal what is going on beneath and behind appearances, to disorient young people and to help them find ways to re-orient themselves. A liberal education aims to accomplish these things by questioning assumptions, by inducing self-reflection, by teaching students to think critically and analytically, by exposing them to the sense of alienation produced by encounters with radically different historical moments and cultural formations and with phenomena that exceed their, and even our own, capacity to fully understand."[1]

The ecoMOD collaborative process can certainly be unsettling and disorienting at first for some students, so my goal is always to make sure it provides enough structure to allow for reflective/critical thinking, and therefore to allow the team to coherently organize themselves for the success of the project. I often tell ecoMOD students (or ecoMODers, as we have come to label ourselves) that it is best to be both resolute *and* flexible during the collaborative design process—determined enough to be willing to stand up for what you believe in, and flexible enough to recognize the importance of giving in when someone has a better solution. Successful participation in the project requires the development of an ability to set priorities, and the recognition that no one person has the right solution for everything. I'm always trying to get everyone to take collective responsibility for finding the best solutions—the simple,

collective thought process that generates the objects is much harder to define and document. Yet this process is far more important. As anyone who manages a team knows, each team develops a collective personality—which may or may not align with the strongest personalities in the team. This other participant—*the team,* as opposed to the individuals that make up the team—has to be managed carefully. The best teams are ones that can collectively use their highest-level creative and critical thinking at the same time. Fortunately, there is considerable overlap between the qualities of an "ideal critical thinker" and the characteristics of a top performing team. These include curiosity, open-mindedness, flexibility, and honesty. It is also important to make sure everyone in the overall team trusts each other, that we maintain a certain level of organization without becoming rigid, and that all team members become deeply involved in some aspect of the project. Getting every single person to take real responsibility for a task or area of research seems to be the best way to encourage a productive team dynamic. Everyone owns a part of the collective project, and all contributions are important. Getting students to think beyond their own egos and strive for solutions that are for the good of the project is always difficult.

The ecoMOD collaborative process is simultaneously intra- and interdisciplinary, which makes the challenge that much more difficult. Students and faculty are forced to learn each other's language—and to collectively reach conclusions. By definition, the design does not come from the mind of a single person, but from the coordinated efforts

elegant, and effective strategies—no matter who initially proposed them. Good ideas are hard to find, and while some people excel at proposing them, others excel at identifying them or developing them. Some students who struggle to find their voice in the early stages will flourish towards the end, and some have the opposite experience. My goal is to find a way for everyone to be effective in every stage of the project—yet I'm realistic enough to recognize that goal is unattainable.

While the result of the ecoMOD design process is a tangible object—a building—the of many. The ecoMOD teams also work with outside advisors who, depending on the project, might include architects, engineers, contractors, fabricators, subcontractors, prefabrication experts, landscape architects, affordable housing developers, housing counselors, planners, historic preservationists, environmental scientists, building department officials, business people, and sustainability experts on daylighting, material selection, indoor air quality, energy efficiency, and renewable energy. The feedback these professionals provide is essential to the success of the project. Even a brief interaction with the right professional can significantly impact the trajectory of the design. These outside experts report that they often learn as much from the process as they bring to it. To be freed from their own relatively narrow focuses is appealing for many. The primary expert on modular construction who has been involved with our student teams since ecoMOD1 has had the chance to learn a lot about sustainable design—something he had not directly addressed previously. The contractor responsible for the Herculean preservation effort on the historic house for ecoMOD3 found himself stretched by the students' energy, research capabilities, and willingness to explore iterative versions of designs. Yet his calmly expressed professional opinions were an extremely important tempering force. The project has been extremely lucky to find so many local and national experts willing to share their advice, and several have reported that they really enjoyed participating because of the chance to interact with such an energized and enthusiastic team of students.

Decision Webs

A significant number of current students are already familiar with a range of environmental issues, and when they become involved in ecoMOD they want to make the right choices when it comes to sustainability. Yet these choices are complicated by the need to be also concerned about aesthetics, the budget, keeping the rain out, the ability of a modular builder to replicate what we put in the prototype, and the social impact of the overall project.

The design teams use "decision webs" to

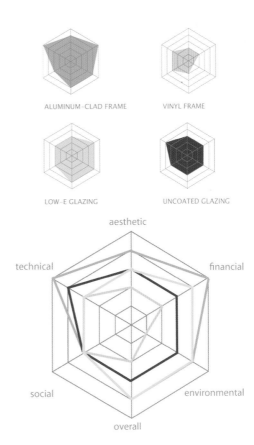

ALUMINUM-CLAD FRAME   VINYL FRAME

LOW-E GLAZING   UNCOATED GLAZING

aesthetic

technical   financial

social   environmental

overall

facilitate the collaborative process. The webs are a graphic device to help track thought processes and recognize the complex array of issues affected by each decision. The individual design subteams do not always agree, and decisions occasionally become compromises. The decision webs help resolve conflicts, and they often evolve over time, as the teams do further research into contested issues. The webs are inspired by spider diagrams and similar graphic strategies used in product marketing and management consulting. These strategies have been used in various ways, ranging from comparing leadership styles for managers to assessing the subtle flavors of scotch whiskey. We use them to choose from among more than one material, system, or strategy option by comparing the choices using the following general categories: aesthetic, financial, ethical, technical, and social. The "right" choice is the one that is able to make the largest web. Although the ecoMOD decision web is graphically somewhat similar to the Sustainable Project Appraisal Routine (SPeAR) diagram used by the well-known interdisciplinary practice Arup, the best choice with SPeAR is found by aiming for the center, whereas in the ecoMOD process the goal is to reach to the outside of the web.[2]

Group Genius

Somewhat unexpectedly, the business literature/business self-help aisles of bookstores with their subsections on team building and team management have yielded lessons that have directly influenced the project, including through Keith Sawyer's *Group Genius,* which

Paxton Marshall introduced to the team, and Patrick Lencioni's *The Five Dysfunctions of a Team.*

One of the dangers of collaboration is the potential of group think, whereby a team makes decisions that are the lowest common denominator, or the decision to which they can all agree. Often this is the solution that no one particularly likes, or the idea that doesn't particularly offend anyone either. It typically means that some people are not fully engaged in the process. They are choosing to hold back and not voice their real opinion, and it is important to drag their opinion out of them —to make sure they at least have their say, even if the majority of the team doesn't agree with them. The most mature of these students are more likely to reengage in the project if they at least get to honestly express their opinion before the entire group. By making their best case, but remaining open-minded, they can become the best collaborators.

The challenge of encouraging each eco-MOD student to be an "ideal critical thinker" is a difficult one. It requires a certain amount of discipline from the faculty, to ensure we are doing our best to act as appropriate role models. In this sense, the ecoMOD project is more like a professional design team—with architecture, engineering, and landscape architecture firms collaborating and working with additional outside consultants. The role of faculty is similar to that of a principal in one of these firms, with the exception that our motivations are educational, environmental, and social, and inherently not focused on earning a profit for the design team. It is essential to give the students real responsi-

bilities in this process and not make decisions for them, but it is also important to lead them in an effective process.

To lead the studios and seminars within the ecoMOD project, I have tried to craft a strategy for emphasizing guiding principles, while making sure the students develop critical thinking skills for their own individual design processes. This method is refined each semester, but at its core is the idea that it is more important to listen and ask questions than to provide students with preconceived answers. From year to year, the forms and finishes of architectural design change quickly, just as the definitions of an environmentally or socially responsible architecture evolve continuously. So rather than present information in the form of precise answers (as some students

would prefer) ecoMOD assignments and activities are structured to ensure that students are constantly asking tougher questions of themselves. A mature knowledge of the process of design can help form the foundation of a long-term career.

Looseness as a Strategy

In addition to listening and asking questions, another way the ecoMOD project encourages critical thinking during the design and build phases is by working in teams to collectively address challenges. The teams are formed according to interest, and the structure is always somewhat loose. Each individual is typically on more than one team, so that they might take a leading role in the structural

design team, and only play a secondary role in the material selection team. The teams set goals and deadlines, so that each individual is responsible to their small teams and to the overall ecoMOD team. Sometimes these teams work really well together, and sometimes despite the best efforts of the best people, the team never really makes any headway. This is where the looseness of the teams is essential—allowing me to reconfigure or dissolve teams when they are no longer useful. I am also largely dependent upon the managers I've selected from within the group to advise me on how things are going—their ears are much closer to the ground, especially during the late nights leading up to deadlines.

This looseness strategy extends to the over-all project. Real-world projects are inherently unpredictable, so a certain degree of built-in flexibility is essential for success. A rigid attitude about schedule and deliverables might make the team more focused and efficient, but it does not necessarily make the project any better. An autocratic leadership style is not the best way to allow students to swim in the waters of the project. If simply told what to do, the team misses out on the opportunity to find the brilliant ideas that can emerge from a successful form of group genius. In addition, students can sense when they are empowered to impact a project—and if they seize that opportunity by working hard to push the project forward, their passion for the success of the project will be that much stronger. With ecoMOD, students are thrown into the deep end of the pool, with suggestions offered from the side. We only give them a life preserver when they're drowning.

Notes

1. Faculty of Arts and Sciences, "Report of the Task Force on General Education" (Harvard University, 2007).
2. Alisdair I. McGregor and Cole Roberts, "Using the SPeAR Assessment Tool in Sustainable Master Planning," http://www.arup.com/_assets/_download/download129.pdf.

Additional References

Lencioni, Patrick. *The Five Dysfunctions of a Team: A Leadership Fable.* San Francisco: Jossey-Bass, 2002.

Sawyer, Keith. *Group Genius: The Creative Power of Collaboration.* New York: Basic Books, 2007.

TROJAN GOAT: THE 2002 UVA SOLAR DECATHLON TEAM

The Challenge of Creating an "Off-the-Grid" Home

The template for the ecoMOD project comes directly from the University of Virginia's participation in the Solar Decathlon competition. From 2000 to 2002 a team of UVA architecture, engineering, and landscape architecture students participated in the first-ever version of the event, a national competition organized by the U.S. Department of Energy (DOE) and the National Renewable Energy Laboratory (NREL). The challenge was to design and build a house (no larger than 800 square feet) powered entirely by the sun. The Solar Decathlon brought together fourteen universities from across the U.S. to compete in ten events focused on energy-efficient house design. For three weeks in the fall of 2002, the teams assembled their houses on the National Mall in Washington DC.

Over the course of two years, more than one hundred students spent countless hours designing, debating, and building. They collaborated on all aspects of the process—from schematic design to construction, from fundraising to equipment specification. The School of Architecture and the School of Engineering and Applied Science integrated the project into our curricula, so that students could work together in and out of the classroom to put theories of sustainability into practice. Along the way, we were forced to question our ideas about sustainable design and what it takes to create an off-the-grid house.

Since the first event, the competition has been held three more times—in '05, '07, and '09. In all four competitions, the impact of the event in the media and on the local community has been enormous. The Decathlon has raised the profile of renewable energy in residential construction and encouraged the next generation of building industry professionals to develop a sophisticated understanding of these issues.

Government Guidelines

One of the first challenges for the UVA team was to respond to the competition guidelines, mostly written by government engineers with little interest in or knowledge of the architectural design process. The organizers were constantly refining their criteria in an effort to make them more "objective" even when the result would actually increase the environmental impact of the competition. Because of this interest in verifiable fairness, they sincerely believed there was a way to objectively judge architectural design—preferably with a checklist. It's fair to say that some of the organizers were less than enthusiastic about creativity in architectural design and expected the final designs to resemble standard single-wide trailers, ranch houses, or early twentieth-century cottages. Several of the fourteen schools lacked representation from architecture students.

I questioned organizers about whether it was possible to hold a university house design competition without the required participation of architecture students. Wouldn't all teams benefit from collaboration between the disciplines? It seemed to me that all teams should also be required to address the issues inherent in the disciplines of landscape architecture and planning. Shouldn't water use in the typical American yard be as much of a concern as energy use? Isn't the issue of density versus sprawl worth discussing in a national competition?

Perhaps most surprising was the fact that the event organizers seemed mostly focused on demonstrating renewable energy—in the very specific form of photovoltaics (PVs). There were no points for other forms of renewable energy, or natural ventilation, or passive storage of heat gain, or daylighting of interior spaces (although light levels generally were measured), let alone use of materials with reduced environmental impact. The houses built by UVA, the University of Texas at Austin, Carnegie Mellon University, Virginia Polytechnic and State University, Auburn University, the University of Puerto Rico, and the University of Colorado were the only ones to rigorously take a broader interpretation of environmental responsibility than the one offered by the DOE. It could also be noted that each of those schools included architecture students in their teams.

And what about affordability? We spent over $350,000 to design, build, and transport our 750-square-foot house. That's over $460 per square foot. How does anyone justify that kind of spending for anything other than a prototypical design in a university competition intended to demonstrate expensive technology? We were not able to convince the DOE officials to consider affordability in the final guidelines. Ultimately, we made a conscious choice to take on the competition guidelines quite literally. We hoped to prove we could play their game on our terms, and we were able to raise enough money to do so. All of the teams recognized that it is difficult to define what is truly sustainable. We only had provisional strategies for making decisions on environmental issues. The DOE guidelines were certainly not definitive, but neither were those of any university team.

I took it upon myself to insist that architectural ideas be more integral to the competition than they were in the first draft of the rules. Although I had hoped to have an equal balance of points for architectural and engineering issues (the first draft had 100 points for "design and livability" of the original 1000), it was immediately clear that I was not going to convince the organizers. I succeeded in getting them to double the architecture points (making it 200 out of 1100 points in the final rules). I pushed for respected designers to be included in the architecture jury. Ultimately, the organizers selected judges with sophistication on environmental issues in architecture, three of whom also have national or international reputations as designers—Steve Badanes, Ed Mazria, and Glenn Murcutt.

Despite my misgivings and frustrations, the DOE and NREL officials always gave me a fair hearing, and often sought my opinion. While it was easy to stew in frustration, the complex challenges the DOE and NREL faced putting the event together became much more real when we arrived in Washington and met the individuals face to face. It was much easier for us to make suggestions for improvements than it was for them to sort through those suggestions from fourteen teams and come to a fair and equitable solution. I do not think anyone from any of the teams ever once

questioned the fairness of the competition administrators, and none of us envied their jobs. There is no question that they have a good message.

Design Process

Design and build a house powered by solar energy no larger than 800 square feet. This was the primary challenge of the Solar Decathlon. On the surface, it sounds like the kind of assignment you could complete in a semester, with a summer for construction. Yet the complexity of the challenge required the concerted effort of over a hundred students spread out over three and a half semesters and two summers. The design of the house was required to be:

- Transportable to and from Washington DC
- A clear demonstration of the integration of renewable energy into a house
- Sufficiently energy efficient to compete against other teams in a rigorous week of monitoring
- Sophisticated enough to appeal to a jury of renowned architects
- Innovative enough in architecture and engineering to meet the standards of our team
- Completed on time, and within our budget (i.e., whatever amount we could fundraise)
- A worthy representative of our university and our disciplines

The team collaborated on every aspect of the design process to resolve countless dilemmas and produce a self-sufficient, transportable house. In the process, they discovered there are few choices that are clearly right or clearly wrong within design. Instead, they found themselves in a pluralistic process requiring great patience, tact, and honesty. Throughout design and construction, the team was often embroiled in debates that occasionally threatened to dissolve a hard-won sense of collective decision-making. As the architecture faculty advisor, I anticipated the process of making design decisions as a team would be difficult. I assumed one student's design would become the obvious choice, and we would move forward on that basis. Architectural education

(and much of contemporary practice) is about the brilliant individual solving a problem on his or her own terms. Yet my initial assumption could not have been more wrong. To my surprise, it became clear that under certain conditions, collaborative design is possible. More than anything, it takes a talented and mature group with the willingness to be both opinionated and open-minded.

Early in the design process architecture students began working with a small team of engineering students. Given their differing educations, it is not surprising that the students spoke different languages. As the engineers talked about optimization and efficiency, the architects were more interested in ambiguity between building and landscape. While the engineers tried to move in a linear fashion through a set of decisions, the architects made great leaps forward and backward (and sideways). Taken to the logical extreme, the engineers' solution would have been an upgraded single-wide trailer with a lot of additional insulation, two small windows, and PV panels on the roof. For the architects, the most "out there" scenario involved a building idea composed of a series of petals that opened and closed according to the season—vaguely resembling a multilayered taco shell. Somewhere in the midst of the complex dialogue, the architects began to develop designs that the engineers could recognize as buildings, and the engineers became more open to the importance of spatial and conceptual ideas.

During the early weeks of the first semester I asked the students to measure themselves performing a domestic activity and create a drawing of this analysis. As they considered

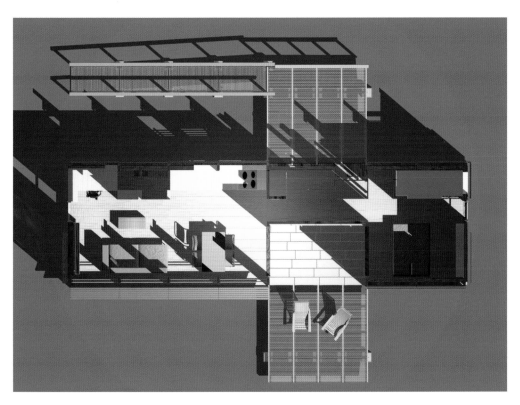

themselves sleeping, cooking, showering, dressing, and so on, they became more aware of the scale of a human body. Next I asked them to design an abstract fragment of a house to perform those activities. These fragments helped generate ideas later in the semester, and the kernel of some of those ideas even made it into the house's final design: one student's sensorial shower concept eventually became the bathroom; another student's fascination with adaptable dining tables and window frames led the team to design and build an adaptable rainscreen panel system. In the final stages of detailing, the students ultimately figured out how to make the concept a reality by using reclaimed wood shipping palettes, all milled, cut, and assembled into panels. They also analyzed relevant architectural precedents and investigated engineering principles.

As the design process began in earnest, students worked in four teams of three, each team collaboratively creating twelve separate designs. The concepts, built as tiny ¹⁄₁₆" scale models, became collectively known as the "babies." Each baby was unique, and was born of a specific thesis or idea. The design team voted on favorites, and teams were reconfigured several times. After each vote the winning houses were completely redesigned by the time of the next review, becoming more thoughtful and rigorous hybrids of the original designs.

Eventually the final winner was selected. The design packed all the "service" elements (plumbing, mechanical, kitchen, bathroom, storage) into a zone to the north of the house, leaving the remainder of the house open for living spaces. With the entire team now working on one design, it was inevitable that the house would continue to change. The floor plan from that stage in the project resembles the final built house, but the interior relationships and the articulation of the exterior form are significantly different. Throughout the semester, as the teams got larger, the designs became more sophisticated. Ideas that were hard to defend fell away, and good ideas remained.

Insurgency

Soon after the entire studio came together to work on one design a small insurgent group of students became dissatisfied with its rigid quality, and late one night temporarily "took over" the design. I had assigned the studio a ½" section model of the building—a small slice. The insurgent group decided to take the ½" model requirement to the next level. Instead of building a small section, they built a 1" model of the entire building—but their interpretation of it. They used the same floor plan, but completely changed the exterior expression of the building—with hinged and sliding panels flying all over the place. The model was so quickly and poorly crafted that it was easy to dismiss. Yet it had a power—as well as a subtlety and spirit—that the previously final design lacked. During a long review and discussion, the studio came together and decided to incorporate many of the insurgents' ideas, but refine them and organize them into a rational system. It was painful and difficult, but everyone felt the building was going to be better for it. It also helped the students realize that they each had an equal voice in the project.

A Goat Ethic

At this critical stage in the project the house got its nickname. A student and I were talking about how the newly suggested sliding and hinging louvers and panels could form a climate-responsive skin around the entire building. I said that it reminded me of the Trojan Horse, in the way the building could arrive with a mysterious wooden wrapper, and then unfold to reveal its true intentions. Another student had a long-standing and oft-stated obsession with goats, extremely adaptable and efficient animals that can survive on most any food. Similarly, we hoped our design would be adaptable. "Goat" had become an adjective for anything cool or interesting within the studio, and thus as we discussed the Trojan Horse, it almost immediately became the "Trojan Goat."

The Trojan Goat identity clarified the ethical framework of the design. The students decided they wanted the building to be ecologically responsible, but on their own terms. It didn't need to be polite as much as clear about its intentions. It was to be like the animal it was named after: climate responsive, adaptable, resourceful, determined, intelligent, comfortable, highly evolved, but maybe a little rough around the edges. Hence the house was to be refined, but visibly handcrafted.

Toward the end of that first semester, it became clear to me that these values were even more important to the students than the form of the building they had designed.

Each student had to give up on a design idea at some point in the collaborative process, which meant the building design was no longer precious or untouchable. They were headed for graduation, and knew another group of students would be taking the project through completion. They cared deeply about the building they had designed, but they were even more concerned about the ideas that helped determine its form. In an effort to smooth that transition, we had two long discussions about the development of a written document stating the ideas and goals of the project. Everyone had to agree on the content. More than making an aesthetic object, they wanted to elaborate an enduring goat ethic.

Refinement

The next major challenge was to transfer the intentions of the original studio to another group of students. In the fall 2001, I co-taught a construction detailing class with my engineering counterpart, Professor Paxton Marshall, and part-time research scientist Dan Pearce. It was a conventional class (as opposed to a design studio), held in the architecture school, but with equal representation of architecture and engineering students. The architecture students were mostly graduate students, with a few undergraduate architecture and graduate landscape architecture students. The class was divided into interdisciplinary groups, focused on specific topics such as structural design, electrical controls, landscape design, and daylighting. The students prepared presentations on their issues and worked toward resolving the house design.

The challenges of interdisciplinary collaboration, which had been an undercurrent all along, became a major source of both concern and inspiration. There were differing expectations about what a house should be. A few of the new engineering students were surprised by the unconventional look of the design. They could not understand why it was not similar to a typical single-wide trailer, which is easy to transport, easy to build, and if well insulated can be energy efficient. The new architecture students had to defend a house designed by their predecessors. Rather than attempt to redesign the house, the architecture team became protective of both the building form and the ethical principles behind it. Fortunately, the design's well-proportioned module was simultaneously flexible and rigid, allowing for refinement of the interior spaces and exterior skin without a complete rethinking of the building form.

The process of questioning design decisions forced the new design team members to take a close look at the drawings and identify weaknesses and strengths. The engineering team expressed two major concerns: 1) the flat roof and 2) the almost complete lack of insulation or solid wall along the south, east, and west walls. The architecture team succeeded in defending the former, and the entire team found an effective compromise on the latter.

The flat (or more accurately low-slope) roof was important to the architecture students for two reasons. It allowed occupation of the roof, with one quarter of its area set aside for a green roof. Since the house size was limited to 800 square feet (ours was actually 750), the designers wanted to expand the house by including the surrounding landscape and making a direct connection between the built form and its unbuilt context. The flat roof also maximizes the interior space of the house, which had a strict 18' height restriction from the DOE. With sufficient floor and roof structure to travel on a federal interstate and a 9' interior ceiling height in the main living spaces, there was not room to put in a conventional sloped roof and mount the PV panels at the ideal angle. Therefore, the PVs had to fold down to fit under highway bridges. In addition, the team had decided to build the house as one structure (rather than several pieces that would be put together on site) and unless a separate gable was attached once in place in Washington (and later removed to transport again), a conventional pitched roof

would carve into the clarity of the interior spaces by bringing the ceiling height down. The engineers were convinced.

As for the lack of solid walls, the architecture students did not deny the legitimacy of the engineering students' concerns. Full height glazing for over half of all the vertical surfaces of the building is not the most energy-efficient way to enclose a house. Yet the original design intent was to maximize the ambiguity between inside and outside—and to critique the typical trailer-style impenetrable box. With a full-height glass wall, the occupants benefit from a more direct connection with the adjacent exterior space.

During the height of summer, heat gain would be significant, but the architecture team had already addressed this with a flexible exterior skin—the sliding, hinged, louvered wood panels. In the final design, the panels could be adjusted to block all heat gain. However, the architecture students had not adequately addressed heat loss during winter. The ultimate solution was two-fold: the majority of the east and west walls, as well as the easternmost quarter of the south wall (the bedroom) would become mostly solid and fully insulated. This arrangement had the added benefit of providing privacy. For the remainder of the south wall, the architecture team committed to a minimum thermal resistance factor (R-value) of 17. The engineering team agreed the architecture team could keep their full-height of glass on the south wall as long as they met the absolute minimum standard for thermal performance of a conventional solid wall. This was a major compromise on their part, as the thermal resistance for the remaining solid walls of the Trojan Goat is an unusually high R-35. The architecture team resolved this by finding a window company that makes high performance fiberglass frame windows (Comfortline) with an R-value of 10—extremely high for windows. They also designed a customized thermal curtain for the south windows with two layers of Thinsulate, an efficient and cost effective insulator. In the end, the effective R-value of the south wall is just under the R-17 goal—R-16.5 with the curtains pulled closed.

The resolution of the exterior wall insulation issue is the perfect example of the advantages of interdisciplinary collaboration. The final result has a selective and tactical use of glazing and a more thoughtful aesthetic. The engineers got their insulation, and the architects got their spatial continuity where it matters the most—in the living and dining room spaces. Aesthetics and ethics are balanced and intertwined.

It was during this second full semester that the team added landscape architecture students. Ideally, this would have occurred in the beginning, so the dialogue between inside and outside would have equal voices. The small team of two graduate landscape architecture students formulated their own goat ethic, and even considered bringing a live goat to chomp on the grass of the National Mall in Washington DC. They established principles for design on both the site in Washington (a movable landscape, in every sense of the word) and the intended final site for the house on the grounds of the university (although it did not end up there). It was an upward battle for the first landscape team members, as they at-

tempted to challenge the architecture students and work with engineering students who were less than clear about the nature of landscape architecture.

It was a difficult semester in many ways, but by the end of it, engineering students became protective of the building form. One even expressed concern about a minor change to the building section that would affect the proportions of the structure. For their part, many of the architecture students were beginning to take seriously the ideas and issues expressed by the engineering team. They were looking for performance criteria in their material selection process, and reading up on air infiltration.

Resolution

In the spring of 2002, the architecture team expanded again with a second fourth-year undergraduate studio, collaborating directly with graduate students participating in independent study. I started the studio with two simultaneous assignments: a thorough, collaborative progress report on the house design, with a candid assessment of the Trojan Goat's strengths and weaknesses, and a short collaborative design/build project—a small temporary shelter, to be assembled from reclaimed materials, set up in three hours, and occupied during a cold winter night.

These assignments allowed the new team members to become familiar with both the design of the Trojan Goat and the underlying principles of passive design. To put together the report, the new students interviewed engineering, architecture, and landscape archi-

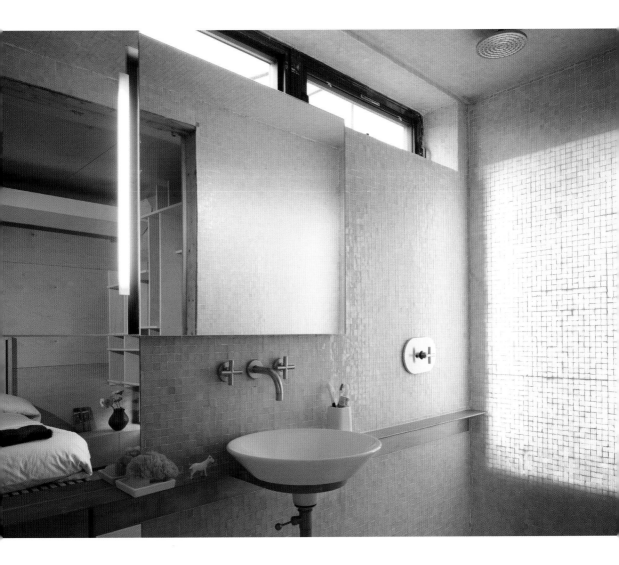

tecture students from the previous semester—only some of whom were continuing on. They collaborated on summarizing the opinions expressed, and compiled a coherent package. In the process of designing and building their small sleeping shelter, they learned about solar gain, insulation, and thermal lag. Their understanding of these issues would have a direct impact on their own sleeping comfort.

The design process had been underway for over a year before this new group of students came on board, and yet each of them became intimately involved in the final resolution of the design. They were assigned tasks based on their interests—from window and door design to rainscreen wall detailing, and from bathroom refinement to cabinetry design. They had to collaborate with team members who (initially) knew the house better than they did, and work within constraints that sometimes appeared capricious. Yet their work, in combination with the engineering and independent study architecture students, made the final construction possible. They put together a coherent set of construction drawings. They researched environmental materials; resolved the placement of mechanical, plumbing, and electrical systems with the engineering team; set standards for the refinement of the cabinetry; and made a definitive 3-D computer model. They respected their predecessors' ideas and overall strategy, and still found a way to make the building their own.

Conflict

As summer approached, many students were itching to get their hands dirty and start building. After a long process of refining, verifying, and finalizing the structural design, we were ready to place an order for lumber. The team had elected to use composite wood joists and framing—commonly known as engineered lumber. As opposed to steel framing, which would require professional welding, the use of engineered lumber made it possible for even the most inexperienced team members to participate in the framing process. The lumber is not cut from solid tree trunks, but instead utilizes smaller shreds and shards of wood, pressed and formed together with adhesives. Compared with standard lumber, engineered lumber is stronger, and is generally perceived as a more ecological product due to the use of wood material that might otherwise be con-

sidered scrap. However, some environmentalists, architects, and engineers question the environmental impact of the adhesives. The team researched the issue carefully and decided the benefits outweighed the disadvantages.

Weyerhaeuser–Trus Joist agreed to donate all the joists and framing members, and also helped us verify our structural assumptions and calculations. We sent them a list of products and waited for the order to arrive. On the day of the first delivery, an error on Weyerhaeuser's part sparked the most heated and interesting debate of the entire project.

The house rests on two 4" x 16" x 48' beams along the bottom of the south and north walls. They carry all the live and dead loads and are connected to two other beams on the east and west walls. After careful consideration by several graduate architecture students it was decided to specify non-pressure-treated lumber. In locations where wood might be directly exposed to moisture, lumber (both conventional and engineered) is typically treated under high pressure with a toxic recipe of chemicals. At the time, the most common method of pressure treatment, known as CCA, included arsenic, and was under careful review by the U.S. Environmental Protection Agency. It has since been outlawed for use in single-family homes, playground equipment, and child care centers and is being phased out. This is based on evidence that arsenic and other chemicals leach into the ground, and that the material is potentially dangerous to handle—particularly during the construction process.

Our Weyerhaeuser representative mistakenly assumed we wanted pressure-treated lumber for the perimeter beams. When the beams arrived, we had to decide whether to use the material or ask that it be replaced. If we had purchased the material, it would have been a nonissue—we would simply return it. But since it was donated, we could not easily ask Weyerhaeuser to exchange the order.

I sent an email to the team asking if we should use the pressure-treated beams or send them back. We could offer to pay for the new material, or at least the shipping costs. We couldn't really afford to pay for anything that would otherwise be donated, and we certainly didn't want to offend our donors. We had just sent in a grant proposal to the Weyerhaeuser Foundation requesting additional funding for the project, making the political quandary more complex. For over two weeks the emails flew back and forth, breaking largely into four overlapping camps: 1) those who wanted to use the material even if it wasn't ideal; 2) those who felt untreated engineered lumber should never have been considered; 3) those who felt the environmental concerns outweighed the technical and financial issues and wanted to buy the new material; and 4) those who wanted to get Weyerhaeuser to replace the material at no cost. Passionate emails cited dense EPA reports on CCA, articles from *Fine Homebuilding* and *Environmental Building News* about the subject, and personal experiences of working with pressure-treated lumber.

In the end, we reached an elegant compromise. We elected to keep the precut short beam pieces, as they could not be used by anyone else and might otherwise end up in the waste stream. I successfully convinced Weyerhaeuser to replace and restock the two long CCA-treated beams with untreated beams. To address the potential of arsenic leaching from the treated beams and the concern about moisture with the untreated beams, the team researched and purchased "environmentally responsible" sealants and finishes. One of the treated beams was encased in a durable sealer and the other left exposed. Ferns that are known to remove arsenic from soil—a form of phyto-remediation—were planned to be planted adjacent to the exposed treated beam. As for the untreated beams, one was painted with a durable, opaque finish, and the other beam received a transparent finish that will need to be renewed every few years. Each of the products selected is considered ecologically benign, with little or no off-gassing from volatile organic compounds. In short, the Trojan Goat became a living laboratory for research on alternatives to pressure treatment and methods of mediating the effects of CCA.

Construction began in an asphalt parking lot in Crozet, Virginia, during an unusually hot and humid summer. The parking lot was on loan from a local developer who also owned several neighboring industrial buildings—including a former frozen food plant. The closest neighboring building was filled with frozen turkeys that summer. Several "goats" dreamed of visiting the turkeys on the hottest days. The design continued to simplify and change as funding ran low and the students realized the complexity of some of the design ideas. They learned it is often easier to draw than to build.

Goat Migration

The process of getting the house to Washington had long been a topic of research and design. Although the building was built to be mobile, it could not move in the same way as a manufactured or modular home. The Trojan Goat was informed by the team's design ideas and optimized for the DOE design guidelines —neither of which conformed to the building proportions of conventional manufactured housing. In the end, the Virginia Department of Transportation deemed the house a "super load"—too long, too wide, too tall, and too heavy to travel under a normal modular house permit. We employed the services of two companies to help us transport it—a regional house moving company to lift and lower the house in Crozet and Washington and a national heavy hauling company to provide the trailer.

Once the house was strapped in place, the professional driver carefully maneuvered it out of the frozen turkey plant parking lot late one night to the cheers of the team as

well as several local residents watching from their front porches and windows. A couple of students and I traveled behind the Goat all the way to Washington, at speeds of up to 65 miles an hour. The truck made a scheduled overnight stay in Northern Virginia (arranged to give us some flexible time, in case something went wrong) so it could cross into Washington DC after dark, and begin to tear up the well-groomed lawn of the National Mall at precisely 12:01 a.m. the next morning. The organizers had carefully planned the arrival sequence—like an awkward ballet for oversized boxes.

It was our first chance to see the houses from the other universities. After two years of figuring out our own design, it was exciting to see the products of other teams and how they approached the same challenge. One favorite of mine was the elaborate component-based modular design from the University of Texas at Austin. They had designed and fabricated a series of modular parts and pieces that arrived in semi-trailers. That first night, the only aspects visible of their design were neatly stacked piles of structural and panelized pieces. During the first week of the competition, as we were to complete the final assembly of the house, the form of the UT Austin house emerged and was attached to a nicely renovated Airstream trailer, housing the kitchen and other plumbing elements.

The Final Push

Meanwhile, our house was supposed to simply arrive in one piece, allowing the Trojan Goat warriors to sit in lawn chairs and watch the rest of the teams, but in reality we were a little behind schedule. The house was fully enclosed and had most of the exterior and interior fittings in place. But things always take longer than planned, and we had a long list of small tasks to complete.

We kept up a frantic pace during the final week before the event opened—working well into the night. The Marriott hotel chain put us up in a hotel just across the Potomac River, but we seldom saw it that week. On the last night before the public viewing, the entire team stayed up all night one last time and "finished" the house. I have two striking memories from that night—one was working with a student to sand and finish the bamboo floor with a palm sander (as nothing else was available); the other was the sense that in the waning hours of work, distinctions between architecture, engineering, and landscape architecture students disappeared. The students knew each other so well at that point that the final push seemed like a carefully choreographed performance. Team members were effortlessly trading tools, finding lost drill bits, and stepping over each other as if they could anticipate everyone else's moves.

The next morning, as the public began to arrive and several members of the team awoke from naps on the back deck, no one was prepared to share the newly completed Goat just yet. We wanted to pause and appreciate our two years of work, yet people were showing up by the thousands. The DOE estimates that well over 100,000 people visited the "solar village" during the official public days, with over 400,000 hits on the Solar Decathlon website each day of the event. Lines soon formed

to tour the houses, and the team quickly became tour guides. We had many questions about the copper cladding, but mostly people said they loved the house. Many noted the bright, spacious feel of the interior, and more than a few were convinced the house had to be more than 750 square feet.

The first event was the judging of Design and Livability—the architecture category. The judges included Steve Badanes, Dr. Douglas Balcomb, Dr. Ed Jackson Jr., Edward Mazria, Glenn Murcutt, and Stephanie Vierra. They visited each house and spoke with the team. When the winners were slowly announced, we kept expecting to hear our team. We had almost given up when Glenn Murcutt announced we won first place. The judges spoke highly of the project. Murcutt said, "There was little question that Virginia had the most inspired house. Virginia had a design that showed that a solar home is not just about plunking a panel on top. It must be as poetic as it is rational. It must consider every aspect of sustainability, from the building materials to the insulation and ductwork to the way light is used. It must be whole-building sustainable design, and all those components must be integrated in an elegant way." It was a very proud moment for everyone on the team, and made all the hard work seem worthwhile. We learned later it was a unanimous decision.

A problem with the control of our hot water systems and a broken dishwasher presented challenges for us in a few of the nine other (mostly engineering-based) events. The engineering students spent most of the fully monitored week running up and down ladders to the mechanical spaces (the architecture students had insisted the loft was the best place for them . . .) tinkering with the system. Eventually gaining control of the systems, and making use of a borrowed dishwasher, we slowly began to work our way back from ninth place (our lowest ranking, despite our first place in design). By the end of the week, everything was working smoothly. On the last day, we were amazed to learn we came in second overall, not far behind the team from the University of Colorado at Boulder.

Washington Post architecture critic Ben Forgery praised the design, and wrote, "The University of Virginia team hand-crafted its long box as if it were a jewel, reshaping recycled materials as ordinary as wooden shipping pallets and as unusual as [bluestone] panels discarded from the terraces of Thomas Jefferson's Rotunda." After two challenging years of inter- and intradisciplinary collaboration with an incredible group of students, the comment that especially pleased me was that of architecture jury chairwoman Stephanie Vierra: "The UVA team attempted to integrate more solar strategies and did it more successfully than any other team. The work of the architecture and engineering students complemented each other in a way that set them apart from the other teams."

Final Note

In addition to finishing first in architecture and second overall, the UVA team tied for first in the Energy Balance category, was awarded a special citation from the American Institute of Architects, and received the BP Solar Progressive Award for the most

forward-thinking team. In 2003, the UVA team's website received an Honor Award in the student category of the 2003 Entablature Website Design Awards. The website team was managed by my fellow architecture professor Jason Johnson.

Paxton Marshall's engineering students continued to tinker with the systems after the house returned to Virginia. All the systems have been monitored, and several students have prepared a thesis based on their research. After several attempts to find a permanent home for the Trojan Goat, I eventually negotiated with UVA officials to donate it to Piedmont Housing Alliance (PHA), a Charlottesville nonprofit housing organization and our partner for the first ecoMOD project. After some delay, PHA sold the house to a local family to raise funds for their low-income housing programs. The family moved the home to become a rental cottage on their rural property in Albemarle County west of Charlottesville. It currently rests on a permanent foundation, but has undergone some changes. The "environmentally responsible" finish we used on the wood reclaimed from shipping palettes (and assembled into the climate-responsive rainscreen system) did not hold up very well, and peeled away unevenly. Much of the cladding was removed to reveal the perfectly durable copper siding underneath—although the Goat does seem to be missing its coat. In an interesting twist of fate, the first permanent occupant of the Goat was one of the project managers for ecoMOD4.

Information on the contests of the 2002 Solar Decathlon and all the events since then can be found at www.solardecathlon .org. The UVA team's website has not been updated since 2002, but can still be found at www.faculty.virginia.edu/solarhome/ and is also linked through ecoMOD's website at www.ecomod.virginia.edu.

TROJAN GOAT DESIGN FEATURES

SUNSPACE The sunspace serves as both an exterior and an interior space, depending on the season. Opening and closing a series of sliding and hinging doors can change its relationship to the outdoors, allowing it to serve as a terrace during the summer and an enclosed solar heat-gain space during the winter. Oriented to the south, the sunspace can be shaded with a sliding panel to block solar gain or left exposed to collect heat. The thermal mass of the dark stone holds heat, which can be drawn into the house with miniature fans located in the air space behind the stone wall. The bluestone on the floor and wall of the sunspace is reclaimed from a terrace renovation at the University of Virginia's Rotunda, designed by Thomas Jefferson. The team designed the pattern of the stone and cut it themselves.

INTERIORS Wood is the home's dominant interior finish. The ceiling and walls are lined with birch-veneer plywood, a material containing layers of wood that are rolled from a tree rather than cut; the process yields more product and reduces waste. The floor is finished with bamboo, a cost-effective alternative to wood flooring. Bamboo grass matures in three to five years, and its strength is comparable to red oak. However, the bamboo flooring was imported from China.

The bathroom is clad entirely in translucent, recycled glass tile. On one wall, the tile is installed over a large sheet of glass, which is placed a few inches inside of an operable exterior window. This detail allows for a continuous tile surface and a large area of glowing natural light. At night the same area glows from an artificial light hidden in a slot and accessible only from outside the window.

RAINSCREEN The Trojan Goat's rainscreen is a porous layer of wood slatted panels, deflecting cold winds, shading from the hot sun, and keeping most of precipitation away from the copper siding beneath. The panels transform

a waste product into an exterior skin. Wood shipping palettes were disassembled, planed and milled into usage lumber, and assembled into custom panels. The rainscreen also embodies the conceptual basis of the Trojan Goat. The house arrives on site as a mysterious and closed box, as in the ancient story of the Trojan horse. The real intentions of the building are revealed when the rainscreen panels open and transform into decks, louvers, and window shades. Like the highly adaptable and resourceful goat, the house with its rainscreen is able to adapt to any site and a variety of climatic conditions.

INSULATION The house's insulation is a spray-applied polyurethane foam installed by Creative Conservation of Richmond, Virginia, and provided by Comfort Foam. Comfort Foam has an R-value of 7 per inch, the highest of all readily available, cost-effective insulations on the market at the time. The walls of the Trojan

Goat range from R-33 to R-70, significantly higher than a conventional wall with batt insulation. Hydrochlorofluorocarbons have been largely removed from the process but not completely. Although staggered studs reduce the conduction of heat through thermal bridging, at some locations where framing touched inside and outside surfaces it could not be avoided. To resolve the matter, the walls have a second layer of insulation outside of the plywood sheathing. This layer is composed of ¾" rigid board insulation that adds an extra R-5. The foil layer on the outer side of the board reflects heat, helping to keep the house cool in the summer.

COPPER SIDING Beneath the rainscreen, the house is sheathed with copper siding reclaimed from the demolition of a roof installation. The standing seam roofing had to be pulled apart, with the edges hammered flat. Once flattened, the copper was bent again to a new interlocking horizontal lap detail appropriate for wall siding. Copper is durable, corrosion-resistant, and highly recyclable.

STRUCTURE The structure of the Trojan Goat incorporates engineered lumber, a product that optimizes wood fiber utilization, thereby reducing waste and the deforestation rate. Composed of laminated or compressed layers of wood, engineered lumber can replace any standard use of wood and is stronger than pine or spruce members. Its use encourages the lumber industry to utilize forest resources more efficiently.

LANDSCAPE Linked to the green roof via a water collection system, the landscape at ground level, a "permanent" landscape for a movable solar house, posed a unique challenge. The Trojan Goat lived on the Mall in Washington DC for three weeks and then returned to Charlottesville. Due to the house's itinerant nature, its landscape was represented in Washington as a series of adaptable concepts for any location. The cisterns collect rainwater for irrigating the garden and flushing the toilet, and in turn the garden provides vegetables for the home. Like the house, the landscape attempts to transform waste into a resource. The tire planters are microclimates tempered by the soaker hoses that wrap them. Custom wire mesh baskets inserted in the tires separate the plant material from the tires and allow for easy transplantation and transportion of plants. The organic vegetables grown in the planters were consumed as part of the required meal preparation aspect of the competition.

GREEN ROOF The Trojan Goat traveled with its own landscape. One quarter of the roof is comprised of a green or planted roof. Drought

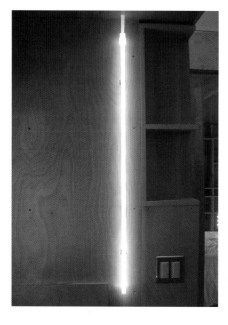

resistant plants, such as sedums, keep the area green throughout much of the year. The green roof measures only ten by twelve feet, yet it serves as an inhabitable garden, a storm water reservoir, a producer of oxygen, and an insulator of the house.

PHOTOVOLTAICS All of the electricity used in the house is produced by a rooftop PV array, consisting of sixteen 330-watt PV panels produced by ASE Americas. The PVs are connected to produce a 24-volt DC output. Excess electricity is stored in a bank of sealed Concord AGM lead-acid batteries.

LUMINAIRE The house makes use of the world's first residential scale luminaire. Working with the Oak Ridge National Laboratory, architecture student Ben Spencer built a domestic scale version of an emerging technology that provides natural daylight at locations far from a window. A mirror dish on the roof of the house tracks the sun and concentrates it into a polished glass fiber cable to deliver the natural light directly into the house's bathroom and entry hall. The glass fiber is attached to an etched glass tube in the entry and bathroom. The texture of the etching makes the light glow. In the future, electrical lights could be attached to the dish of the luminaire, to mimic natural light after the sun goes down. (The luminaire was destroyed during a serious wind storm in 2007, after the house had been moved to its final home. The wind pulled up one of the solar panels and slammed it against the polished mirror dish—damaging the dish beyond repair, though the PV panel survived.)

CABINETRY The cabinetry was composed of a limited palette of materials, chosen for economy and workability. The materials include birch-veneer plywood, sustainably forested (FSC certified) maple butcher-block countertop, and solid birch edge banding. The team designed the cabinetry as a single plane that was punctured at varying scales—maintaining the appearance of a single mass, while allowing for carefully composed flexibility. The design integrates storage and appliances, while maintaining flexibility for future uses.

SMART[W]ALL Smart[w]all is a prototype for a new method of understanding, interacting with, and controlling the energy efficiency of a house. The wall glows different colors to indicate the temperature of the house—red when it's warm, blue when it's cool. The wall also provides information in the touch screen computer interface.

FURNITURE The furniture was designed and built by students in architecture professor Theo van Groll's Architectural Crafts class. The students used sustainably forested lumber to build a platform bed with integrated storage base, a kitchen table with silverware drawers, and a foldable deck chair.

MECHANICAL SYSTEMS The Trojan Goat heating and cooling systems are silent, energy efficient, ductless, and draftless. These characteristics are important to the livability and comfort of the house, while also reducing

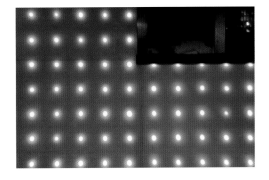

electrical loads compared with a forced air system. The heating of the house is achieved with passive solar design complemented by a radiant floor. This system utilizes water heated by solar thermal collector panels and can be supplemented by hot water from a geothermal heat pump.

Likewise, the house utilizes passive cooling methods, including shading and natural ventilation. When ventilation isn't sufficient, the heat pump chills water to cool and dehumidify the house through a valance cooling unit located along the south edge of the ceiling in the dining area and bedroom. The valance is similar to a radiator heating system, except that the fluid is cold.

**STUDENT ESSAY
BY ADAM RUFFIN**

Adam Ruffin, MArch '02, was the graduate architectural project manager for the UVA Solar Decathlon team, and currently works as a project manager for Thomas Phifer and Partners in New York City.

Joining the design process nearly a year after the project had begun, and after some very innovative and thoughtful designers had given it the ethos and identity of the Trojan Goat, I had to really focus on the collaborative spirit which John had intended the project to embody. Like everyone else, I had become accustomed to working alone, guided by my own interests and approach to design. The Goat, however, was the collective idea of another group of students, most of whom had now graduated, and this idea had to be completed and made better by an entirely new group, adhering to a philosophy we had inherited.

Managing this process of collaborative development of a shared philosophy was initially the most difficult aspect of the project; we learned to let go of the usual modes of ownership and intellectual investment in order to accept and claim existing ideas while embracing the ideas and talents of others working for the same goal. We built a management structure with teams of students focused on various aspects of the project. We produced schedules and budgets and analyses of every system we had in place to make the building work. We developed working drawings that we would have to interpret and from which we would have to build. We devised remarkably elegant strategies for accomplishing the architectural, sustainable, and educational goals of the Goat. And we had to learn to put the bulk of the thing together with our own hands from raw materials or with the aid of professionals in various industries who could help us apply their trades to our project. Throughout, we were constantly making decisions based on input from local authorities, budget shortfalls, time constraints, and workforce limitations, frequently compromising to make progress but never weakening a clear design idea and a well-defined goal.

The Trojan Goat taught the students who invested so much of themselves in it that architecture is made by many people over a long period of time working with constraints completely unfamiliar to us. It was architectural education made manifest in all the ways that studio was not and it taught us more than any other single project could have about the importance of collaboration and intense belief in a shared goal. This is the legacy of this project for the university and it is the true strength of the Goat.

STUDENT ESSAY BY DAVID CLICK

David Click, BSEngr '00, MSEngr '02, was the graduate engineering project manager for the UVA Solar Decathlon team. He has worked at Solar Design Associates for leading solar architect Steven Strong, and is currently at the Florida Solar Energy Center.

Working on the project was far more rewarding than I'd expected, and the process was a great opportunity to integrate my own experience and knowledge with that of others. Typically my team projects at school meant that I'd be working with two to four other engineers. Any difficulties encountered never approached the challenges of working with a hundred engineers, architects, professionals, and industry experts. And with this larger group, we were able to solve many issues that were difficult enough to deal with in isolation—but with a house that integrated so many systems, every decision involved a lot of thought, discussion, and compromise. Although we were initially hesitant, we engineers found that through this collaboration, we were developing higher-quality engineering systems that led to a stronger product on the National Mall. For example, we initially insisted on heavily insulated walls with few windows to make the interior space easier to heat or cool. After a number of design revisions that developed through collaboration between many disciplines, we had a beautiful interior space with plenty of windows (and even skylights!) to make our 750-square-foot house seem surprisingly spacious—and thermal performance was hardly impacted thanks to a high amount of thermal mass, an insulating curtain, and movable louvers that could control the amount of direct solar gain without compromising daylighting.

I had just received a job offer from Lockheed Martin when I realized that I'd have a lot more fun seeing the house through the rest of its design, construction, and competition rather than working on satellite communications systems. Therefore, I decided to stay at UVA for my master's. At the project's beginning, I attended a presentation by solar pioneer Steven Strong, which eventually led to my joining his design firm, Solar Design Associates, in Massachusetts. In my work with SDA (and in my current job at the Florida Solar Energy Center), I've often found myself working with developers, architects, and other engineers to help them understand the benefits of solar technology and how they can integrate solar and other energy-efficiency upgrades into their buildings. Bringing such a disparate group together and helping them accomplish a common goal without compromising their architectural vision is easy, thanks to my experiences in the Solar Decathlon. The Decathlon experience has made me a much better (and happier) engineer, and every day I apply the lessons it taught me in critical thinking and interdisciplinary collaboration.

ecoMOD1: OUTin

Shifting Gears to Focus on Affordable Housing

During the Solar Decathlon experience, one of my frustrations was that the competition was not focused on affordable designs that could easily be replicated in the prefab housing industry. At the core of my interest in starting the ecoMOD project was a return to those issues. I didn't want to do another one-off design that we could make "affordable" simply by getting material donations and using student labor. I wanted to create designs that were easily replicated and adapted to different circumstances—and I wanted to refine the educational aspects of the experience, to ensure everyone the maximum benefit from the project. I didn't realize it at the time, but these new challenges would be even more difficult than the Trojan Goat. Even though we built the Goat and displayed it on a national stage, the reality of having an affordable housing client, with a real budget and a real site (or three different sites before the first design was completed) made the process that much more complex.

I knew I wanted to make the project iterative, so we could learn from our mistakes and eventually figure out how to succeed at this process. For-tunately, I was able to find an anonymous funding organization that understood my vision and was willing to support the administrative aspects of the project. Several people, including the donor, recommended I contact Piedmont Housing Alliance (PHA) and Habitat for Humanity as potential partners, and by chance I approached PHA first. I met with PHA executive director Stu Armstrong and project development manager Mark Watson, as well as other members of their staff.

Their interest in a partnership was immediate, and both Stu and Mark seemed to understand the potential of the project for both PHA and UVA. Ever since that first meeting in 2003, even during some of the most difficult times of the project, PHA has been able to effectively explain their vision while recognizing the importance of the project for the students and the housing industry as a whole.

Piedmont Housing Alliance: Affordable Housing Partner for ecoMOD1 and 3

Piedmont Housing Alliance is a regional non-profit organization with a mission to address affordable housing and community development needs in Charlottesville and the sur-rounding communities. Officially, it is a Community Housing Development Organization, making it eligible for certain forms of federal and state funding, and while it has only been known as Piedmont Housing Alliance since 1997, its roots go back to 1983. The organization's focus is on affordable and fair housing counseling and education, as well as affordable housing development. PHA is also certified as a Housing Counseling Agency by the U.S. Department of Housing and Urban Development, a Homeownership Education and Counseling Agency by Freddie Mac, and a Community Development Financial Institution by the U.S. Department of the Treasury. The overlap of these roles allows PHA to address local housing issues in a comprehensive way, and to receive government funding as well as support from a variety of companies, individuals, and philanthropic organizations. It manages the Mainstream Voucher Program for HUD locally, to provide housing assistance for disabled people. It rehabilitates and manages affordable rental complexes in the area, and also develops new homes intended for sale to its affordable housing clients.

What separates PHA from most similar organizations is the emphasis they place on community outreach with their education and counseling programs, and on green building and innovative financing with their development projects. A part of PHA's agenda is to support low income as well as moderate income or "work-force" housing in the region. This means that in part it serves a more financially well-off demographic than does Habitat for Humanity. Occasionally I have heard criticisms from low income locals who openly wonder what *affordable* means when they hear about PHA homes selling to market rate clients or to PHA affordable housing clients for $200,000 plus. Sometimes these individuals don't realize the affordable housing clients receive subsidies for financing and down payments, to bring the homes in line with what they can afford. PHA aims to sell homes at appraised value (but subsidized) for affordable housing clients, with the intention of building wealth within local communities. This has become much more difficult over the last ten years. Land and home values in the area have increased so much that PHA has had to come up with creative ways of financing their development projects.

One recent project illustrates how PHA has

responded to these challenges through a series of homes built and renovated in the Tenth and Page neighborhood of Charlottesville. Located within easy walking distance of the University of Virginia, the Tenth and Page neighborhood is a traditionally African American community made up of nineteenth- and twentieth-century single-family detached homes. Many of the residents of the area have low incomes, and some of them have deferred their home maintenance—making their homes less valuable than one would imagine given the convenient location. The longtime residents of the compact neighborhood have a strong sense of pride, in part because of the sense of community that has built up over the years. Nearby, the Westhaven public housing project is home to many families that were driven out of a nearby traditionally African American neighborhood, Vinegar Hill, when it was demolished during the "urban renewal" days of the 1960s.

Topographically, the Tenth and Page intersection is a low point in the area, and it directly abuts wealthier nineteenth- and early twentieth-century neighborhoods on higher ground. This higher ground has transitioned from almost exclusively white owner-occupied homes to various forms of student housing. Some of the nicest homes in that area have been torn down to build generic student apartment complexes. Tenth and Page is largely cut off from direct access to these neighborhoods—few of the streets connect and high fences also deter pedestrian traffic. Only recently have the children from Tenth and Page been allowed to take the most direct route to the nearby Venable School, when a chain link fence was removed around a newly renovated community center. Needless to say, children in the traditionally white neighborhoods had no such access problem.

Given the serious development pressures on neighborhoods near the university, PHA decided to purchase several empty lots and dilapidated homes and to renovate them or replace them with new homes. Because of current building codes, the new homes are slightly larger in scale than their neighbors. Most of them include green building strategies, and one of them is the first EarthCraft-certified affordable home in the state. Of the thirty-one homes in the project, one quarter of them were going to be sold at market rate to help offset the cost of building the similar affordable homes. However, as home values soared in the area during the first half of the '00s, PHA had to increase the percentage of market-rate homes to one third to keep the remaining homes affordable.

The project is not without controversy. Some local residents have complained the homes overpower the neighborhood, and that the neotraditional designs are "candy-colored cartoons." There has also been concern that the homes are not meant for people who have always lived in the area—because they are too expensive. This has been compounded by the fact that property taxes for those living near the new and renovated homes have increased, in part due to PHA's efforts—yet property taxes have increased by a similar percentage throughout the city. Gentrification is a legitimate concern in neighborhoods like this, and the search for the right balance of mixed income housing is always a significant challenge. Yet in many ways, it is clear the project accomplished its goals. According to information provided by PHA, the subsidies for the low income units average over $40,000, plus subsidized low interest mortgages as low as 3.5 percent fixed for thirty years. The average annual household income for the affordable homes is 47 percent of area median income—$28,000 per household when the project was completed in 2005. The new homeowners are not uniformly African American, but 65 percent of all buyers (combined affordable and market rate) are minorities, including new immigrants to the country.

As Tenth and Page was underway, the ecoMOD1 team and PHA were starting to plan the first ecoMOD project for the Fifeville neighborhood, about a mile from Tenth and Page. The idea of using modular housing was not initially planned for Tenth and Page, but as PHA got more involved in ecoMOD, they became interested in testing a modular version of their conventional neotraditional designs. To make it happen, PHA worked with Virginia-based Mod-U-Kraf to create three of the homes as two-piece, two-story modular homes. The test project was a success—the homes sold as easily as the others, and the quality of construction was very good. The cost per square foot was comparable to many of the other homes, but higher than ecoMOD1 (completed at the same time) largely due to unforeseen problems with excessive water on the low-lying lots. There is no reason to think those homes could not be replicated at a lower cost on a normal site.

In many ways, PHA has been a terrific partner for the ecoMOD project. They have

been very open-minded about using contemporary design, and about trying to push
sustainability beyond the measures they
had already started to implement. While I
think some members of the PHA staff were
concerned the ecoMOD homes might not
sell as quickly as their standard homes, they
have been pleasantly surprised that all the
units have had offers on them very quickly.
Stu Armstrong and Mark Watson refer to

ecoMOD as the research and development
arm of PHA—where we test strategies and
technologies before they are adopted more
broadly within PHA.

The Design of the First Prototype

The first PHA house, ecoMOD1, called the
OUTin house, was designed, prefabricated
off-site, and sited in the Fifeville neighborhood of Charlottesville on 7½ Street. The
2,196-square-foot, three-story building was
sold as a two-unit condominium, with the
basement unit sold separately from the upper
two floors. The features of the 1,464-square-
foot two-story, three-bedroom upper unit
include a potable rainwater collection system.
It collects rainwater from the roof, then stores,
purifies, and distributes the water throughout
the house. Other house features include a
solar hot water panel, low impact finishes, and
a landscape of native, drought tolerant plants.
After considerable debate, the team selected
sustainably forested poplar for the flooring,
supplied by Appalachian Sustainable Development. The walls and roof are constructed
from structural insulated panels (SIPs) made
from expanded polystyrene foam sandwiched
between two layers of oriented strand board.

The primary design strategy of the OUTin
house is to make the entire site habitable and
usable. Rather than a rectangular box without
functional outdoor spaces, the OUTin house
is designed to merge outside and inside.
Sunlight, breezes, vegetation, the earth, and
the surrounding context are brought into
the house through passive design strategies
and shifted modules that define outdoor/

indoor spaces. OUTin's design strategies are grounded philosophically and formally in the design team's clearly stated ecological mission: they wanted to make ecology legible for the inhabitant.

During the fall of 2004, the first ecoMOD design studio was held in the School of Architecture. The group of twelve graduate and undergraduate students—representing architecture and landscape architecture—were

a diverse group of individuals drawn to the project for a variety of reasons. Some were committed to affordable housing, others were mostly interested in sustainability, and still others wanted to participate in a tangible project with a built result. In reality, they were all interested in at least two of these themes, if not all three. I structured the studio in a similar way to the initial Goat studio, but I felt I wanted to adjust some aspects. Unfortunately, the engineering participation that first semester was pretty light. Paxton was on board with the idea of ecoMOD, but initially would have preferred participating in the next Solar Decathlon. As an associate dean in the School of Engineering and Applied Science, his administrative workload was significant, and during that particular semester he couldn't commit the same amount of time as we put into the Goat. He was still working with students tinkering with the systems of the Goat and monitoring it, and some of them were interested in ecoMOD too. But it wasn't until the second semester of the design process that we began to have regular contact with engineering students.

I asked the studio to begin with student presentations on relevant prefab and ecological case studies, and design studies that addressed specific activities within the home. This led to preliminary design studies as the team worked individually and then collaborated in small groups. The groups were regularly shuffled in order to minimize the potential of isolated subgroups. Landscape architecture students worked alongside architecture students, and were often participating in the same assignments. The overlap

between the UVA architecture and landscape architecture graduate programs is much more significant than at most universities, and a significant percentage of graduate students participate in dual degree programs between two of the four disciplines in the school—architecture, landscape architecture, urban and environmental planning, and architectural history. Both of the landscape architecture students were pursuing dual degrees with architecture and using the studio as one of their core required landscape studios. Accordingly, landscape architecture faculty members Chris Fannin and Julie Bargmann advised the studio throughout the process.

Participants in the first studio were paired with planning students for an analysis project on the neighborhood for the first house, the traditionally African American Fifeville. A neighborhood development workshop taught by planning professor Nisha Botchwey offered the context for this collaboration.

Although the students welcomed the possibility of interdisciplinary work, the results of analysis did not live up to Nisha's or my expectations. Analysis of urban context takes on very different forms in the two disciplines, and the students found it difficult to collaborate within their interdisciplinary subgroups within the limited time frame we gave them. However, the most positive aspect of the early collaboration with the planning students was the ensuing discussion about the broader agenda for the project. Planning student subgroups were asked to frame a set of guidelines for decision-making during the design process. Most participants were surprised that the lists prepared by the planning students overlapped with the collaborative list developed by the architecture and landscape architecture students in the context of the studio. However, one planning student subgroup suggested that the design ought to replicate the existing architectural language of the neighborhood.

A heated discussion on this topic helped all parties better understand and articulate their positions. Nisha effectively navigated the discussion to ensure all voices were heard. Needless to say, the design students did not agree with the suggestion, but more importantly did not agree with the assumption underpinning it—that a contemporary design would not be accepted by the homeowners or the neighbors. In the end, the interdisciplinary group did not reach complete agreement about how to handle this relevant and controversial topic, but it certainly helped them understand each other's disciplines and points of view. It also led to a self-imposed commitment by the studio students to present their design ideas to members of the Fifeville Neighborhood Association (FNA). Intended as a way to receive feedback about their preliminary design ideas, the meetings with the FNA became an essential part of the design process.

The students were concerned that a few of their early design ideas might not align with the opinions of the FNA membership, but they found they were not so far apart. The participants in the feedback sessions (four sessions over a period of six months) never questioned the contemporary nature of the designs presented to them and mostly responded to functional issues. The most heated discussion in the FNA meetings related to the appropriate location for the kitchen—nearer the street or nearer the backyard. By the very end of the design process, the designers found an effective middle ground, with the kitchen in the middle and a clear line of sight to both the street and the backyard. The students also interacted regularly with professional members of the local community—from building department officials to local contractors and consultants. These conversations helped the team develop the design further.

As we neared the end of the first semester, the studio had developed a very elegant design that was perhaps going to be more expensive to build than what PHA could afford. Although PHA had intentionally been somewhat ambiguous about the budget in order to let the scope of the project evolve, that ambiguity was not helpful at this stage. But another more pressing problem was about to shake up the whole process. During that fall semester, PHA had acquired an existing house with a small cottage behind it—immediately adjacent to our site. Their intention was to tear down both the house and the cottage and put up another house next to ecoMOD1. Both buildings were in a serious state of disrepair and had been condemned. The foundations for both buildings, which were probably not adequate to begin with, had been undermined by the constant flow of water off the higher-set street. The buildings were leaning over, and the cottage in particular could have fallen over in a major windstorm. As we neared the end of the semester, PHA began to consider the possibility of working with the city (which was supporting their efforts in Fifeville) to redraw the lot lines and create three affordable houses on the site instead of two. This would require that the width of our lot be significantly reduced. The house, as designed, would no longer fit. The official decision was not made until after the semester was over, which was probably for the best because it allowed the team to complete something, even though it would not get built in that form.

The spring semester included many of the students from fall continuing on, as well as an entirely new group of graduate and undergraduate students. The enlarged team set about redesigning the house for the new narrower lot, and reducing the cost at the same time. The elegant but potentially very expensive translucent stair tower was shoved most of the way into the building, while other things were reconfigured. The landscape team had to start over because the new narrower lot was also on a different part of the site. The team had a choice of any of the three newly proposed lots, and elected to build on the northernmost one because it was the last on the dead-end street. This allowed the landscape strategy to more directly connect to a larger idea the team had for connecting pedestrian paths through the block to the immediate vicinity. The site change significantly delayed the development of the design, but forced the team to address the adaptability of the design to various sites.

I selected a team of student managers who worked with the studio, myself, and Paxton to collectively make important design decisions. Choices that required a comparison of multiple possibilities were facilitated with decision webs, as discussed earlier. In concept the webs were meant to help the team with the decision process, but in reality the webs were mostly treated as a documentation of the team's choice. The students were not enthusiastic about the decision webs at the time, but later began to appreciate the graphic representations of their collective thinking.

In the middle of April, two weeks before the official end of classes, and just before our deadline to order the SIPs, another major change impacted the project's design. Back in February, as PHA was proceeding with the demolition process of the two homes, the city neighborhood services office declined the demolition for the one nearest the street (but not the cottage behind it). Apparently it had been individually designated as an important historic property in the city, and while the neighborhood was not a historic district, the designation had the effect of putting the demolition and any potential new construction on the site under the purview of the Board of Architectural Review (BAR). At first we were in a state of disbelief, since the house was in such bad shape and was difficult to imagine as having any historic value. It appeared to be occupied by squatters and used as a crack den after the previous owner had moved out. PHA proceeded with the hearing before the BAR in March, and when it also denied the demolition permit, PHA decided to asked the city council to weigh in on the matter. After all, the city had been the ones that asked PHA to purchase the site and develop affordable housing there, and it was the city's administrative procedures that failed in allowing PHA to buy the property in '04 without learning of its historic designation until the spring of '05. If the house needed to be retained and restored, it would undoubtedly cost PHA a lot more money than a new affordable house, especially if it needed to meet the guidelines of the BAR for historically designated properties. I had assumed the situation would resolve itself, but as the April city council meeting approached, the studio and I learned that the historic designation was based on some evidence that the house dated from the mid-nineteenth century, not the mid-twentieth century as we had all assumed, and there was reason to believe the original core of the house had been built as a slave quarters.

When it became obvious in the meeting

that the city council was unlikely to overturn the decision of the BAR, PHA withdrew the demolition permit request. That evening I sat in the council chambers wondering how we were going to handle the situation, realizing the status of the entire three-site proposal was thrown up in the air, and it might take PHA awhile to figure out how they were going to respond. Yet I had a team of students getting ready for graduation, and many of them had committed to sticking around for the summer to build a house. I approached Mark Watson as he was leaving the chambers and asked him if he had any other sites. Fortunately, he had one that they had no current plans to develop on—it had been a part of their "land bank" from before the organization was renamed PHA, and was in another part of Fifeville. I stopped to take a look at the potential new site on my way home that evening, and within two days PHA moved us to this alternative location. An awkward-shaped bit of land that straddles a constructed stormwater stream, the lot is also adjacent to a wooded area that a developer is expecting to turn into a major development once they can get financing and approvals. (See chapter 2.5 for the rest of the story about the historic house, which became the setting for ecoMOD3 two years later.)

The students responded well to this second site change—despite the impending deadline. In some ways it was a little easier than the first site change because the reasons were very clear and the design had come a long way. However, the topography at the new site was much steeper than the previous one, and it also had a different solar orientation. Our aspiration for a modular design that could adapt to various topographic and climate conditions was immediately put to the test as the team had to scrap the landscape design a second time, integrate a walk-out basement that became a second housing unit, and flip the house to accommodate the new solar orientation. The new site on 7½ Street is also a very different urban context. There would have to be a lot more open space adjacent to the house, as it sits next to a constructed drainage stream and up against a wooded area, and unfortunately it would appear much taller than its immediate

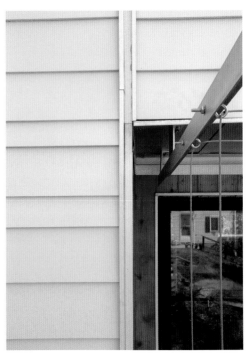

neighbors due to topography and the height of the nearest buildings. What was designed as a two-story urban infill underwent some gyrations and became a three-story building (only two stories from the front) on the side of a hill with the roof higher than the nearest neighbor on both sides.

The team designed the layout of the basement but did not build interior stairs, so that it could eventually be finished by the homeowner and rented as a studio apartment to supplement their income. But when the house was appraised (at the very height of the real estate boom) and the value was higher than a family that qualified for affordable housing subsidies could afford, PHA made the decision to finish off the basement themselves and sell it as a two unit condominium—the first of its kind in Charlottesville.

Build Phase

Because of the last minute site change, the start of the construction process was delayed by nearly two months. The team refined the design to fit the new site, and designed the new structure and plumbing layout for the basement level. By July of 2005, the students began fabricating eight small modules for the upper two stories in a decommissioned airport hangar owned by the university, and transported them to the infill site in early September. Unlike conventional modular houses, the students' modules were designed to fit the proportion of urban infill sites and to be easily transported along narrow streets. The modules were less than half the typical size, allowing for the use of a less expensive

crane and the possibility of moving the modules to the narrowest streets with the tightest turning radiuses. The original site was on a very narrow street, with restricted access that necessitated this strategy, but we chose not to change the module size when we ended up on a wider street. However, we did put two modules on each trailer.

The majority of the design studio students elected to stay in town after their graduation and participate in the construction process. Most of them had little or no building experience. The team worked through all the logistics themselves, including coordination between various building trades, material procurement, and transportation. They also built the entire house, with the exception of the basement/foundation and the final installation of the plumbing, electrical, and mechanical infrastructure. PHA hired Roger Rothwell, a local developer/contractor, and his son Roger Jr. to build the foundation and coordinate the site and utility work. He also handled the building permit process and advised the students on several issues. The foundation was more complicated than expected, as the remains of a previous home on the site were discovered during excavation and the site had a very high water table. This necessitated additional excavation, gravel, and a French drain system to keep the basement dry. Ted Marrs, a project manager with one of the top homebuilders in town, Abrahamse & Company, also advised the team. I was invited to a prefab conference organized by *Dwell,* where I met a modular building expert, Greg Sloditskie, who has been an advisor to the project ever since.

The funding for the tools and a significant

percentage of the summer student fellowship money was provided by the grant from the anonymous organization. I raised the remainder of the funding required for student fellowships and green upgrades via grants and donations. Field trips to modular home factories confirmed that most of the required tools and equipment were within our budget—although we could not afford some of the more sophisticated equipment used to increase productivity in most modular facilities. The field trips also helped us to mimic the standard modular home fabrication process, and to refine the structural and module "seam" details based on our observations. The students devised strategies to work around the lack of automated equipment. For example, one company uses pneumatic devices to allow the modules to float or "hover" as they move along the assembly line. The students built the eight modules in a single line in the hangar, and only moved them when it was time to transport them at the end. For this purpose, they designed and fabricated a set of "house skates" using leftover framing material on wheels to reposition the modules when necessary, and then used conventional car jacks at each corner to raise the modules high enough to roll a trailer underneath and lower them onto the bed. It was fun to watch three or four people easily push the modules around while on the "skates"—as long as there weren't any stones or fasteners on the floor.

Soon after the SIPs arrived in early July, a couple of team members were frustrated with the difficulty of lifting the heavy panels to attach them on both sides. For the first few panels, they were laying them on the floor framing, attaching them together on one side, and then awkwardly flipping the partially attached panels over to fasten them on the other side. One evening, the two students invented a contraption that allowed them to slide the panels along rolling slices of cardboard tubes while holding them upright. The SIPs were fastened together on both sides through a gap in the vertical supports, and then slid along to

make room for the next one. Overnight, the "SIP Master 3000" was born.

With the delay in the start of the construction process, it was inevitable that it would go later than the end of the summer. Two months after the delivery of the SIPs, the inexperienced team completed enough of the work on the eight modules to move them to the site. In early September the students, who had already graduated, were expecting to be finished with the project, and needed to start their prearranged jobs or find gainful employment. We pushed hard to move the modules before the

students started to leave. The module move day was exciting and nerve-wracking for everyone, but it went off without a hitch.

After the modules were on-site, students slowly started to leave town over the next two months, until we were down to two hard-working team members by the end of the fall. With help from Roger and Roger Jr., we were able to substantially complete the interior finishes in time for a ribbon cutting, but small scopes of work continued for the last two volunteers for another couple of months. The last 5 percent of work always seems to take

50 percent of the time, especially when you only have 5 percent of your workforce.

My goal, naive in retrospect, was to have the house cost less per square foot than a comparable one built by PHA at the same time. In the end, we met that goal, but just barely. The additional cost of having Roger and his crew work on an hourly basis to help finish parts of the house that the students had been hoping to complete themselves increased the budget. I had figured that since the students were being paid by money I raised, we would save on labor costs, but the delay meant we came in just barely under what the homes in the Tenth and Page neighborhood cost PHA—approximately $114 per square foot for the building itself, and $123 per square foot including site work and sidewalk.

Evaluation and Current Status

During the 2005–6 academic year, the evaluation team researched the affordability and environmental impact of the materials and

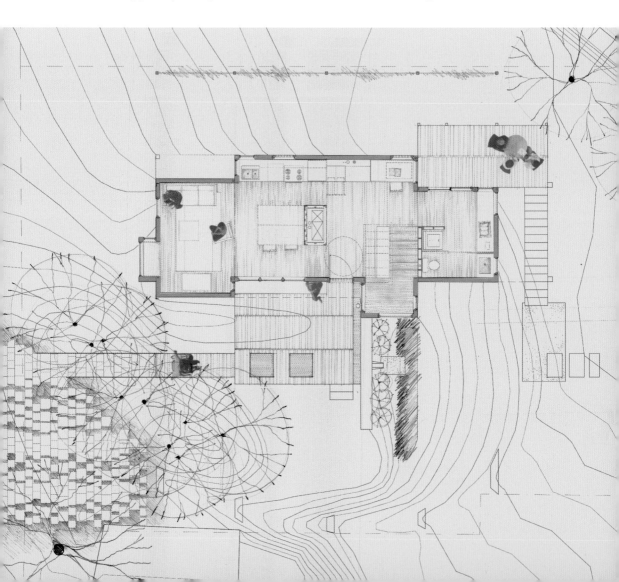

construction methods used on the house. Prior to the house going on the market (as the lower unit was still being finished by PHA) the evaluation team installed a monitoring system throughout the upper unit. The system measures temperature, humidity, and indoor air quality, and it also includes devices to track the power used on individual circuits at the electrical panel.

As the delay for PHA's contractor to finish off the basement continued, the evaluation team was able to get good steady-state read-ings on the performance of the building without occupants. They are a useful baseline for comparison to the life of the home with people inside. The analysis of the collected data is being used to produce recommen-dations that are informing later ecoMOD projects and their teams.

During the evaluation phase of ecoMOD1, students discovered that the first version of the monitoring system had an overabundance of sensors. This has caused some problems with monitoring because of overlapping data being

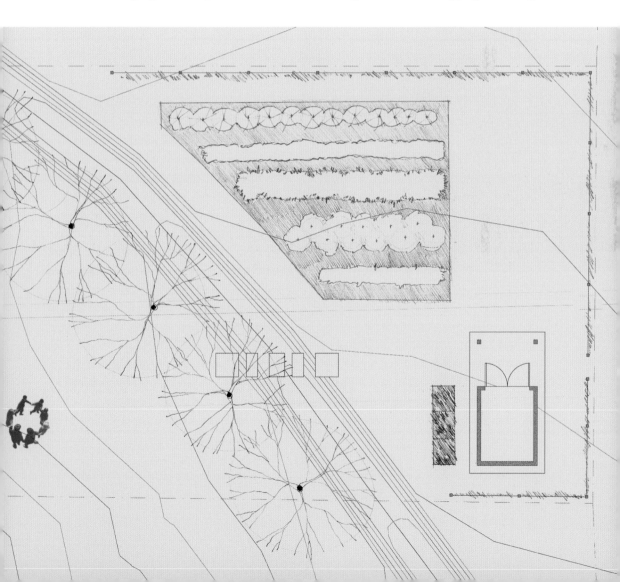

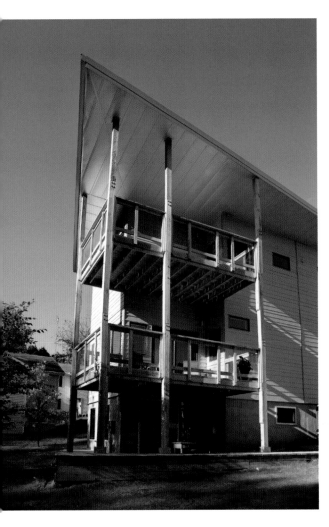

recorded. These findings were helpful in the design and layout of the monitoring system for ecoMOD3. Reducing the number of sensors also saves on fabrication costs and time.

As soon as the basement was finished and the condominium filing was complete, the two units went on the market. Very quickly the upper unit of ecoMOD1 was sold to two young people, and an older gentleman initially purchased the lower unit. After living there for almost two years, he died in 2007, and when his survivors could not pay the mortgage, the property was repossessed and sold at auction. That process has effectively removed the housing unit from the affordable housing market, because the constraints against simply selling the home for a profit were void after the property was repossessed. PHA bid on the unit in an attempt to keep it affordable, but they were outbid.

The people in the upper unit have given the evaluation team enthusiastic feedback about the home. They were attracted by the contemporary design and the sustainability agenda, and report that they find themselves trying to live more responsibly since becoming the owners. The negative feedback has been minor—some of the storage isn't convenient, and there have been a few lingering punchlist items. Data from the monitoring system helped the evaluation team discover that, unfortunately, two of the major systems were not working properly—the rainwater collection system and the solar hot water heater. After a few attempts the solar hot water heater was fixed, but it took the team some time to figure out exactly what was wrong with the rainwater collection system. Eventually, after excavating around the tanks, we discovered the plumbing leading to the collection tanks was not sloped appropriately to them. The team reworked the plumbing, and temporarily the system worked properly. In 2010, another problem emerged regarding the pump, which appears to have been improperly sized. Without a warranty for the overall system, it was difficult and expensive to address these issues.

There have been four semesters of evaluation since the modules were moved for eco-MOD1. The first two were focused exclusively on ecoMOD1, and the later two also evaluated ecoMOD2 and 3. Each evaluation team carefully considered the choices made by the design/build team. In addition to monitoring, the evaluation teams have considered life-cycle assessments of the materials and construction process and completed a post-occupancy evaluation with the homeowners, including questions about thermal and lighting comfort, as well as evaluation of the design hypotheses set out in the design phase. Planning students prepared an affordability analysis comparing the cost of both the prototype and the eventual production model to other homes and an architecture student did an assessment of the design's suitability for production with a major manufacturer.

Preliminary conclusions indicate the following:

- While the potable rainwater collection system will save the homeowners money

and reduce the home's environmental impact, the cost of the filtration equipment negates the efficacy of recommending it for locations where the municipal water supply is relatively inexpensive (the cost of the equipment was funded separately by ecoMOD, and not by PHA).

- Stricter guidelines need to be established to make sure the emphasis on reducing material waste at the hangar during the off-site construction process is not lost during the final phase on site, where a large dumpster was available, and a little too convenient.
- While the design addresses shading from the summer sun, the shade device above the large south facing windows does not have vines growing on it as expected, and therefore heat gain is not reduced as much as it ought to be; also the passive design strategy does not appear to sufficiently address the potential positive contribution of solar heat gain during the winter months— there is not sufficient thermal mass, such

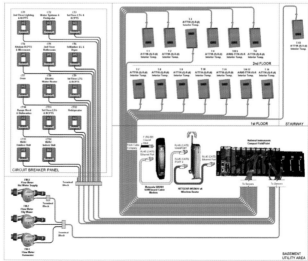

as stone or concrete, to hold the heat from the sun.

- The material life cycle assessments support the design decisions, but additional research is required into a comparison of the no-VOC interior paint (as selected for ecoMOD1) versus low-VOC paint, which is more durable and doesn't need to be repainted as often.
- The centralized air handler and ductwork—located in the middle of the conditioned space—appears to contribute to the energy efficiency of the mechanical system.
- The combined effect of the energy efficient wall and roof system (SIPs), the equipment, and the passive design strategies seems to indicate a minimum of a 50 percent reduction in energy costs for the homeowners. In some months the reduction is closer to 65 percent.

- The preliminary market analysis by commerce and economics students indicates that if the ecoMOD project were a for-profit business venture, it would be able to successfully find its niche in the largely underserved market for environmentally responsible, prefabricated, and affordable housing.
- Two major modular manufacturers could replicate the design for between $80 and $110 per square foot (including foundation).
- PHA's policy to always sell homes at their appraised value contributes to the growing recognition at PHA that single-family affordable homes are no longer a viable option in the Charlottesville area. With house prices and construction costs skyrocketing in the last four years, PHA is increasingly looking to multifamily complexes. The ecoMOD1 house appraised $40,000 higher than comparable homes built by PHA, despite the fact that the costs per square foot were the same or lower than these homes. This was largely due to the location of the property and had nothing to do with the sustainable design features. Therefore measures need to be established to minimize the appraised value of the house—at least at the time of the initial appraisal. The appraiser indicated that some of the appraised value was related to the generous exterior decks.

Although the student evaluators did not address it, my personal assessment of ecoMOD1 is that the system of modules is not as intrinsically flexible as the team intended it to be. Each of the eight modules is unique, which certainly keeps the home from becoming a generic box, but when the house had to move to a different site, we had to change the modules in ways that might be difficult for a nondesigner to do without assistance. While it was a good first step, the mass customization strategy and modules developed for ecoMOD3 and ecoMOD4 are more flexible systems, and would not require the same level of adjustment to make the home site specific.

The copyright registration for the design of ecoMOD1 has been processed by the UVA Patent Foundation, including four adaptations to various solar orientations and topographies.

The monitoring is continuing as long as the homeowners are willing to allow us to keep the equipment in their home. They've been very helpful so far, and are interested in the results. A preliminary analysis of the data collected so far indicates the home continues to outperform the simulations. It is believed ecoMOD1 uses 50 to 60 percent less power than a comparable home using conventional construction methods, despite homeowners that due to their conflicting work schedules are often in the home around the clock. In 2007, analysis of the home's energy performance showed that in the categories of HVAC, laundry, kitchen, outlets, and lighting, ecoMOD1 is consistently outperforming the average home in efficiency. Low energy output in ecoMOD1 is due both to the efficient systems of the home and sensitivity towards energy usage that these systems create in the home's residents. The annual energy bills of the ecoMOD1 residents in 2007 was more than $500 less than the annual energy bills of the average American home.

ecoMOD1 DESIGN FEATURES

STRUCTURAL INSULATED PANELS The SIPs used for the walls and roof are made of two layers of oriented strand board with a core of expanded polystyrene foam. The supplier was R-Control in northern Virginia. The system creates a superinsulated roof and walls, and is structurally stronger than conventional stud frames. Buildings made with SIPs can be framed in a shorter time than required for normal stud-framing, and air infiltration and thermal bridging are reduced.

POTABLE RAINWATER COLLECTION SYSTEM The potable rainwater collection system is the first in the modern era in the city of

Charlottesville. The water is collected using a single wedge-shaped roof, which allowed the design team to cover both the house and the rear porches and direct the water into a single gutter, and a side-by-side pair of oversized downspouts—collecting all the water in one place. The roof water is stored in two 1,750-gallon tanks below the front deck, and a sophisticated filtration system located just inside the entry door provides clean water to the entire house. The system, sold to us as components by Rainwater Management Solutions, provides roughly 35 percent of the water needed in a year for a family of four. The system did not operate properly at first (due to some plumbing in-stallation and other problems) and potential buyers of similar systems are strongly encouraged to get a warranty for both parts and labor, and to use a plumber familiar with these systems.

SUSTAINABLY HARVESTED WOOD FLOOR The flooring is from sustainably managed forests in Virginia. Bamboo was eliminated because of the embodied energy impact of shipping it from China. The wood is poplar, a species found throughout the mid-Atlantic region of the U.S., and a relatively soft wood not always used for floors. However, the budget was very tight, and poplar was the only affordable choice at that time. The wood is from the Sustainable Woods program of Appalachian Sustainable Development (ASD), a Virginia-based organization dedicated to the support of local economies and sustainable forest management. ASD is part of the Sustainable Woods network, and uses standards designed to ensure long-term diversity of the forest and protection of water resources. These standards are very similar to the principles of the Forest Stewardship Council (FSC) and in 2009 (after the project was finished), ASD became an official FSC supplier. The ASD drying kiln, located in southwest Virginia, is solar and wood-waste powered.

ENERGY STAR APPLIANCES To help the home-owner save on utility bills, the design team selected all Energy Star appliances. The Energy Star program was created by and is managed by the Environmental Protection Agency and the U.S. Department of Energy, and continues to evolve each year. Energy Star appliances have been selected for ecoMOD projects, and while there are recent news reports about the rigor of Energy Star testing, the ecoMOD teams have always sought the highest efficiency appliance in the price range.

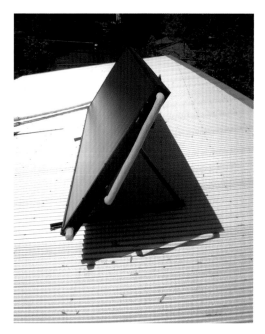

LOW/NO-VOC INTERIOR MATERIALS Volatile organic compounds (VOCs) found in paints, varnishes, sealants, and primers can impact indoor air quality and potentially harm the health of the home's occupants. The ecoMOD teams try to avoid interior materials with VOCs whenever the budget allows it. The interior paint, caulks, sealants, and flooring finish were all no- or low-VOC products (and this is true for all ecoMOD designs). The ecoMOD1 team could not afford entirely VOC-free cabinetry.

SOLAR HOT WATER HEATER The solar hot water system used on ecoMOD1 is a conven-tional flat plate system with antifreeze running the plumbing so the pipes don't freeze in the winter. The heat collected in the system is transferred to the domestic hot water, and also stored until used. The system reduces the

water-heating costs for the occupants by $300 to $350 a year. Initial problems with this system were resolved by the subcontractor who installed it.

DAYLIGHTING Each room has at least two windows on two different walls to allow natural light to illuminate the interior spaces. Effective daylighting can reduce annual energy costs by 20 to 30 percent, and the layout of the house gives important primary spaces more sunlight.

STUDENT ESSAY BY CAROLINA CORDERO

Carolina Cordero was a research assistant for ecoMOD1, later transitioning into a project management role as the construction phase dragged on. She has worked in Sri Lanka and Haiti on post-disaster relief housing for the Red Cross and other organizations.

Being part of the ecoMOD team has been one of the most satisfactory experiences of my academic and professional life, although not without sacrifices. All of us who worked on the OUTin house had very low income for quite some time and worked long hours—from hot summer days under a metal hangar to cold February mornings in the snow. We struggled at times to keep the team together, motivated, and focused. We spent hours debating the impact of using one material or system over another, hours stretching the budget to its limits, ridiculously long hours trying to define sustainability and affordability, and some more developing methods to apply those concepts.

I left the project site in March '06 having a long list of satisfactions: contributing to the development of an intelligent system for affordable housing; seeing the OUTin house rise from paper to brick and mortar—or rather OSB and foam; knowing that we had built an efficient house, beautifully designed and detailed; understanding the impact of a project of its nature to the university community, the Fifeville neighborhood, and the housing sector as a whole. But more importantly I left knowing that the experience of managing this project would significantly impact my future—professional and personal.

I discovered things about myself and my attitude toward work. I understood then that I am most comfortable at the job site, that working under challenging and sometimes restricting conditions makes me strive further, and that I am happiest and most focused when my work involves high levels of social responsibility.

Although it has proven difficult to find projects that compare to such an ambitious and comprehensive program as ecoMOD, my career since has been quite interesting and challenging. I am lucky to have been able to work for organizations concerned with some of the same principles. I often think about my time at ecoMOD and I find myself going back to those drawings, essays, and photos to draw lessons for my current work. I know that others who participated do as well. So the concept and principles evolve beyond the OUTin house, and I believe that is the key proof of the program's remarkable potential.

**STUDENT ESSAY
BY CHRISTOPHER
BROOKS**

Christopher Brooks was a
construction manager for
ecoMOD1, and currently
works as an assistant
project manager for Bovis
Land Lease in Chicago.

I arrived at UVA after spending a couple of years working full time in Chicago in an architectural practice. Admittedly, I viewed the year away from the profession as a sabbatical of sorts; an opportunity to flex my design muscles and to thrive in the spirit of Mountain Dew and all-night design studio work. The expectation was to knock out a few design projects, take supplementary courses, build up a killer portfolio, and return to the profession with another prestigious degree and get back on the fast track. The plan changed when I sat in an auditorium in Campbell Hall while the respective instructors were giving the design studio presentations. It would be wrong for me to say that the other courses were not relevant to me, but there was something about the hopeful yet progressive nature of the ecoMOD project John Quale spoke of that afternoon. I knew it was going to be real and I wanted to be a part of it.

Every day was a new challenge and I really learned that having a good idea just isn't enough. What was most important was learning how to communicate goals to the team members, how to listen to people, and how to find out what makes a person uncomfortable and figure out how to help the person through that task.

Working on this project gave me a better glimpse into what I was capable of doing and raised my expectations for myself. All of us were able to leave the university and be more than entry-level contributors at whatever offices we landed at because we actually built something that was real. There would be more than a portfolio of drawings and computer renderings to show to prospective employers, there would be someone's home. We would share stories of shoveling gravel for drain tile, being yelled at by Sally Ann the plumber, lifting incredibly heavy SIPs sections (who ever thought OSB and foam would be so heavy?), marathon design decision meetings, navigating city officials trying to obtain permits, countless trips to the building supply stores, and so on. We were a true family that summer and I definitely miss the group.

ecoMOD2: preHAB

Responding in a Small Way to a Natural Disaster

Originally focused exclusively on housing for central Virginia, in late 2005 the ecoMOD project was invited to ship a home to southern Mississippi for the Operation Home Delivery program with Habitat for Humanity of Greater Charlottesville (HFHGC). With more than 200,000 homes destroyed by hurricanes in 2005, the Gulf Coast region is in the midst of a long rebuilding effort. Hurricane Katrina alone is the single most destructive and costliest natural disaster in U.S. history. To help address the resulting building crisis, the ecoMOD project expanded its scope to partner with Habitat for Humanity in the devastated gulf coast of Mississippi. In Mississippi alone, Katrina destroyed 70,000 homes and another 65,000 were very significantly damaged. HFHGC sent five conventional panelized homes to Habitat for Humanity of the Mississippi Gulf Coast (HFHMGC), and the ecoMOD2 team designed and built another home. The opportunity came about because legal-thriller author John Grisham and his wife Renee decided to give money to HFHGC to support these homes. The Grishams lived in Mississippi for many years, but currently reside in the Charlottesville area.

The preHAB house, ecoMOD2, was shipped in the spring of 2006 as a flat-pack panelized home using an innovative superinsulated steel and foam panel system instead of a conventional wood-stud frame. The preHAB house was installed in an established neighborhood in Gautier, Mississippi, for a family displaced by Hurricane Katrina. The site is a 1960s affordable housing subdivision just north of the area flooded by the initial deluge of Katrina. Several houses in the subdivision were

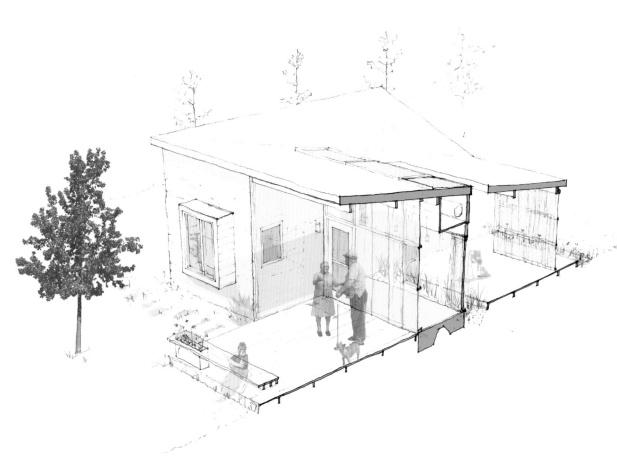

very significantly damaged, but the part of Gautier that was essentially erased is two miles south—directly on the coast. This particular house was an opportunity for the design team to test and investigate contemporary design, environmentally responsible strategies, and prefabricated construction within the constraints and mission of Habitat for Humanity.

The ecoMOD policy, when working with PHA, was to avoid donations or discounts for baseline materials to ensure the designs could be easily replicated by affordable housing organizations and modular builders. However, in light of the difficult situation after the hurricane, ecoMOD2 seemed to require a

slightly different response. We raised money to subsidize material upgrades and sought equipment donations and discounts. To align with Habitat for Humanity's mission, Habitat and university volunteers completed all of the work. The 1,087-square-foot, three-bedroom home was built for approximately $65 per square foot, although exact costs for individual HFH homes are difficult to track because of donated materials and volunteer labor.

The design is intended to demonstrate the potential of prefab for Habitat affiliates. HFH was already pursuing panelized construction with their Operation Home Delivery project focused on delivering wall panels from around the country to be set up in the hurricane-devastated Gulf Coast region. The program was heavily promoted by Habitat at the time—the news personalities of NBC's *Today Show* built a home in front of Rockefeller Center, and the president and First Lady helped assemble a home shipped from elsewhere in Louisiana. Unfortunately, the scale of the disaster meant the process was not very well organized, and some homes were received that could not easily be assembled as intended. I know anecdotally of at least a few situations where the prefabricated frame walls and roofs were disassembled so the lumber could be used for other homes.

The goal of the preHAB (i.e., prefab for Habitat) design was to take this strategy one step further, by developing a home that can be prefabricated in various ways. With this project we imagined future disaster relief efforts where Habitat affiliates from around the U.S. could enlist their volunteers to build house panels, modules, or components without taking too much time or money away from their own local building efforts. The perception among Habitat officials is that prefab construction conflicts with HFH's local volunteer labor strategies. Typically, Habitat affiliates use conventional on-site wood framing strategies with a volunteer workforce, often including the future homeowners putting in their "sweat equity." Habitat officials see the value in the dramatic scene of a crowd of volunteers hammering conventional walls together to energize the community and maximize fundraising opportunities. Yet, with a carefully designed prefab house system,

HFH affiliates from across the country could also contribute to very worthy relief efforts outside their own area. By offering a range of opportunities for their level of involvement, this prototype house strategy could include the efforts of smaller Habitat affiliates without the resources to ship a complete home to a disaster area. The shipping distance is a factor to consider with prefabricated components. In the context of Hurricane Katrina, HFH affiliates in the states adjoining Mississippi and Louisiana could contribute modules. Affiliates within 800 miles could produce wall and roof panels, and others could ship smaller and simpler components. This idea can be likened to the way thousands of Americans prepared first-aid dressings in their homes for injured soldiers during World War I.

Habitat for Humanity: Affordable Housing Partner for ecoMOD2 and 4

Habitat for Humanity International (HFHI) is a nonprofit organization founded by Millard and Linda Fuller in 1976. The Fullers became involved with a "housing ministry" in Georgia in 1968, and later went to the Congo for three

years to test-drive their strategy for a home-building process with the direct involvement of the future occupants in the construction. Based on these experiences, they established Habitat for Humanity as an international organization to address the global housing shortage. The mission of HFHI is to create simple, affordable housing using volunteer labor and the "sweat equity" of the homeowners. The residents purchase their home with the sweat equity applied to their down payment, but the price is significantly reduced compared to similar homes in the same areas. The owners also receive interest-free financing.

HFH was founded as a religious organization, and the Christian principles espoused by the Fullers still influence many of its decisions. Yet Habitat homes have been built by and lived in by people of all faiths, and religion plays no part in family selection. Habitat typically keeps the aesthetics of their homes simple and practical so that they can focus their funds on the construction of as many new homes as possible. In 1984, when former president Jimmy Carter and his wife Rosalynn first participated in a Habitat work trip, the profile of the organization began to expand significantly. The Carters remain actively involved in Habitat to this day—and many outsiders mistakenly believe they founded the organization. HFH builds homes in a variety of countries, and is the fifteenth largest home-builder in the United States. HFH has provided homes for more than a million people in over 250,000 houses—distributed in more than 3,000 communities across the globe.

Much of the real work of Habitat occurs at the level of the local affiliate. Affiliates work within a flexible structure set up by HFHI that allows the affiliates to respond to the unique culture and specific needs of a community. Larger affiliates tend to have paid staff, including fundraising personnel to bring in material and cash donations to fund their local homes. While the standard photo opportunity with a group of volunteers at a Habitat house framing is an important aspect of the work, the back-room coordination to pull off these events is considerable. HFH affiliates depend on staff and regular volunteers to manage the home-build events intended for the media, as well as not so glamorous tasks like credit counseling, loan coordination, material procurement, and family selection. The media-oriented events

with weekend volunteers putting in a few hours to pound nails are essentially fund-raisers—structured to maximize free publicity and spread the word about the organization. It should be no surprise that some of the most consistent and generous donors to HFH have been introduced to the organization through these building events. It is a fine example of a worthwhile organization using the news media for the public good.

The conservative nature of the architectural design of most Habitat homes has presented an interesting challenge for architects in the last ten years. Habitat homes in the U.S. are often conventional ranch homes, like so many other ranchburgers across the country. The only difference is that the homes tend to be a little smaller, and, to keep costs down, there is never a garage. Architects and architecture students have long been intrigued by the possibility of rethinking the standard Habitat house. Design competitions have been held (often without any involvement from HFH) and architecture design studios taught to challenge designers to work within the size and cost constraints of Habitat. The results are varied—some of the designs offer considerable architectural sophistication, but would be too expensive or too complicated for normal Habitat volunteers to construct. Others simply shuffle the rooms and windows around a little, but offer no particular advantages. Occasion-

ally, a designer is able to find a solution that is elegant, affordable, and easily constructed. Other organizations that are interested in the same ideas, but don't want the constraints of HFH, have created alternative processes for creating affordable homes. Design Corps, run by Bryan Bell in North Carolina, is a compelling example. Design Corps provides design solutions to underserved communities in a way that gets them invested in design, and in their future. Design Corps funds recent design graduates to work as design fellows in local communities to address relevant challenges, often related to housing. A design agenda is important to Bell, who seeks to raise the profile of design and social issues simultaneously. Bell's work with migrant labor housing is of particular note. Although structured in a very different way, the socially responsible projects and competitions organized by Cameron Sinclair and Kate Stohr's Architecture for Humanity are another important example.

Another twist on the standard Habitat home is the relatively recent emphasis on sustainability at HFHI and many of the local affiliates. HFHI now provides guidelines on sustainable construction on their website, and quite recently has started to officially encourage this kind of thinking. Outside organizations have taken these ideas further by working directly with a local Habitat affiliate to build demonstration homes using alternative materials and strategies and renewable energy technologies. The Oak Ridge National Laboratory built several almost net–zero energy Habitat homes using superinsulated construction and PV panels, and later went on to

monitor their performance. As evidence that such homes can be built within the context of Habitat, they are an important next step—despite the fact that the homes are as architecturally conventional as any stock building design Habitat offers on their website.

Design Process

The normal cycle of the ecoMOD project includes an academic year plus a summer for design and construction, and then an academic year of evaluation. However, for ecoMOD2, this was significantly reduced to fourteen weeks for design, overlapping with about six broken-up weeks of construction by the design/build team, and several intermittent weeks to complete the home by the design/build team and Habitat volunteers in Mississippi. Because of the shortened time frame for design, I generated the schematic design in late 2005 and handed it to the design team at the beginning of the spring 2006 semester. It was a simple massing of the building, with some basic ideas about how it could be adjusted to different sites, but it included nothing about the character of the interior or exterior spaces, the materials, or the architectural ideas about shading or storage—both of which became primary elements of the final design. The team adjusted the design to meet the specifics of the site and to fit with their own ideas. While the mass of the building remained substantially the same, the texture and materials of the home were created by the team—and by the end of the process, they owned the design completely. This is the one time that I have taken such a heavy hand with a design for ecoMOD—and while I recognize this method limits some of the learning opportunities of the team, the schedule would not allow us to start from scratch in January 2006. I required the team to critique and adjust the building however they wanted to—and I can honestly say the design belongs to them. Yet I think it is important to reveal this information because much has been made of the design role of faculty in other student design/build projects (including several Solar Decathlon teams), and I want to clarify my intentions in this unusual situation and state that it is not my preference to work in this way.

The preHAB home was designed with an emphasis on natural ventilation, thermal efficiency, and cost-saving strategies for materials, including the use of reclaimed materials from buildings destroyed in the hurricane. It was also designed to meet the U.S. Green Building Council LEED for Homes standard; however, the $3,000 cost of participating in the pilot phase of LEED for Homes, and the scheduling

of the design and construction, kept the team from registering the project with the USGBC. Both ecoMOD3 and 4 participated in LEED for Homes.

Through the use of sustainable design, materials, and technologies, our hope is this home will educate homeowners, Habitat officials, builders, and architects in the region and provide support for the development of sustainable goods and services by increasing the market for these products. By designing hurricane-resilient housing using precautionary principles, another goal of this demonstration effort was to help mitigate the creation of building debris in future disaster recoveries. Media in the region took interest in ecoMOD2, providing an opportunity to communicate the potential of the design. The house was featured on local television stations, in newspapers, and on a few area websites. It was also included in an exhibit of Gulf Coast rebuilding efforts that traveled through the region and was exhibited in New York City.

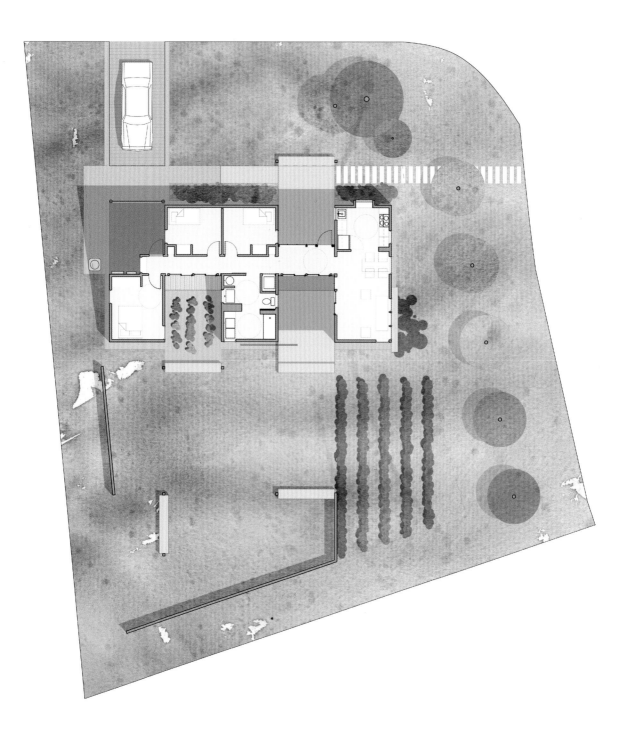

The design team followed the strict Habitat requirement to create a three-bedroom home no larger than 1,100 square feet. However, we were interested in creating a design that met the letter of law but not necessarily the intent. We wanted to expand the apparent size of the house with more generous exterior spaces. At 1,087 square feet, ecoMOD2 appears to be almost 2,100 square feet because of the covered porches and outdoor spaces brought into the perimeter of the building. Each of these four spaces serves a unique purpose: entry, screened-in outdoor dining, private terrace, and a covered storage area to substitute for the garage that Habitat does not typically provide but that is common in the neighborhood.

The team created a house that is adjustable to the climate of southern Mississippi. The contained exterior spaces are an integral element of the home and help to passively cool it. The team's goal was for the family to be able to leave the air-conditioning off during all but the very hottest days of the year—a strategy that is highly unusual today in that part of Mississippi. The south-facing outdoor spaces and the windows on the east and west facades were meant to incorporate shading elements that are able to both protect the home from harsh sunlight and adapt to become hurricane protection devices. Unfortunately, only some of these screens were installed because new wind-load requirements established after Hurricane Katrina made it difficult for the team to appropriately document the structural capacity of these elements. All the windows and doors are carefully placed to balance the needs for daylight, natural ventilation, and

privacy. The single shed roof with the high point facing the north also encourages natural ventilation. With breezes coming from the south and southwest, north-facing windows are high on the wall to facilitate stack effect and cross ventilation.

The house incorporates a PV solar panel array and a heat pump/heat recovery system that will provide domestic hot water. With the PV array in place (a gift to the family from funding secured by the UVA team), the home can operate without electricity from the grid if the air-conditioning is turned off. Unfortunately, Mississippi is not a net metering state, so the homeowners won't be able to bank any excess capacity for other days.

During spring break, about halfway through the semester, the architecture and engineering students had the option to travel to visit the site in Mississippi. Several students were able to attend, and it was an important opportunity for them to see the scale of the disaster by visiting parts of Mississippi and Louisiana—including the most devastated parts of New Orleans. All of us took part in

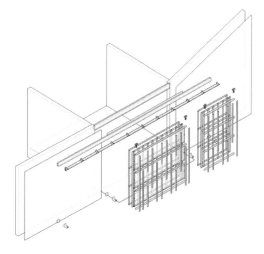

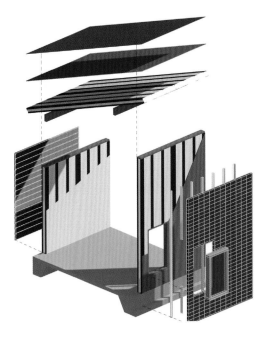

volunteer reconstruction efforts during the week—which at that stage were still focused mostly on removing debris or stripping homes of the materials that were wind-damaged or water-logged during and after the storm. While it was clear there was slightly more actual rebuilding going on in Mississippi than in New Orleans six months after the storm, there was still visible evidence of the hurricane everywhere. In some areas of New Orleans and right along the coast of Mississippi, it appeared the storm had only gone through the week before. As I was preparing for ecoMOD2, I visited the region in early 2006—four months after the storm (with HFHGC official Kelly Eplee and some volunteers to help a local affiliate)—and was shocked by what I saw. Yet when I visited again in early March, I had expected to see significant progress—and surprisingly little

had changed. We stayed in a FEMA tent city for our first visit, and a church-sponsored one for the second, and as we interacted with locals, the true impact of the situation revealed itself in conversations about their daily lives since the event. I was struck by the combination of dazed exhaustion and genuine resolve to retake control of their lives. During our many hours volunteering to help move the demolition and reconstruction effort forward, we heard many sincere expressions of gratitude, even when our efforts seemed meaningless in the context of the huge task before the communities affected.

It is more than 900 miles from Charlottesville to Gautier, so it made much more sense to ship panels rather than modules. The house is built from an innovative steel and foam panel system (provided by ThermaSteel of Radford, Virginia), which is highly energy efficient and resists hurricane-force winds as well as mold. The ecoMOD2 team convinced ThermaSteel to sell their leftover panels for a significantly reduced cost—less than wood-stud framing. Typically ThermaSteel engineers and prefabricates the panels to fit each project. However, the purchase of the remainders meant the ecoMOD2 team had to cut and reassemble the wall panels into the correct configuration for the preHAB design. Because the exterior spaces are partly covered by the roof, which is susceptible to uplift in high winds, it was necessary to ensure the hurricane-proof structural performance of the exposed areas, so the ecoMOD2 team had ThermaSteel make custom panels for the roof. All the panels for the house were shipped on a flatbed truck to the empty lot in Gautier.

Sweat Equity

For the construction of the home, the eco-MOD2 team partnered with various groups from Habitat for Humanity including: HFH International, HFH of Greater Charlottesville, HFH of the Mississippi Gulf Coast, and a team from HFH of Coastal Fairfield County, Connecticut, that made regular trips to Mississippi to help finish the house. Through these partnerships the team was able to demonstrate for themselves, Habitat officials, Habitat volunteers, and local people value-added construction using sustainable and reclaimed materials. The benefit of partnering with Habitat for Humanity was not just the invaluable cross-fertilization of ideas and skills between the students and volunteers, but also the ability to lower overall production costs. The prefabrication occurred over nine hundred miles from the final site of the house, so the challenge of responding to on-site issues was a difficult one. Since the team could not permanently oversee construction during the entire period, on-site time was valuable and became a critical concern.

The construction phase started before the end of the one semester devoted to design, meaning students were drawing and making models at the same time they were assembling walls. The adaptation of the ThermaSteel remainder panels proved to be more difficult than we imagined. Cutting the panels and adjusting them to correspond to our wall layouts was labor intensive. There was a significant learning curve as the team began to figure out the most efficient way of completing the work. Eventually, the team devised a method,

and they worked in shifts to accomplish the task.

Site visits prior to shipping the panels were an excellent opportunity to educate myself about the impact hurricanes have on buildings. I found myself playing detective with buildings—trying to figure out whether flooding or high winds caused the damage I observed. It was a relevant topic because many local citizens were involved in disputes with their insurance companies over this exact issue. The insurance companies were arguing that families whose homes had coverage for storms but not flooding should not be covered unless there was clear evidence of wind damage. The more nuanced and accurate explanation was that, for many, there was a combination of factors, but this was not a part of the discussion. Nor was the fact that the flooding would not have happened without the hurricane.

As I tried to read the devastation for clues, one building stuck out as an example of how a seemingly minor construction error, and lack of proper oversight by a building department official, can have destructive results. In a small subdivision just north of the railroad tracks in Pass Christian, Mississippi, a series of houses sustained substantial damage, but they were just far enough from the coast to avoid the complete erasure of buildings that occurred half a mile away. The storm surge that wiped away homes and businesses impacted the entire region, but most of the water receded soon afterwards (in contrast with the flooding that created the most serious problems in New Orleans and stayed for several weeks). However, this subdivision was on low ground,

and with the slightly elevated railroad tracks nearby, the flooding stayed for several days. Fortunately most of the homes were built in the last ten years and were sitting on high foundation walls, so the water only engulfed the first floor of these buildings—although a lot of them were only one story. While the flooding meant the homes had to be completely gutted inside, most of them were fine structurally, and a few of them even had mostly intact roofs.

There was one home that had been stripped from its perch on its foundation and had migrated as a mostly intact volume onto its neighbor's yard, partly damaging the front porch of the other house. It appeared that only two small trees kept the house from moving further and completely destroying the neighbor's home. As I worked with Habitat volunteers to gut and then start installation of new drywall on the adjacent house, it took a day or two for me to notice that there was something strange about the house off its foundation. When I began to look more closely at it, I realized that its foundation was in almost perfect condition. At first I had assumed the hurricane had blown the house off its foundation, but that didn't correspond with the damage to the neighboring houses. And if wind caused the house to come off its foundation, then certainly that wind would have been strong enough to push over the relatively small trees the house was resting against. So the house must have floated off the foundation during those days of high water—but why would that happen to only one home in the subdivision, where all of the homes appeared to have been built at the same time? Eventually, by looking at the bottom of the frame of the house, I discovered that it did not have the requisite hurricane straps—steel strips used to join a wood-frame house with the foundation. The floor framing appeared to have been attached to the wood sill plate on top of the foundation with only toe-nails—a series of nails pounded diagonally into the bottom of the piece of wood. Yet the sill plate appeared to have been very firmly attached to the foundation wall with the correct bolt, and the bolt appeared to have been properly grouted—set into mortar—into the concrete block foundation. It's difficult to say for sure, but it looked like the builder knew enough about residential construction to properly install the sill plate, but forgot to attach the floor framing to it, which would have locked the system together. When the flooding started, the house simply floated up as if it had been sitting in dry dock before the hurricane. The house "sailed" until it touched the nearby trees, and landed on its new location after the waters receded. There were many examples of this situation throughout Mississippi and Louisiana at the time, but most of them were homes built prior to the establishment of the hurricane strap requirement. Needless to say, we went overboard with hurricane straps for ecoMOD2—even though we were required to build the foundation as a slab on grade, which meant it was not legally obligated to have hurricane straps at the time of construction.

During one of the early trips, I stopped by the planning department for Jackson County to inquire about building code issues and the process of getting a building permit. I wanted to make sure our design and our

drawings lived up their expectations. What I experienced was a department slowly starting to gear up for a massive rebuilding effort, but without the funding or staff in place to make it happen. The people were incredibly helpful and friendly, but at times they were not able to respond to basic questions like which building code should be used. Each county in the state is allowed to select their own code requirements, which meant that for the communities along the gulf coast of Mississippi guidelines differed and none of them seemed to have the kind of strict wind load and flood plain requirements that you would expect from a hurricane-prone region. Sometime after the storm, the state government used an emergency measure to temporarily adopt the International Residential Code (IRC) for the southernmost counties until the state code commission could come up with a more consistent policy. However, during the spring of '06, we were forced to guess which direction this might go, and therefore used the strictest requirements we could find by blending some of the BOCA code and the original Jackson County requirements with IRC and the Florida Hurricane code. Fortunately, after we submitted hurricane-force wind test reports for the ThermaSteel system to the building officials, they were willing to let us use the system.

The team also built the custom cabinetry, including the various built-in storage boxes designed for the wall between the small bedrooms and main corridor, as well as the cedar-post frames and panels intended for use as shade devices and privacy screens. As the end of the semester neared, the team sourced

as many of the building materials as possible, since we were unsure whether some items would be commonly available in that area. Building material shortages, which were heavily reported soon after Katrina, were no longer a problem, but some of our choices were a little unconventional—for design or sustainability reasons—and we knew they were much more likely to be utilized if they were brought with us and were sitting on-site.

After graduation, a majority of the team drove to Mississippi—with two large rental trucks filled with cabinetry (both custom and IKEA), building materials, tools, and equipment. A shipping company transported the panels on the back of a flatbed truck. When the team arrived on-site with the panels, we expected to set up the wall and roof panels within two weeks. Unfortunately, the Habitat officials had tried very hard but were not able to get the slab poured prior to our arrival. This set our schedule back significantly, but also helped the team understand the nature of construction on the Gulf Coast eight and a half months after the hurricane. The plumber had not shown up to install the supply and waste lines that are embedded in the slab, so the concrete subcontractor had to wait. We would have preferred to build preHAB on something other than a slab on grade, but this was a requirement for building in this subdivision—and the site had been donated to Habitat.

One of the major problems along the gulf coast at that time was not lack of building materials, but lack of skilled labor. The Lowe's store just down the road stocked just about everything we could find in Lowe's in Charlottesville, but finding an available plumber was a real challenge. This was an ironic problem for Habitat, as an organization built on skilled and unskilled volunteer labor. Yet some tasks need to be performed by skilled professionals. With a good supply of volunteers rotating in from all parts of the U.S. for a week or so at a time, HFHI and HFHMGC had enough people to handle most of the house construction. It was more difficult finding mechanical, electrical, and plumbing professionals. With the massive rebuilding effort along the gulf, general contractors working on the large casinos were able to control a lot of the MEP subcontractors by offering wages and construction contracts far more lucrative than most individual homeowners or Habitat could offer. So while there were more mechanical specialists, electricians, and plumbers in the region during that time than there ever have been, it was extremely difficult to get them to focus on single-family homes—especially low-budget Habitat homes.

This unexpected delay is one of the reasons the project took so long to complete, but one of the positive outcomes was the opportunity for the student team to learn more about plumbing and concrete. Several team members corrected minor errors that had been made in positioning of plumbing, and then helped the plumber with the work. They also helped the concrete subcontractor, while another set of students emptied the rental trucks at a Habitat warehouse and helped another Habitat crew on a different house.

As the team was volunteering their time, and hotel rooms were still filled with evacuated families, as well as construction personnel temporarily in the region, our team stayed at a tent village in the backyard of a large church a few miles away. With a reasonable donation to the church, we secured bunk bed space in army-style tents, complete with air-conditioning fed through huge flexible

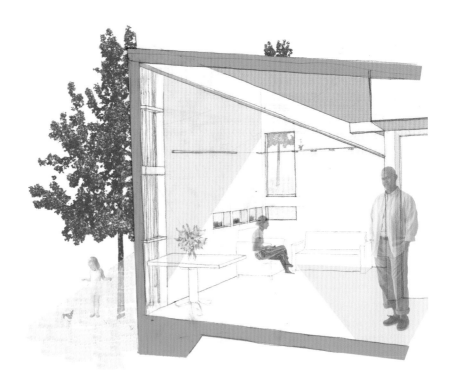

ducts. Except for the air-conditioning, the atmosphere was a little like a summer camp, with meals in the church cafeteria; showers, toilets, and sinks in semi-trailers behind the church; and free time spent playing guitars and basketball. An incredibly diverse crowd of volunteers from around the country kept the church parishioners busy with meals and management of the community.

By the time we had to leave, the walls were up, but we had only just started on the roof panels. HFHMGC with assistance from the Habitat group from Connecticut completed the installation of the roof panels. By the time we needed a framing inspection, the building officials who approved the ThermaSteel system had left the department and newer people needed to be convinced. A time-saving strategy to place electrical wiring in a fire-rated

steel channel (generously donated by the Wiremold company) attached along the bottom of the wall was first approved at the permit stage, but later rejected by an inspector. The same was true for the attachment of the ThermaSteel roof panels to the roof frame—which meant the Habitat construction manager, Victor Alfsen, had to work with the building officials to figure out a way to adjust the detail. This is just one of several situations Alfsen had to respond to—and his dry, restrained sense of humor made him well suited to the position. Despite his gruff exterior, nothing seemed to really bother him—it was just another hurdle he had to jump, one of thousands he has faced in the region.

The house sat untouched for months on end, as HFHI negotiated with the three local affiliates to combine them into the HFH of the Mississippi Gulf Coast, and geared up for a huge push to build new homes. Occasionally week-long visits from the Connecticut-based Habitat crew that adopted the house, and the former ecoMOD2 students taking time off from their new jobs, pushed along the interior and exterior finishes. Finally the house was

substantially completed in the summer of 2007. During the last stages, a Habitat family visiting the completed Habitat house next door saw ecoMOD2 and asked if they could take a look. Apparently they liked it immediately and were selected as the homeowners. The last major delay was getting a building inspector to make the final inspection. By then, the already overwhelmed planning department had lost several inspectors to jobs in the burgeoning construction industry.

Evaluation

Given the distance between UVA and the site in Mississippi and the lack of funding to support travel, the evaluation phase for ecoMOD2 was cut back, limited to post-occupancy

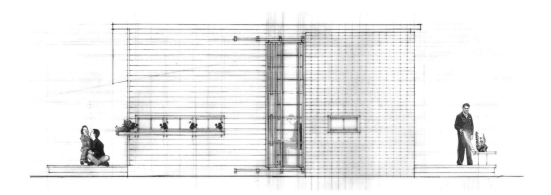

evaluations and a brief material assessment. A small monitoring system was installed, but the ecoMOD engineering teams have not been able to get any data from it because the homeowners have not consistently had internet service.

We had hoped for a more thorough evaluation phase, but in the end we were limited to more personal observations about the ability to translate the ecoMOD2 project to other similar situations. One of our primary observations is that, while a region responding to a natural disaster and housing crisis makes a good testing ground for alternative methods of providing housing, working in such an area requires a great deal of patience and flexibility. Furthermore, we found that sustainable, prefabricated housing is compatible with the mission of Habitat for Humanity; however, instituting it on a widespread basis will require a significant commitment from Habitat staff and volunteers.

The extreme nature of the Hurricane Katrina disaster is the biggest challenge facing the rebuilding effort. The National Low Income Housing Coalition estimates that 71 percent of the destroyed units in the affected areas were affordable to low and very low income households. According to the Congressional Budget Office, the recovery process from Hurricane Katrina will take longer than it otherwise would because workers have no place to live. According to the Brookings Institution, median house prices in New Orleans have increased since Katrina and the limited supply of housing is pushing up ownership and rental prices to the extent that entry-level and other working families may have difficulty finding affordable housing if and when they return. The commonly held expectation that New Orleans may only reach 60 percent of its pre-Katrina population over the next several years is very possible if affordable housing is not available. Clearly in this scenario the Gulf Coast will shrink in its economic capacity, tax revenues, and ability to maintain housing stock that is no longer habitable or in areas that are truly at grave risk and uninsurable. This data confirms that affordable housing is a necessity and the Gulf Coast is in desperate need.

Inadequate support and infrastructure directly affects the rebuilding efforts. Existing local Habitat for Humanity teams were typically producing two homes per year in this region before the hurricane. Post-Katrina that number has increased to a goal of two hundred homes per year. The initial lack of infrastructure to support such a large rebuilding effort proved to be a very significant challenge. In the end, HFHI took over a lot of the responsibilities typically reserved for local affiliates and provided a major influx of cash through donations. HFHI also combined county-based Habitat affiliates into the more robust regional HFH of the Mississippi Gulf Coast. When the ecoMOD2 team first arrived in Mississippi less than six months after Katrina, both HFH and the local building department were operating with small staffs and just starting to make headway towards an organized response to the situation. What was a patched-together operation has transitioned into a much more organized and effective team of Habitat professionals leading their efforts.

The difficulties of taking on the preHAB prototype in this context were significant. At the time, HFH was having difficulty completing conventional wood-stud structures such as they have built all over the country. With ecoMOD2, we were asking them to help with a very different design and a very different type of structure. The collaborative team learned that if ecoMOD participates in another disaster relief effort, it is important to completely solve all issues before shipping to the site so that the on-site construction can be completed on time. In addition, the team should have assumed each phase would take at least twice as long to complete as it would under normal circumstances.

As for the design itself, the team already knows that if the design is built again, it should be simplified somewhat, to ensure any Habitat team can complete it without a lot of head-scratching. Unfortunately, changes were made to the home in the middle of construc-

tion because the HFH teams didn't understand the design intentions. A complete set of construction drawings were available inside the house, but one group misunderstood an exterior open "skylight" in the outdoor dining area and a bay window in the kitchen, and removed them both. These elements would have enhanced the livability of the home considerably. In addition, the ecoMOD team should have prepared a clearer list of locally available and acceptable materials to be appended to the construction drawings, to allow for last minute substitutions. For example, all the ecoMOD teams typically try to avoid PVC/vinyl products, due to the toxic nature of their production and the challenges with recycling them. The local Habitat builders ignored the suggestion of a commonly available aluminum eave and window-trim product when they found there would be a slight delay in receiving it, and vinyl—standard for Habitat homes—was installed instead. Also, most of the old-growth cypress wood reclaimed (with permission) from destroyed buildings in nearby Bay St. Louis was not assembled into the front entry deck and outdoor-dining deck as planned because the local Habitat workers didn't have the right equipment, and the wood was left on the ground for an extended period of time—where it turned into a breeding ground for insects. What would have been a beautiful deck of free material was replaced with concrete. Of far less importance but notable nonetheless is the unnecessary addition of conventional interior trim at cabinetry edges and door openings; the design team had labored to create simple, clean details, but failed to put large notes on them when leaving

town so that the local workers would know nothing more was required.

In this sense, the completed home is less than what the team intended, but these lessons are important ones. With the projects in Charlottesville, the teams have almost complete control over the built efforts, but even with ecoMOD1 and 3, the final buildings could have been simplified without reducing the quality of the design. Recognizing and acknowledging these problems is an important part of refining the ecoMOD design process.

Current Status

As previously mentioned, the local HFH affiliate received a lot of interest in the house, and a family was selected near the end of the summer of '07. The birth of a new child in the family delayed their closing on house, but in the spring of '08, the family finally moved in.

The UVA Patent Foundation has registered the copyrights for ecoMOD2. As with the other designs, they have also licensed the designs to Modern Modular. Estimates from modular builders show the prototypes can be replicated at a lower cost than standard site-built housing. However, we do not have clear evidence that this is true in the context of the heavily subsidized and donation-dependent world of Habitat for Humanity construction. Further research into this is difficult, given the challenges of tracking hard costs with a single Habitat home, but it is an important question for the viability of the preHAB design. In the end, what can be definitively stated is that a team of architecture and engineering students learned a lot about sustainability, prefabrication, and disaster relief housing; Habitat for Humanity staff and volunteers were exposed to more sustainable methods of design and construction; and a family lives in a home that they like, and that will cost them less to operate than the one next door. Perhaps that's enough for now.

ecoMOD2 DESIGN FEATURES

PHOTOVOLTAICS Approximately half of the electricity used in the house in the summer season is produced by a rooftop PV array. The eight-panel, two-kilowatt system is provided by Schott, and was installed without a battery backup to simplify maintenance for the homeowners.

RECLAIMED WOOD The team reclaimed highly durable lumber from a home destroyed by Hurricane Katrina in Bay St. Louis, Mississippi. The owner of the property runs a reclaimed materials business—the Green Project

—and allowed the ecoMOD2 team to use some of the wood at no cost in exchange for sorting and stacking much of the materials that remained on the lot.

DESUPERHEATER The highly energy efficient heat pump system has a heat recovery/ desuperheater system attached to it, to collect the waste heat from the heat pump and use it to preheat the domestic hot water. For under $500, the easily installed desuperheater technology will pay for itself in southern Mississippi within a couple of years.

in the summer. The plan is organized to give each interior space at least two exterior walls —to maximize daylight and breezes. The window placements and slope of the roof were designed to encourage displacement ventilation and cross breezes.

THERMASTEEL PANELS The walls and roof are constructed of an innovative steel and expanded polystyrene foam panel system made by the ThermaSteel company based in Radford, Virginia. The panels are extremely light and framed with steel studs, some of which are turned ninety degrees from their conventional orientation to minimize thermal bridging. The team adapted the panels from remainders in the yard at ThermaSteel and purchased them at a deeply discounted rate.

PASSIVE SOLAR DESIGN As described above, the house was designed to respond to the hot, humid climate of the gulf coast of Mississippi. The team used overhangs and covered porches to provide shading and prevent overheating

STUDENT ESSAY BY AMY LEWANDOWSKI

Amy Lewandowski, BSArch '03, MArch '06, was one of the project managers for ecoMOD2. She currently works at an architecture firm in Seattle, and has also taught design studios as an adjunct lecturer in the UVA School of Architecture.

My involvement with preHAB as project manager has influenced how I think about my role in design, how I work as a professional, and how I teach architecture. In a short window of time, it gave me the opportunity to push past my comfort zone to take on a leadership position that guided me towards a better understanding of the role architects can play in addressing important social issues.

Through the project and my continued work in the field, it has become clear to me that architects can make a great impact on the health and well-being of both individuals and communities. By considering the larger impact of design, architects serve to provide not only shelter, but also a quality of life. With the use of simple and inexpensive materials we can manipulate space and light to design environments that have the power to build community and a sense of well-being.

Taking on the role of project manager was a great leap for me during my semester with the ecoMOD project. With only a semester to design and build a house, it became very clear that keeping to a schedule was going to be crucial to making the ideas become a reality. I learned how to keep a handle on the big picture of what needed to be done while working with the team to make sure we moved through the necessary details of the design and fabrication of the house. Even within a time constraint we knew it was important to spend the time and effort to seek out new sustainable materials, find low-cost alternatives, and achieve a high level of design through the spaces we created rather than the expense of materials and construction. This knowledge has been carried into numerous projects I have worked on in professional practice where quality is the goal but budget is the reality.

**STUDENT ESSAY BY
RASHEDA BOWMAN**

Rasheda Bowman, BSArch '06, was the construction manager for ecoMOD2, and soon afterwards became an AmeriCorps volunteer. She is currently an intern with RRMM Architects in Norfolk, Virginia.

I did not truly understand the many layers of architecture until ecoMOD2. The project allowed me to gain hands-on experience in understanding the many complexities of the design and construction processes. There is only so much you can learn from books, lectures, and studios; until that point architecture was only a 2-D drawing. From construction safety to difficulties with window ordering, every step taught me more than I ever thought I'd learn as a student.

At an early age I developed a fascination for the built environment. However, this fascination was inspired by the spaces in which I had personal experiences. I grew up in several subpar housing units that were the only places my family could afford. There was one place that physically made my family sick. I always felt that there was a level of unfairness about the situation. It was as if we were being punished for not having money. Serving as the construction manager for ecoMOD2 has allowed me to dispel some of those thoughts. I had the opportunity to help to improve the quality of life of someone else by giving him or her something I never had.

This experience has allowed me as an aspiring architect to become more sensitive toward not only the user, but also the environment. John was the first person to really introduce me to sustainable design. I learned the significance of using recycled and recyclable materials and renewable energy. The ecoMOD2 project has helped me to realize solutions to issues by improving already existing methods. Thinking outside the box drove the design process. I am almost positive that some of the house's features will never be duplicated. The long-term benefits of sustainable design completely outweigh the initial costs. Through our design, we were able to save the family money that they necessarily did not have.

Before ecoMOD2, my interest in architecture and my passion for improving lives were two separate entities. I knew what brought me to the field, but I did not know how to apply that reason to carve my own path. After graduation, I joined the AmeriCorps program and worked for a nonprofit organization helping to renovate a house for a men's transitional home. The house served a significant purpose within the community. It allowed men who had been incarcerated to successfully transition back into society. I was able to apply the skills I learned while working on the eco-MOD project, such as making and keeping track of the budget and ordering materials, to help further the project along.

I am grateful and proud to be a member of the ecoMOD2 team. It is definitely an experience that I will never forget. I can honestly say that it has helped me to refocus my initial intent of becoming an architect and compels my passion now. The experience allowed me to push myself in ways that I had not before; and it has instilled in me the commitment to never settle for the average, but always strive to go to the next level.

STUDENT ESSAY BY MICHAEL PILAT

Michael Pilat, BSEngr '07, was a leader for the engineering teams of both ecoMOD2 and ecoMOD3. He is currently working for Lockheed Martin in New Orleans.

As I progressed through my engineering education, I craved to be a part of a hands-on team project. Although I attended information sessions for various teams, nothing clicked with me until Brian Hickey mentioned an opportunity he had heard about in the winter of 2005. From then on, the ecoMOD2 project consumed much of my free time—by choice. I feel very fortunate to have been part of a project that allowed me such latitude and responsibility in design coupled with the satisfaction of constructing the final product myself. As much as I might have impacted the project, I know that the ecoMOD project has greatly shaped me by educating me about affordable housing, sustainable development, and renewable energy. It is not an exaggeration to say my entire outlook on the world has been changed by my participation in this project.

When Brian and I first entered Campbell Hall (the architecture studio), we were quite impressed with the organization and high level of detail in the models and drawings that the architects created. We initially communicated some of our design ideas with the entire architecture team, using their models to demonstrate positions of systems. But we began to realize how precious our time was in the studio, and soon transitioned to having specific discussions with individual architecture students about how our system might interact with their particular design area. During other periods in the week, this individual could contact the engineering team for more details or could relay the information to the rest of the architecture team for further discussion. Generally, middlemen are viewed as ineffectual, but in eco-MOD2, this technique was not only very helpful, it was absolutely necessary to be time effective.

**STUDENT ESSAY BY
CAROL SHIFLETT**

Carol Shiflett, BSArch '06, participated in the evaluation of ecoMOD1 and was a project manager for ecoMOD2. She is currently working at MulvannyG2 Architecture in Bellevue, Washington.

From the outset, I was completely excited about participating in the preHAB project. I had seen bits and pieces of the Trojan Goat project and OUTin over my first three years in the School of Architecture, and I really wanted to get involved with a project that was actually going to be built *and* was going to have a direct positive impact on the affordable housing crisis.

One of the greatest challenges that I found while working on preHAB was collaboration. Working with a project team comprised of members from multiple fields (in this case, architecture students and electrical engineering students) is not a skill that people typically learn in studio. I certainly hadn't learned anything about this type of collaboration up to that point. We quickly learned that we, the architecture students, had our priorities for the project that we were designing, while the engineering students had their own priorities. Not only were there differences of opinion between architecture and engineering students, but also amongst the architecture students. In particular, I remember the placement of the house on the site—a pretty critical design decision—became a lengthy discussion for the whole studio. We were able to come to a decision as a group that both met our design intentions and provided the best positioning for our engineers to mount the PV panels, but finding that middle ground when you are sure that your concerns are the most important can be quite difficult.

Knowing that the project was going to be built also required that we move beyond theory and literally start to understand the nuts and bolts of construction. If we designed it and didn't know how to build it, we had to find out. I think the team did a fantastic job learning how to use the materials that we had in order to build the wall panels, the interior framed walls (with some help from the local Habitat crew), and the interior storage/cabinet pieces. I think we all learned a lot about how the details we draw when we are sitting at our studio desk significantly impact what happens in the field. Also, if we don't detail it when we are at our desk, someone may have to make up their own solution in the field, and it does not always line up with the designer's original intentions.

I am very fortunate to have come away from preHAB with a better understanding of the importance of communication and clearly defined intentions when collaborating with a group on a project.

ecoMOD3: SEAM

Joining Old and New

Two years after having to move the site of ecoMOD1 to another part of Charlottesville—soon after it was discovered that the dilapidated house on the original site was protected as a historically important building—we returned to Fourth Street, SW, in the Fifeville/Castle Hill neighborhood for ecoMOD3. The historic building was in such a serious state of disrepair, and had been layered with such a hodge-podge of materials and room additions, that it was difficult to see why it had any value. The previous owner and many of the longtime neighbors were surprised to learn it had received the historic designation more than twenty years prior. Several of the neighbors felt the home was an eyesore and should be torn down to make way for more affordable housing. This was the Piedmont Housing Alliance's plan, but as discussed in my account of ecoMOD1, the city government would not allow demolition. In the gap between 2005 and 2007, PHA considered a variety of solutions to the problem of being stuck with a historic property without the budget to restore it. In the end, Mark Watson at PHA asked me if I would be willing to return to Fourth Street, to take on both the historic preservation effort and the construction of a new modular addition behind it. I was hesitant, but willing to take it on. The idea that there is no building more sustainable than the one that already exists was part of my thinking. However, it was pretty clear that we would have to remove so much of the fabric of the building to stabilize it that the final result would essentially be a new building.

In addition to the historic preservation, Mark and I had previously

accessory rental unit   bedroom addition   historic house

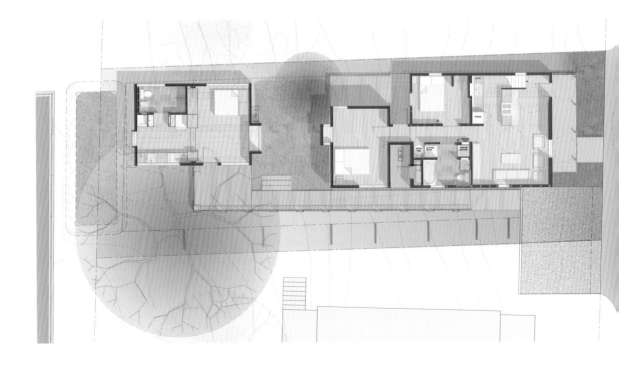

discussed the possibility of an ecoMOD project focused on housing the growing population of older people in the community. Gordon Walker of the Jefferson Area Board for Aging had encouraged us to consider this, and we liked the idea. Paxton was also interested in housing for the aging, in part because of the possibility of integrating a building monitoring system with some form of noninvasive medical monitoring—possibly in partnership with the UVA Medical Automated Research Center, a leader in these technologies.

So the idea for ecoMOD3 started to come together, and as we began the design phase in the fall of 2006, the plan was for the student team to 1) research the history of the old house; 2) design the historic preservation effort with a heavy emphasis on green renovation strategies; 3) design and build a modular addition to the back of the house; 4) test the recent zoning changes to encourage the development of accessory dwelling units in the city; and 5) evaluate the two housing units that would result. This solution appealed to me because it would allow ecoMOD to expand to include renovation and return an existing affordable house to the market with significant improvements while also adding another one on the same site. In addition, the student team and group of advisors would expand to include the disciplines of architectural history and historic preservation; and with a modular system geared toward additions, we could imagine ecoMOD3 modules attached to any home.

In the final built result, the two housing units include the historic house with a modular bedroom addition, and behind it a de-tached accessory rental unit comprised of two modules. The historic house has two bedrooms and a loft, and the accessory unit is a rental studio apartment. Both are fully handicap accessible (except for the loft).

The fall semester began with a fourth-year undergraduate design studio, a mixed graduate and undergraduate engineering class, and a graduate architecture, landscape architecture, planning, and historic preservation seminar. It was a smart team, with diverse backgrounds and interests. The entire group met once a week to discuss team issues, give presentations, and make decisions. However, with almost fifty people involved, it was sometimes difficult to keep the weekly sessions relevant for everyone, and even more difficult to effectively manage the team. It is largely due to the enthusiasm of the team that we didn't lose too many people along the way. Paxton and I went into response mode for a good part of that semester—doing our best to keep everyone moving along and fully engaged in the work.

One strategy that helped with this expanded team was the use of an online collaboration tool. Paxton and I had received a joint Teaching and Technology Initiative fellowship from UVA to test-drive the Sakai software recently adopted by the university. We figured we were a good test case because our process was spread out between two schools at the university and required instant access to information from a variety of people. With the smaller teams for ecoMOD1 and 2, we had survived mostly by emailing documents and drawings back and forth to each other—a hopelessly inefficient way to communicate. The Sakai platform, branded as Collab at UVA, not only offers the ability to post drawings and other files online, with access limited to team members, it also includes other tools such as team emails, scheduling, a chat tool, a discussion blog, and a place for team announcements. Perhaps the most useful component has been the wiki tool—an online software that allows one to post and edit text and images in a real-time collaborative environment—similar to the best known example of the software, Wikipedia. The ecoMOD wiki has become an essential documentary vessel for the project. Many shared documents—from team and contact lists to evaluation reports—exist primarily or exclusively in the wiki environment. While the transition to Collab was somewhat painful, at this point, I cannot imagine another way to capture the ideas and documents created by the team. The only problems we've had so far are that the upload process is somewhat slow, and while the UVA computer technologies team has been generous with the data storage space, it does have its limits. Therefore, for now we have had to continue the use of local servers for most of the architectural work—drawings and images in particular—because they tend to take up the most space. The ecoMOD3 team got around this by posting only the highest level drawings and only after deadlines—unless someone had a special request.

As the fall semester got into gear, several themes were floating around in the students' heads: the challenge of *bridging the gap* between disciplines, made more seamless with a digital tool; the *connection* between the historic building and the new addition; the *generational gap* between young and old with the potential of a home for someone who wants to "age in place"; and the resurgence of a common theme for architecture students, the potential *overlap* between the inside and the outside. All these themes became fused together when we began to discuss the possible solutions to the construction joint between the modules as they are placed next to each other on the foundation. This gap is always a little bit of a challenge because even when you've built the modules perfectly, with everything plumb and level, the two modules tend to be slightly different from each other—not surprising when they travel down the highway at 65 miles per hour. A ¼" misalignment is not unexpected. Soon we began to discuss an architectural solution to this problem, involving a zone of plywood and cabinetry where the modules meet that would allow us to avoid drywall in that area and hide any misalignment. Eventually all these themes were blended together when the team came up with the name the SEAM house. Some of the SEAM ideas even found their way into the interior of the historic house—including the undulating plywood seam that forms the kitchen countertop and guardrail at the loft.

Initially the team was working under the assumption that under new zoning regulations in Charlottesville, we would be able to attach three 12' × 16' modules to the rear of the historic house—using one module as a bedroom addition, and then creating a fire separation between that one and the accessory unit in the other two modules, which would have a separate entrance. This strategy had the least impact on the site and was the most efficient way to add on to the house. Unfortunately, by the end of the semester, PHA had realized that the elegant solution is not always the lawful one. While the new zoning regulations were intended to encourage greater density and the use of accessory units, after discussions with the city, it became clear that the regulations unintentionally made some aspects of this difficult. Although the city was willing to rethink this, it was clear that would not happen in time for ecoMOD3 to stay on schedule, so the design had to be adjusted. Based on a complex formula for determining the possible square footage of a detached dwelling unit and its proximity to the ground plane, we eventually settled on two modules put together as a 24' × 16' detached accessory unit—sitting at the rear of the site—and one module attached as a bedroom directly to the rear of the historic house. The solution was architecturally less clean with the separation of the volumes, and inherently more expensive (because it required the addition of two more exterior walls), but we had no choice. As with ecoMOD1, we had to transition from the fall semester to the spring semester with a major adjustment to the design. The process set us back a bit, but not quite as much as we were impacted by the two site changes for ecoMOD1.

The Historic Smith-Reaves-White House

The historic preservation team (HP team for short) consisted of two graduate students with architectural history/historic preservation backgrounds and four undergraduate archi-

tecture students with an interest in the topic. The graduate students led the effort and were members of the graduate student seminar; the undergraduates were in the studio. We lost part of the team during the construction phase, so another graduate student, with a dual degree in architecture and landscape architecture, took over leadership with one of the undergraduates.

Louis Nelson, the chair of the school's Department of Architectural History, advised the students on research efforts—enthusiastically helping the team decipher both the physical and the documentary evidence. Daniel Bluestone, the director of the department's historic preservation program, also advised occasionally, and was partly responsible for saving the

house. He attended the Board of Architectural Review meetings and the city council meeting in 2005, as a member of Preservation Piedmont. He voiced his opinion that the house probably represents a unique example of an antebellum slave quarters and ought to be saved. The eventual conclusion reached by everyone involved was that while it was unfortunate that the city had not communicated this information to PHA when they purchased the property, the best solution was to learn more about the building and restore it. As the studio and seminar got underway,

it was clear that Louis was very effective at helping students balance the need for rigorous scholarship with the importance of defining an accurate and compelling narrative for a building. He can date a building with elements such as nails and saw marks, and there were plenty of those to observe as the team removed some of the layers of the building in researching its history.

The team mined the city property records and historic records to find information—but the history of African American neighborhoods is often unrecorded. Available historic

of when the land was transferred from John Barksdale, a white slaveholder, to Armistead Smith. Smith clearly owned the property after the Civil War, as the deed was transferred to his adult son upon his death in 1870, and his son paid some of the remaining debt on the property to Barksdale. The physical evidence of the earliest phase of construction suggests that an educated builder, who used methods common to slave quarters, built the structure. Smith may have been one of Barksdale's slaves. Though there is no documentary evidence of this, it was not uncommon for freed slaves to purchase their homes from their former masters in the era immediately after the war.

A common strategy in historic preservation is to establish an important date in the history of the house, and gear the renovation effort towards remaking the building in that year. The team rejected this strategy because the exact year of construction is not known and, with the multiple layers of additions and materials, it would be difficult to design to any one year with confidence. In addition, the HP team recognized that there was value in the many layers of history, and while the renovation required most of the more recent materials to be removed, we didn't want to beautify the building into something it never was. The various materials and construction strategies represent a wide range of skill levels and a "repair as you go" attitude. The creative reuse of materials to patch walls, floors, and roofs, together with the additive nature of the building, meant that its precise history would never be known, but we felt the spirit of this "make-do" strategy should be revealed in the final product. To the degree that it was

records were mostly limited to deeds, and despite the very close proximity to Charlottesville's Main Street and the downtown area, the building did not appear on any maps until the late nineteenth century or in any publicly documented photographs until the 1980s. A well-known Charlottesville photographer documented a significant percentage of the city during the late nineteenth century and early twentieth century, but predominantly African American Fourth Street, SW, was not included. The earliest documentary evidence was missing—there is not a record realistic, the team wanted to save the earliest materials and the quirkiness of the building. Rather than sanitize and clean up the design of the building by removing all the awkward traces of unskilled home improvement, the HP team aspired to a process of selective editing—with complete removal of something only when doing otherwise would affect the budget or the environmental impact.

As we began our design and research efforts, the Fifeville–Castle Hill neighborhood was being considered for historic designation—something most communities would welcome with pride. However, many residents were concerned the move would encourage more gentrification of the neighborhood and push more longtime residents out. In addition, they expressed concern that all construction in the community—including minor renovations—would have to be reviewed by the BAR. However, the form of designation being considered did not require that, only that there would be oversight for the demolition of buildings—and, as an incentive, state tax credits would be available for some renovations. Yet, in my opinion, the community was rightfully suspicious. Only a couple of years earlier, the city approved a large high-end housing development for the edge of Fifeville nearest the Amtrak train station. The neighborhood association was only partially involved in the planning process—though they did request the site design be better integrated into the community. Many of their concerns and requests were ignored, and the final result is a mostly gated community without any interior roads that directly connect with the nearby city grid. The development towers over

parts of Fifeville, and can only be accessed from one dead-end road. The only "benefit" to the surrounding community is the increase in real estate taxes.

The individual historic designation of the house on Fourth Street required that we present our drawings to the BAR. The students created a package for the BAR on three occasions, and I presented their design for them each time. Generally the board was supportive, as most of them recognized that we were all fortunate that PHA was willing to restore the building given its state. The BAR guidelines seemed capricious at times, but the board has latitude to approve designs on a case-by-case basis. Fortunately, the BAR guidelines generally require an addition to an historic structure to make obvious that it is not part of the original building (ironic, given the difficulty we had discerning the scope of the additions on the house), and that anything new be easily removed in the future. The massing of the addition must also be shorter and narrower than the original, which limited the addition to one story (while the original was two stories, the nineteenth-century ceiling heights would not be allowed today). After a preliminary meeting in the fall, and a request for more detailed information on a few items during the second meeting, the project was approved during the third meeting—much to everyone's relief. As required, the modular addition is very clearly different, but we also proposed joints and material differences to demark the earlier additions that had been masked over time. For example, we placed vertical trim pieces between the new exterior siding at the joint between the early phases of construction.

Extensive analysis reveals that the house was built in five phases spanning from the early 1860s to the 1980s. The historic preservation team produced extensive visual documentation of the home, including 2-D and 3-D drawings as well as a 3-D scanning process that captured all of the ins and outs of the rooms after some of the interior wall finishes had been removed. The team worked with Louis to carefully identify the vintage of many elements of the home and formulate a story of its construction. The multiple additions made this difficult, and we will never know exactly the form of the house at each stage of its history. We found plenty of contradictory evidence in the building. Most notably, the hand-riven lath found underneath the original plaster in the living room, which if seen in isolation would date the building to 1820 or 1830, contradicted a few saw marks on the roof and wall framing that indicate an earliest possible initial construction phase in the late 1850s or early 1860s.

With assistance from Louis, the team formed a hypothesis that the front portion of the home was built in two phases—with a slender stair-room addition on the north side added later. This was based on the odd separation of the stair as a separate room—probably indicating that the wall closing it off from the main living area was a structural wall—and the fact that if you sliced away that segment, you would be left with a nearly perfect example of a 16' square slave quarters of the early to mid-nineteenth century. The odd asymmetry of the front windows and doors reinforced this interpretation, but it was only when the drywall on the roof framing and the wallboard at the downstairs wall were removed that the HP team was able to confirm their theory. We also discovered traces of framing and whitewash finish that suggest a ladder was used to access the upper loft prior to the addition of the stair. Later, the theory was further confirmed when the exterior siding was removed on the front, revealing that the framing of the front window (which would be roughly centered on the facade without the stair-room addition) was originally a door. Later additions include a kitchen at the rear and a bedroom. According to the last owner, the back porch (probably early twentieth century) was filled in to make an interior bathroom and mechanical closet in the 1980s.

The most difficult decision the team made in the effort to design the new interiors was the choice to remove the wall between the living room and stair-room/entry. The narrow space was unworkable as it was, but we hated the idea of removing the wall that we had only recently discovered was an exterior wall in the original scheme. Yet the home would have been almost unmarketable otherwise.

At only 644 square feet on the first floor, there wasn't a lot of extra space for the extravagance of honesty in historic preservation—the family needed a kitchen, two bedrooms, a bathroom, and a living room, all handicap accessible. Besides, there was some evidence that the kitchen was simply going to return to its original location prior to the stair and kitchen additions. So the team did the next best thing—they saved the wood studs from the wall and put them together like a column at the two end points of where the wall once stood. The ceiling was removed under the loft framing in this area, to expose the difference in framing on the two sides of the wall. Since the original flooring had to be removed so we could lift the house and install a new foundation, when it went back down, we changed its orientation along the wall line—further reinforcing its location.

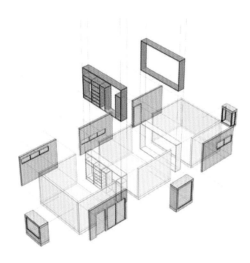

The design team carefully considered the best way to balance historic preservation with sustainable design. The roof of the historic house was insulated with highly energy-efficient foam insulation, and the walls with wet cellulose. Energy and water efficient appliances, equipment, and plumbing fixtures were used throughout. An evacuated tube solar hot water system sits on the roof above the bathroom, coupled with on-demand water heating. To allow for the original roof framing and decking to be exposed in the bedroom, we placed new structure and insulation on top of the roof.

The unique and intricate history of the Smith-Reaves-White House tells the story of vernacular affordable housing in the Fifeville–Castle Hill area of Charlottesville, as well as the social and cultural conditions in this traditionally African American neighborhood. From the core of what was probably a slave quarters, to the addition of an interior stair and kitchen in the era of Reconstruction, to the addition of a first floor bedroom in the Jim Crow era, to the enclosure of a bathroom after the civil rights era, the house is something of an occupiable textbook on the history of housing for African Americans in the South. The complete reports on the history are available from the ecoMOD3 section of our website, www.ecomod.virginia.edu.

The Addition Module System and Accessory Unit

Despite our emphasis on the very specific history of the Smith-Reaves-White house, our goal with the bedroom addition and detached accessory unit was to create a modular system that was flexible enough to attach to any home. The team was constantly aware of our

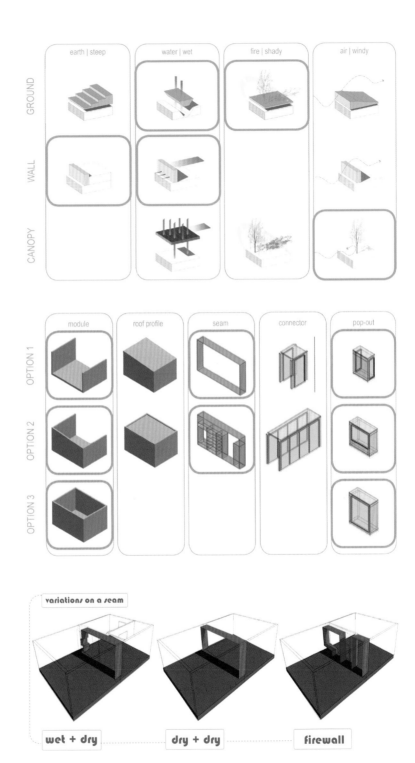

variations on a seam

wet + dry   dry + dry   firewall

immediate context on Fourth Street, but we simultaneously strived to imagine the adaptations that would be required to create a variety of permutations. The team avoided a "one-size-fits-all" solution and instead designed a system that included three module types, two roof profiles, and a variety of window locations and sizes that could be arranged according to climate, solar orien-tation, topography, and the preferences of the homeowner. The 12' × 16' dimensions are a constant, but the modules can be attached to each other in a variety of ways, and can even be stacked. As the most flexible ecoMOD system so far, ecoMOD3 provides potentially endless variations. Therefore the challenge is to make sure that the system is used wisely to minimize environmental impact and efficiently provide the necessary enclosed space.

The concept of modularity also extends into the landscape with the notion of the "seed packet"—a tool for assessing and deploying a set of predetermined elements based on existing site conditions. As the team developed the SEAM system, it became clear that the first step in assembling your home from it will be an analysis of the site. In contrast with a conventional modular home that is plunked down with little consideration of the climate, vegetation, or topography, the team imagined a more sophisticated process in which these aspects are seen as important resources, and therefore fully integrated into the design process. To assist with this analysis, the team developed a landscape kit of parts—the seed packet. It offers a variety of simple strategies that can be deployed to integrate the building with the site, create outdoor places,

minimize the negative impacts of the weather, and correspond to interior spaces. In many ways the seed packet is the culmination of the landscape design efforts from ecoMOD1, 2, and 3. The two previous teams (and even the landscape architectural team for the Trojan Goat) were initially flummoxed by the challenge of a "prefab landscape," but they tapped into the idea that the landscape architectural equivalent of prefab is not modules, but a set of design options that should be adjusted to a place. Although not fully developed yet, it offers a homeowner or an affordable housing organization a simple course in interpreting and designing a site, leading toward the selection of the modules. The ecoMOD4 team developed the system further, and eventually the document recording it will be distributed to all interested organizations and individuals. To advise the landscape team, longtime landscape architecture faculty member Nancy Takahashi joined the group, and, in a similar way to Louis Nelson, she quickly proved to be essential. UVA is a school well known for the integration of landscape and architecture, and an essential aspect of that integration is collaborative teaching. Nancy is particularly adept at balancing conceptual design with the practical issues that need to be addressed in a design/build effort.

During the design process, the team responded to research into aging issues with help from local experts. As a component of the universal design/fully accessible agenda, the SEAM house accessory unit can be supplemented with a medical monitoring system to allow an older or ill individual to be monitored by a relative or a medical professional. The team quickly realized that the older target demographic is as diverse as any other, and age group does not determine preferences. In the end, they decided simply to make the design as flexible as possible and fully accessible for all potential occupants. Energy saving technologies were used, and careful consideration was made of natural light, ventilation, and the use of sustainable, low- or no-VOC materials. The rear accessory unit has super-insulated wall and roof panel construction, low impact materials, a modular green roof system, a large deck with trellis/shade device, a rain garden and a small courtyard space. The sustainable landscape and green roof mitigate the stormwater entering the site, which over the years had damaged the foundation of the historic house. The accessory unit received a LEED Platinum rating within the U.S. Green Building Council's LEED for Homes certification program. The team chose not to explore certification for the historic house because of the complexities of submitting an existing house.

Pushing the Historic House Back into Shape

It was clear from the beginning of the design process that PHA would have to hire a builder with expertise in historic preservation to handle the construction work in the historic house. The house was structurally unstable, and even a very good builder would face some difficult challenges. It was agreed the student team would handle the historical research and design the renovation, and then focus their

construction work on the modules (which were challenging enough), but provide some assistance on the historic house interior finishes. Fortunately, PHA had worked with an excellent builder, Bruce Guss of House-wright Inc, who had completed a renovation for them a block away. He also does high-end renovation/historic preservation work, and is a master finish carpenter. Bruce proved to be essential for the success of the project. He had the right balance of know-how and curiosity, and became an excellent mentor for the students. He was endlessly patient with their ideas and questions, but if they didn't resolve a design issue in time, he was perfectly willing to plow ahead with construction to stay on schedule.

The first major job on the house was to lift it off its crumbling foundation, excavate around it, and replace the old one with a new foundation that pushed the house up slightly higher. The intent was not only to stabilize

the home, but also to minimize the potential of any further water damage. It appeared as though all the rainwater from the street had been directed right at the front foundation wall for the last 160+/– years. To lift it, Bruce and his team had to replace the perimeter beams that had rotted (we saved them and reused parts of them in the house, and later in ecoMOD4), and then use conventional jacks (which we also used to lift the modules) to place the new framing temporarily on steel beams sitting on wood cribbing. After the foundation was complete, they lowered the house onto its much-improved foundation.

The next major task was to stabilize the rest of the wood framing. Ironically, but perhaps not that surprisingly, the older portions of the home were in better shape than the newer ones—with the exception of the perimeter beam at the front wall which had taken on a lot of water over the years. The sequence of construction seemed to indicate a stepping down in material quality and skilled labor as the years progressed, with the latest work (probably from the 1980s) of the poorest quality. I think deep down Mark Watson from PHA and Bruce would have preferred to completely replace all the framing, but the HP/design team had taken the stance of keeping as much in place as possible—even if it wasn't useful structurally. In the end, we removed some of the very worst framing in the newest areas, and in the older areas the existing framing was either reinforced with new material, or supplemented with an entirely new wall or roof essentially sitting partly outside of the original. This strategy allowed us to keep much of the original interior plaster in the oldest part of the building, but make the exterior walls and the roof plumb and level on the outside. The frame was in such bad shape that Bruce and his team spent several days just trying to knock the walls into alignment—almost like a chiropractor. They used "pull along" straps to push and pull the walls, and were constantly frustrated that just as they got one wall plumb, the other would be out by 8 inches. The new framing helped hide the misalignments, and also made the installation of new siding much easier. We had briefly considered the possibility of keeping the original exterior siding, but since it was in such bad shape and was covered with lead paint, to do so just didn't make sense. With the exception of the siding and old roof shingles, we kept

most of the material that was not reused, and did our best to integrate it somewhere. Some of it was left in the airplane hangar where we build the modules, for use on future projects.

During the chiropractic session, the builders discovered a lot of debris and household items in the roof framing and the ceiling framing above the first floor. It was an unusual mix of stuff, ranging from children's toys, to a homemade fishing rod, to early twentieth-century ketchup and whiskey bottles. The most surprising discovery was what appeared to be human or animal bones—including a knee joint (cleanly cut) and some rib and leg bones. We researched the vintage of the items, and selected a portion of them (not the bones) to return to the home on a series of shelves with Plexiglas panels in front of them—as a kind of permanent display in the loft area of the home. We also left half the shelves empty and uncovered, so the new occupants could add their own history.

We did keep two areas of original siding that had been exterior walls many years ago but were buried beneath new interior walls as various additions were constructed. One area in particular had never been painted, and was clearly part of the oldest siding from the section that we assume was a slave quarters. There was evidence of whitewashing that had faded, but it seemed as though the surface had not been viewed in over a hundred years. Our plan was to keep the section, which is in the corner of what was becoming the bedroom, and simply put a clear finish on it to protect the surface but reveal the original color. Unfortunately, a professional painter hired by Bruce did not get this message, and a new coat of paint went over it. It was probably the most

painful moment for the team, as we feel as if we really lost something at that point. Stripping the paint would have simply damaged the wood, so we grinned and bore it.

One of the challenges we faced was what to do with the flooring. Some of it appeared to be in good condition, and some of it was clearly in bad shape. All of it on the first floor had to be removed because the floor framing beneath it needed to be supplemented or replaced. Bruce was concerned about what it would take to reinstall the flooring afterwards, but the HP team was committed to saving as much of it as possible and reusing it in the home. We took the flooring to our fabrication facility—the hangar—and sorted it by size, vintage, and condition. We trimmed part of the good pieces and sent all of the truly bad pieces to a wood recycler, but were able to clean up the vast majority of the material. Reinstalling it was not as difficult as Bruce had imagined, but he did experience more difficulty than he would have with new flooring. We didn't have quite enough of the more recent (perhaps mid-twentieth-century) oak flooring that was going into the bathroom, so Bruce purchased some inexpensive new oak that matched it perfectly. When the floor was sanded and finished, the students felt vindicated because the floor looked terrific— almost too good in that it was difficult to tell it was old wood. As mentioned before, the orientation was changed at the transitions from one part of the building to another— which had the added benefit of directing your eyes to the beautiful finish.

When Louis helped the team identify the original riven lath under the original plaster,

the effort to save most of the plaster began. The chiropractic job on the framing didn't do as much damage to the plaster as you might expect, largely because the plaster was limited to the first floor and was held up from the bottom of the wall where the base molding was, so that by removing the base molding and replacing it later, we were able to let the framing move more freely and allow the plaster to "wiggle" a bit. When the plasterer came in towards the end of the project to patch selected areas and give skim coat to the entire surface to blend it together, the team was temporarily disappointed at the loss of the more raw surface, but quickly realized that its original spirit had been restored.

When we started the renovation, all the windows in the house were inexpensive 1960s or '70s replacements, with the exception of one late 1800s window in what was to become the bedroom. We clearly felt no need to keep the newer ones and replaced them with historically appropriate and energy efficient windows from Pella, but we decided to restore the old window. One student made it her project to research, deconstruct, and reassemble the window—a process that took longer than any of us expected. With help from a few other students, she was able to stabilize and structurally improve the window, but in the end we were not able to make it operable again. To bring the performance in line with the new windows, we added a custom wood storm window, made by the team.

Another major concern was how to properly insulate the historic house. The added thickness of the walls—thanks to the combination of new plumb framing and old

out-of-plumb framing—made it possible to minimize thermal bridges (where wood studs touch both the inside and outside wall surface) and fill the cavity with wet cellulose insulation from recycled newspaper. For the roof, we selected an expanded foam product that would not only minimize any heat gain or loss, but also eliminate the need for ventilating any air space above the insulation, since the foam would leave none. Above the bedroom, where the roof framing needed to be completely replaced and the shape of the roof was somewhat complicated, we were able to simplify the structure and insulation of part of it by using some extra ThermaSteel panels from ecoMOD2. They were installed on top

of the old framing, with some new framing around them, which allowed the relatively weak but still attractive old framing to be exposed—adding to the perception of height in the room. In the end, the insulation went a very long way to improving the performance of what had been a completely uninsulated home up to that point.

Module Construction

After considerable debate, the team selected ThermaSteel panels for the walls and roofs of the modules for ecoMOD3, with conventional floor framing—wood I-joists with a perimeter framing system. While the Therma-

Steel panels are incredibly lightweight, reasonably priced, well-insulated, and resistant to mold, a problem with our shop drawings from the manufacturer led to some errors in the custom panels that were shipped to us. It was only by chance, as we were trying to figure out how to build a detail from a drawing we had originally sent to the manufacturer but to which we hadn't received a response, that we discovered they had not fully engineered our window openings. The headers (the framing above the windows) had not been built properly by the company, and so we had to adapt the panels, which were already mostly in place. The solution involved adding an extra

layer of sheet metal, attached with self-tapping screws. This turned what had been a slightly awkward but not difficult process into the very labor intensive task of attaching the sheet metal (while standing on a ladder or scaffold) through multiple other layers of sheet metal. This difficulty compounded itself when it became time to install siding, which would have been quite easy on a wood system, but was twice as difficult and time-consuming when drilling through multiple layers of steel. While the ThermaSteel system itself made sense financially and environmentally, the error created enough problems that several on the team wouldn't want to work with it

again. In my opinion, it is still a terrific system that didn't happen to work well in this case.

Although only three modules were fabricated for ecoMOD3 (unlike the eight for ecoMOD1), they still took the team a while to construct. The challenges installing the siding slightly delayed the project, but not as much as we were delayed on ecoMOD1, and the team was able to complete 90 percent of the finish work at the hangar, bringing the modules to Fourth Street in August of 2007. Once on-site, the team installed the "ecoSCREEN" deck next to the accessory unit, the SEAM cabinetry zone, and some of the kitchen. The modules were substantially complete before the historic house, but only by a few weeks.

Evaluation and Current Status

An offer was made on the house (historic house and accessory unit sold together) soon after it went on the market in the early winter of 2008. After some delay, the sale was finalized in July 2008. The new homeowner has not elected to have the medical monitoring system installed, but is aware he has that option.

The UVA Patent Foundation has registered the copyrights for ecoMOD3. In addition to the designs, the ecoMOD engineering team hopes to make aspects of their wireless monitoring system available to affordable housing organizations and individuals, so others can get easily understandable feedback on their energy and water usage and the performance of their home.

During the evaluation phase, some initial observations were made regarding the performance of the passive design and green roof systems in ecoMOD3. One of the major energy-saving strategies the ecoMOD3 team used was passive design—meaning that the design of the home takes into consideration siting and local conditions to maximize interior comfort with minimal energy usage. According to an evaluation student's analysis from the spring of 2008—after the project was complete but before the home was occupied—daylighting, thermal comfort, and ventilation are all functioning effectively to provide a comfortable environment in both units. It is not too surprising that the studio accessory unit performed better than the historic home, due to the limitations of wall, window, and door placement in the older unit. When the homeowner and his renter moved in, the team noticed that both seemed to understand and appreciate the passive cooling opportunities of their homes—and used their windows regularly, even when others in the neighborhood had their air-conditioning going. The accessory unit occupant has mentioned to several team members that he really likes the window locations because he always gets a good breeze.

Students have also had the opportunity to monitor the performance of the green roof on the accessory unit. One purpose of a green roof is to reduce stormwater surges, flash flooding, soil erosion, and pollution of the local watershed by retaining water on the roof and allowing it to evaporate without touching the ground. The ecoMOD3 team monitored stormwater runoff data to test the efficacy of this strategy. The monitoring revealed that ecoMOD3's green roof delays the peak runoff time by about 4 hours, and reduces the peak runoff rate by 60 percent while retaining 55 percent of rainfall in comparison to the 10 percent retained by a traditional impervious roof.

During the evaluation class in the fall of 2009, a historic preservation graduate student, with considerable real-world experience, assessed the success of the historic preservation effort. Her conclusion was that it did not strictly follow U.S. Department of Interior guidelines for preservation—in particular in the removal of exterior siding. However, despite this, she concluded the decisions were fair and reasonable, and the negatives were outweighed by the positive aspect of demonstrating that undervalued buildings can be regenerated and returned to the affordable housing market. She also felt that the project was an important demonstration of the fact that historic preservation and sustainable design are compatible.

ecoMOD3 FEATURES

DAYLIGHTING Natural light was used to illuminate the interior spaces in lieu of electrical lighting when possible. This method reduces the electrical load and produces a more natural interior environment. Daylight is delivered through strategically placed openings on each wall—often placed in corners, near adjacent walls, floors, and ceilings to maximize the opportunity for light to bounce off these surfaces.

CABINETRY The cabinetry was mostly sourced from IKEA, a company with an environmental commitment to reduced material waste. The ribbon-like SEAM zones—important in the conceptual understanding of the project— are made from birch-veneer plywood. Given the tight budget, non-VOC plywood to make custom cabinetry was not an option. The design integrates storage and appliances, while maintaining flexibility for future uses.

MATERIAL REUSE Many materials from the historic house were reused in place, or adapted for use elsewhere in the house or in the accessory dwelling unit behind. The reused materials were mostly limited to wood flooring and framing, and contributed significantly to reducing the carbon footprint of the project. Leftover wood framing was later used to build a powder room countertop in ecoMOD4.

MECHANICAL SYSTEMS Both the historic house and the accessory rental unit use a mini-split heating and cooling system. The highly efficient system is ductless, reducing the potential of indoor air quality problems. A passive air inlet and continuously running low CFM bathroom fan ensure fresh air is regularly renewed in both housing units. The equipment and installation cost of the overall system is less than half that of a conventional heat pump system, and the variable speed fan helps keep the system efficient, which will also reduce long-term operating costs.

DESIGN FOR DECONSTRUCTION Design for deconstruction (DfD) is a way of thinking about and designing a building to maximize its flexibility. The design approach is focused on extending the useful life of the building and its building components. The goal of designing for deconstruction is to design elements to be easily disassembled, allowing them to be reused, helping to "close the loop" on construction waste and minimize energy costs. The modules used at the SEAM house address DfD through the following building elements:

- *Green roof system:* Removable planting trays can be cleared out and reused in other green roof systems.
- *ThermaSteel roof and walls:* Steel and foam panels assembled with screws—simple connections lead to easy disassembly.
- *Plywood sheathing:* Screwed into Therma-Steel panels and easily disassembled.
- *Wood flooring:* Reclaimed from historic house, closing the loop on construction waste.

- *Floor framing:* Lumber assembled with screws can be easily disassembled and reused.
- *Adhesives:* Construction adhesives are avoided wherever possible, to ease the disassembly process.

The modules themselves can be separated and moved to another location with a crane and trailer.

The foundation for the modules is constructed with concrete block piers as opposed to a crawlspace, which not only saves money, but also facilitates later reuse on another site. The modules are still considered permanent construction.

GREEN ROOF The prefabricated modules of the ecoMOD3 project—the modular bedroom added to the historic house and the accessory rental unit—have a tray (modular) green roof system provided by a Virginia-based company, Building Logics. The design aims to reduce site runoff. It is a relatively affordable green upgrade and fits into the modular agenda of ecoMOD. The system is composed of a roll-applied waterproofing membrane in combination with pre-grown trays that allow

for negligible maintenance for the homeowner post-installation. Each tray was planted with a wide variety of hardy sedum plants that, once installed on the roof, began to adapt so that certain species become dominant according to climate conditions.

PASSIVE DESIGN While active mechanical systems and appliances are connected to the city grid, consuming utilities such as electricity, gas, and water, passive design relies entirely on readily available natural resources like the sun and the wind. In challenging conventional building methods, the design team sought to make the SEAM house ecologically legible to the inhabitants. Most readily, the modules' fenestration maximizes southern exposure for winter heating and induces natural ventilation through operable windows that are staggered vertically from one facade to another so as to take in low, cool air and exhaust high, warm air. It is possible for homeowners to enjoy considerable monthly savings as a result, and the performance evaluation bears this out.

UNIVERSAL DESIGN The Center for Universal Design has developed a series of minimum dimensions and desirable layouts for those with limited mobility. Universal Design is both a design philosophy and a set of guidelines. Three of the seven principles—"Equity," "Low Physical Effort," and "Size and Space for Use"—have spatial implications. In order to create a space that everyone can use, it is essential to understand the minimum space requirements for a range of abilities. Together with the handicapped accessibility aspects of

the building code, these suggestions guided the SEAM house's initial design phase. With this information, the ecoMOD3 team created spaces that allow for full accessibility through the historic house (except the upstairs loft) and in the accessory rental unit. The accessory rental unit includes a zero-step, roll-in shower and a combined washer/dryer appliance, which eliminates the reaching problem of a stacked washer/dryer without taking up additional space in the very small unit.

LANDSCAPE Because of the many decades of stormwater runoff flowing directly at the foundation of the historic house and seriously destabilizing its structure, the landscape architecture team decided to focus on outdoor spaces that would keep the storm water away from the foundations and that would encourage the recharging of the water into the ground on the site. A small garden at the front of the historic home is meant to collect some water; the gravel courtyard between the housing units and the green roof on top of the modules are designed to collect water and allow it to either percolate into the soil or evaporate into the air. The lowest part of the lot, behind the accessory rental unit, is a fully engineered rain garden, with water-loving plants to collect any water that makes it that far. The plants are all native and drought tolerant.

ENERGY MODELING The modeling and simulation team—composed of engineering and architecture students with faculty advising—simulated the energy and building performance of the historic house and accessory rental unit to support decision-making in the design process. Software was used to simulate a variety of conditions, including the annual energy consumption of the occupants, the solar gain on the roof of the house, the ability to drive natural ventilation, and carbon dioxide emissions. The modeling and simulation team worked closely with the data analysis team to analyze measured data from ecoMOD1. The process helps the modeling team validate a virtual model of the project and have a more in-depth understanding of energy flow.

ecoSCREEN The team designed a steel trellis/shade system for the deck of the accessory rental unit called ecoSCREEN. It provides a seating area, a protected threshold, and a framework for vegetation. The screen addresses many issues that are integral to the SEAM house design, supporting the mobility of an aging client, transitioning between indoor and outdoor spaces, and providing a modular structure that easily adapts to a variety of site conditions.

EVACUATED TUBE SOLAR HOT WATER HEATER Solar hot water heating works on the premise that energy from the sun can be captured and used to heat water for domestic use. While there are several types of solar hot water collection systems that are used in residential applications, the ecoMOD3 historic house features an evacuated tube solar hot water system. A vacuum is placed between rows of double-layered glass tubes to encourage the absorption of solar energy while reducing heat loss due to radiation in the tubes. The system

is engineered to provide easy monitoring functions, pump replacement, and fluid replacement. Any plumber or HVAC technician, or interested homeowner, is capable of replacing the system, and the system's operation is accessible to the homeowner in a small mechanical closet. AltEnergy of Charlottesville installed (with assistance from engineering students) and warrants the system.

LEED FOR HOMES LEED, or Leadership in Energy and Environmental Design, is a green building certification program developed by the U.S. Green Building Council to provide a comprehensive series of guidelines for the building industry that promotes sustainable construction practices, energy efficient buildings, and healthy spaces for occupants to work and live. The accessory rental unit of the SEAM house pursued LEED for Homes certification, the residential green building certification program within the LEED framework. The process necessitates a collaborative effort between architects, engineers, builders, and contractors, resulting in a green building label that publicly reflects the project's conscientious design and construction decisions. The project received a platinum rating, the highest available within the system. The location of the housing unit, in the city, near public transportation and other community resources, contributed to the high rating.

INSULATION AND THERMASTEEL PANELS The historic house uses open-cell polyurethane foam insulation in the roof, dense packed cellulose insulation in the walls, and rigid insulation at the foundation. The foam insulation

out-performs the others, but budget restricted the team from using it at the walls and foundation. The accessory rental unit is constructed of an innovative steel and expanded polystyrene foam panel system made by the Virginia-based ThermaSteel company. This is the same company that created the panels for ecoMOD2. The panels are extremely light and match the foam insulation for performance. Foam insulation was used in the floors of the modules. Foam insulation is a petroleum-based product, something the ecoMOD design teams try to avoid where possible, but the carbon debt of the foam is offset quickly with the improved efficiency of its insulative properties. Foam also minimizes air infiltration because it fills the entire cavity, but the open-cell variety is still breathable in case of

a moisture problem. The foam company that provided the material was Creative Conservation, a Virginia-based company.

MONITORING The ecoMOD3 engineering team designed a comprehensive, feedback-based energy monitoring system for the project that would allow temperatures, humidity, and carbon dioxide levels to be monitored throughout the house. Data can be transmitted wirelessly from each sensor to a central base station. The homeowner initially expressed some concern about having information about his daily patterns accessible to others, and so the team only installed the solar hot water monitoring components into the home. The remainder of the system was installed into ecoMOD1, to allow the new wireless strategy to be directly compared to the fully hard-wired system and determine if the information it gathers is comparable. So far, the data correlates successfully.

MEDICAL MONITORING The energy team also developed a simple, noninvasive home medical monitoring system that records patient vital signs—the original concept of the SEAM design was to make the housing unit available to people that want to "age in place." The team researched housing for the elderly, working with the Jefferson Area Board on Aging and the UVA Institute on Aging. However, the homeowner is not elderly and is sufficiently healthy not to require the medical monitoring system.

STUDENT ESSAY BY BETH KAHLEY

Beth Kahley, BSEngr '01 and MArch '08, participated in the evaluation phase for ecoMOD1, and was a project manager of ecoMOD3. She currently works for Kieran Timberlake Associates in Philadelphia.

The concept of ecologically sensitive design is what first drew me to the study of architecture at the University of Virginia and ultimately to the doorstep of the first ecoMOD house. Yet ecoMOD1 did not conform to the image of sustainability as I superficially understood it at the time. This house was not constructed out of straw bales and used tires. It was not powered by an off-grid photovoltaic array. It was not sited on an expansive rural lot in a bucolic setting. This house defined sustainability in an entirely different way than I had been taught by the natural building books that piqued my interest leading into graduate school. In large part, I credit my ecoMOD experience with this critical evolution of perspective. Looking back from where I now stand reveals the true value of this experience to me: the immense potential for far-reaching change as each ecoMOD student passes though the program and brings its compelling and crucial message to the building industry.

Sustainability, as I learned from ecoMOD, is a vastly more nuanced proposition than I had thought. Implicit in the project is the idea that ethical design extends beyond environmental awareness to social responsibility —good ecological architecture that is not accessible or affordable to the majority of the population is inherently not sustainable. This critical distinction is what launches ecoMOD into new and deeply challenging territory and gives its students a healthy and educated skepticism of the status quo in the housing industry today.

As a project manager of ecoMOD3, the SEAM house, I quickly learned that design is a delicate art of compromise while holding fast to the project's essential principles. It was simply not enough for a material to be safe for the environment. Did it fall within our budget? Was it durable and did it require little long-term maintenance? Was it workable and appropriate for mass production in a factory setting? Could it be beautifully detailed? Each difficult decision brought us one step closer to reaching what we believe is an imperative goal of residential architecture today: to offer quality, healthy, ecologically sound design to people of all degrees of economic means and physical ability through innovative construction strategies.

I am exceedingly fortunate to come away from my education with a more sophisticated understanding of sustainability than when I began. It is not itself an isolated field of study, but the intricate and messy conflation of many important and often conflicting agendas. As I continue to explore this idea at the start of my career, I am deeply indebted to ecoMOD for revealing it to me in a way that inspires genuine passion, enthusiasm, and hope for the future.

STUDENT ESSAY BY CHRIS FANO

Christopher Fano, BSArch '07, was a project manager of ecoMOD3, and currently works for Arkin Tilt Architects in Berkeley, California.

The gap between theory and practice, though not an inevitability, leaves room within architectural academia for rich experimentation. As one of many managers on the ecoMOD project, I have come to appreciate the unification of these two spheres, one that merges the freedom of exploration with the pragmatics of making. One of the most valuable experiences I have taken from my time on the ecoMOD3 house has been an understanding of the fundamentals of construction and material assembly. Our level of participation in every aspect of both design and creation has been invaluable, especially at a time when it seems the architect is becoming increasingly removed from the act of making, the procurement of materials, and the true creative process. This project has given me a greater understanding of how something is made, who makes it, and how much it actually costs, which transforms both my approach and my attitude toward design.

Since I had very little background in the field prior to this project, learning how to relate to contractors and consultants, the specifics of dimensional lumber, and more importantly how to ask questions has also proven invaluable in a professional setting. Learning about detail in a secure educational setting has provided me with a perspective on the vernacular house type and building method that I never would have experienced in a strictly theoretical arena. I've been able to apply and compare new details, building materials, and ideas to personal experiences, which provides a level of confidence that is rare when first entering design practice. Similarly, my management experience has provided a level of confidence in the acquisition of information, which ranges from being able to interpret a set of redlines to calling manufacturers to, again, knowing how to ask the right questions. Beyond the conceptual, I have a greater sense of sequencing, scheduling, and prioritization that transcends individual projects and circumstances.

STUDENT ESSAY BY
TOM HOGGE

Tom Hogge, MArch/LAr
'09, was a historic pres-
ervation project manager
during the summer of
construction, and com-
pleted a dual degree in
architecture and land-
scape architecture. He
taught an undergraduate
design studio during the
spring of 2010.

As student designers, we depend so much on our ability to draw. Conveying an idea, an intention, requires that we communicate spatial experiences and sensibilities that words and their multiple associations would only muddle.

But the intense collaboration of ecoMOD3 revealed that the clarity of such drawings has a minor role in helping complete such a project. More critical are the people making the drawings, making decisions from them, and making things that reflect the intentions embodied in them.

The design ideas that had their genesis with pencil on paper or computer pixels on a screen were edited to their clearest when rubbed onto a door frame with chalk or penned on the construction drawing that was not quite so clear after all. There were not always the group meetings and consultations that attempted to democratize the design process; at ground or sky, water was sole arbiter, whether manifest at the foundation or under the roof.

Where we lacked information, we lacked drawings. We compensated for both deficiencies by making more drawings. But as much as the environment, the expertise of the collaborators was instructive. We each brought different construction skills and experiences, and our impromptu lessons in joinery or machinery, design or detailing, took over where our drawings left off.

It seems a bit trite to conclude that the most learning happened on-site with sketches instead of at a screen with digital visualization. Certainly there is a critical connection between doing and learning. But the project was most instructive when drawing prompted discussion, when sketches generated skepticism—when the conveniences of a neatly decided design confronted the awkwardness of a material situation, backing designer, builder, student, and teacher into a corner, where the only solution could be: draw it again.

Further, it is not design *then* build, but design *and* build. And build and design.

STUDENT ESSAY BY
TARYN HARUNAH

Taryn Harunah, BSArch
'07, was one of the his-
toric preservation project
managers for ecoMOD3,
and participated in both
design studios. She is
currently working in New
York City.

The Smith-Reeves-White house of ecoMOD3 is not like any other historic property located in the Charlottesville vicinity. Looking at the building, which had been condemned and slated for demolition before becoming an integral piece of the SEAM house, it became clear to me, as a member of the historic preservation team, that we would have to work diligently to uncover the almost lost historic treasures laced throughout its deteriorating fabric.

More than 150 years of inhabitant modifications led to a rich and complex layering of building traditions that at times became difficult to deconstruct. The house's perceived cohesiveness is an actual makeup of several separate, overlapping building phases spanning the length of its built existence. Certain fluid transitions between phases, like the one between the earliest two, made it easy to draw premature conclusions based on our pre-conceived notions about spatial construction. In one instance, the seamless transition from the earliest framework, a 16' × 16' pre–Civil War era room, into the adjacent stair hallway made a plausible argument for the entire conglomerate to be the earliest structural phase. Over time and through further excavation, however, it became apparent that while a stairway may connect the upper floor today, the underlying ceiling in the 16' × 16' room revealed that at one point a ladder entryway was used to gain access to the second floor. No other greater indicator would help to solidify the separation between spaces than the discovery of a doorway frame outlining the existing front window of the earliest structure. The discovery brought on a new defining characteristic to the 16' × 16' configuration, with qualities suggesting a type of slave housing endemic to the South.

As the unveiling of such historic revelations composed the building's written history, a greater sense of hesitancy grew on my part about how to responsibly address these discoveries in our preservation efforts. Our handling of the Smith-Reeves-White house would ultimately add another layer to the rich history of the home. A layer that, if executed haphazardly, could easily befuddle and overshadow these same historic elements we worked hard to uncover. Questions began to stir over our approach to the house. How would we differentiate between existing elements and new insertions? Should certain existing elements be worth noting while others were completely ignored? Did it even make sense to call attention to these details? For after all, as one of my teammates so vividly put it, we didn't want the house to turn into a historic *circus* attraction.

The jarring imagery of a potential spectacle led me to believe that perhaps the solution could be found right in front of us all along. The same interconnected complexity of additions that made deconstruction efforts difficult to decipher, also allowed for seamless transition between the different spaces within the home. It seemed that regardless of the size of the addition, each contributor to the house made sure that its purposeful intent was met with subtlety, as can be noted in the two early phases. However, although their efforts for subtlety succeeded, their intentions simultaneously devalue the unusual characteristics defining the home. As a result, it became apparent that our team's best methodological approach would be as a clarifier. The team carefully highlighted important elements within the house to let the building tell its own story.

STUDENT ESSAY BY BRIELLE GALLINELLI

Brielle Gallinelli, BSArch '07 with a minor in engineering, was a construction manager for ecoMOD3, and is currently living in New York City working as a project engineer for Bovis Lend Lease.

For me, ecoMOD was so much more than a single accomplishment. It was a series of mini-lessons, of collaborative moments. I recall standing in the framed-out kitchen trying to figure out how we were going to bring together a piece of cabinetry and lots of electrical wiring in the transition space to the bathroom. Basically, we were trying to fit a lot into a small space—a common dilemma throughout the construction of ecoMOD3. A few of us took it to the drawing board. Multiple perspectives led to many different potential solutions. There were different design priorities for each of us—making sure electrical elements fit, aesthetics, construction quality. A few layers of trace paper later and eventually a great solution was reached right there in the field with the input of electrical engineering, civil engineering, and architectural minds. This is just one example of the collaborative, on-site problem-solving this project afforded students. The ability to communicate with people of different disciplines working towards a common goal has carried over into my professional career. Not a day goes by that I do not use the skills developed during ecoMOD to effectively communicate with architects, structural engineers, mechanical engineers, clients, and contractors.

STUDENT ESSAY BY LORENZO BATTISTELLI

Lorenzo Battistelli, MArch '07, MAH '08, was one of the historic preservation project managers for eco-MOD3. A native of Rome, Italy, Lorenzo has taught at the University of Washington, worked in Philadelphia, and is currently back in Charlottesville.

Unlike its two predecessors, ecoMOD3 tackles the fundamental problem of adding sustainable modules to pre-existing structures. The innate ecofriendliness of building small additions to existing homes, historic or not—rather than demolishing and reconstructing anew—was central to our ecoMOD3 mantra. My role between the fall of '07 and that of '08 was to oversee the correct preservation of the historic house located in Charlottesville's Fifeville–Castle Hill neighborhood as a historic preservation manager.

My first introduction to the Fourth Street house was not a romantic encounter. Abandoned and occupied by squatters, the existing structure did not immediately seem worthy of being saved. After an initial walk through and photographic documentation the historic preservation team embarked on an academic process of digging deep into the home's layers of construction; one that was often equated to the work of a CSI investigator. What originally seemed a disarrayed mass of building additions, some less shoddy than others, soon became logical and, strangely, quite beautiful. Eryn Brennan, a fellow architectural history graduate student, scoured the city records for information on past ownership and building permits, while a team of undergraduate architecture students and I raked through the Fourth Street home with a fine-tooth comb. Once all the dust settled (literally), and after countless discussions over a nail's precise date, we all came to an agreement on a construction date of 1860 to 1866, one that matched both archival and building technology evidence. *Riven lath, circular saw marks,* and *cut nails* were as big a part of ecoMOD3's vocabulary as *green roofs, passive cooling,* and *self-tapping screws.*

For all the students on the historic preservation team who first encountered a crooked and abandoned house, opening day had a special meaning. While the governor of Virginia walked on the house's freshly stained floors, we smiled remembering the puzzled looks of people wondering why we were saving such a disaster. Though the work never seemed easy, we realized the importance of redefining how we live on this earth. To demolish homes rather than rework and add to them is counterintuitive and deleterious to our environment. I was once told that Rome, my home city, can be considered the most sustainable city in the world. I challenged this assumption by stating that one would be hard-pressed to find double-glazed windows, let alone green roofs. I was introduced to a new understanding of sustainability—one in which a city, for the last 2700 years, adapts its way of life to the existing urban condition while striving to maintain it.

ecoMOD4: THRU

Design Process

The ecoMOD4 process began with the possibility of a multi-family housing complex for Piedmont Housing Alliance, but as construction financing became more difficult in 2008, PHA had to delay the project indefinitely. I contacted Habitat for Humanity of Greater Charlottesville, with whom we had collaborated on ecoMOD2—the post-Katrina housing along the gulf coast of Mississippi—and they were enthusiastic about working together again. The city of Charlottesville had subdivided a property near the downtown area—only a few blocks from ecoMOD1 and 3—and they were donating it to HFHGC. HFHGC selected a married couple from Afghanistan as the client family. The couple was familiar with two recently completed contemporary home designs built for Habitat in Charlottesville, and was enthusiastic about getting a different kind of home. As a couple, they only qualified for a two-bedroom unit—which was not to exceed 900 square feet. The urban nature of the site necessitated a two-story design, and the HFHGC personnel let us add square footage beyond the 900 square feet to include the stair and a first floor powder room. The design sequence was similar to ecoMOD3—in the fall semester an undergraduate studio, graduate student seminar, and engineering class; in the spring a combined grad and undergrad studio with another parallel engineering class; both leading into a summer of construction.

Habitat for Humanity of Greater Charlottesville

HFHGC is a well-established and large affiliate, focused on addressing the issue of affordability in the inflated real estate market of an economically stable college town. With several paid staff, and the support of at least one or two full-time AmeriCorps volunteers at any given time, HFHGC is comparable to a mid-sized home construction company. Inspired by the example of other affiliates, HFHGC has established a successful Habitat Store that sells donated new and reclaimed construction materials and furniture. The store also offers shelf space to a local green building material supplier (and supplier for ecoMOD), Nature Neutral, so builders and homeowners can have one-stop shopping for both low-VOC finishes and reclaimed building materials. In addition, the store hosted HFHGC's "how-to" public lecture series on sustainable house construction.

A few years ago, HFHGC had the opportunity to purchase the site of the two-acre Sunrise Trailer Court near downtown Charlottesville. They raised the money to purchase the land, and organized an international design competition to come up with ideas for how to keep the current occupants on the site (in housing they could afford), but mix their units in with other affordable and market rate housing. The land purchase and the design competition—coordinated with the Charlottesville Community Design Center—were significant leaps for HFHGC. In the struggle to formulate a clear response to the significant increase in home values in the area, the transition to mixed income development was a logical next step. HFHGC raised additional money to hire both the first place and second place design firms to develop a master plan for the site, and then another firm to take the master plan further. The final design was developed by another firm, losing several of the original ideas. Construction began in early 2011.

The success of the process, which included several design workshops with participation from Sunrise occupants, inspired HFHGC to purchase the 100-acre Southwood Mobile Home Park near Charlottesville and partner with local developers to start planning another mixed income neighborhood. In addition, HFHGC has set up a for-profit organization—Creative Homes—that develops housing for both the workforce (moderate income) housing demographic and for market rate buyers.

Working with Habitat has been an important experience for ecoMOD. We have had the opportunity to watch a local affiliate of an internationally known organization respond to challenges—and redefine the methods for delivering affordable housing. One of the goals of the ecoMOD4 design is to create something that can be deployed at the Southwood site, and built for them by a modular builder or Habitat volunteers.

A Challenging Site

The fall semester 2008 started with a two-week introductory exercise to design and build a shelter made entirely of reclaimed materials to sleep in for one night. It was very

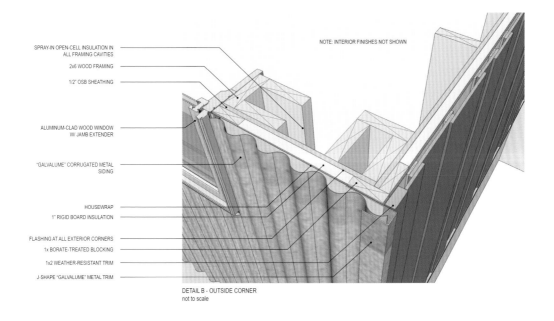

NOTE: INTERIOR FINISHES NOT SHOWN

SPRAY-IN OPEN-CELL INSULATION IN ALL FRAMING CAVITIES

2x6 WOOD FRAMING

1/2" OSB SHEATHING

ALUMINUM-CLAD WOOD WINDOW W/ JAMB EXTENDER

"GALVALUME" CORRUGATED METAL SIDING

HOUSEWRAP

1" RIGID BOARD INSULATION

FLASHING AT ALL EXTERIOR CORNERS

1x BORATE-TREATED BLOCKING

1x2 WEATHER-RESISTANT TRIM

J-SHAPE "GALVALUME" METAL TRIM

DETAIL B - OUTSIDE CORNER
not to scale

similar to the exercise I assigned for one of the Trojan Goat studios. The projects had to be prefabricated as components or panels off-site, and the teams had two hours to assemble their shelter at the final location (my backyard). The students worked in architecture/engineering collaborative teams, and had to collaborate throughout the process. Their total budget could not exceed $10, but most teams built their shelters without spending any money. Passive design was an important consideration, but the project was completed in the early fall, so it was difficult for teams to determine if they should be designing for a hot, muggy night, or a cool, rainy one. The monitoring team used temperature and humidity sensors to measure the comfort level of each shelter during the night the designers slept in them, and in the end, a group of

faculty and Habitat officials judged the shelters and selected a winner. It was an excellent way to encourage the team to get to know each other very quickly, and to require the architecture and engineering students to work together early on.

As the team began to focus on the design of the housing unit, the constraints of the selected site became very clear. The property was sited behind a 1920s bungalow. The older home sits in a historic district and faces a prominent entrance corridor just south of Charlottesville's downtown area. The ecoMOD4 lot had once been the backyard of this home and is significantly below the much higher—and appropriately named— Ridge Street. The ecoMOD4 lot faces the secondary road—Elliott Avenue—and the corner of Ridge and Elliott is a well-known stoplight intersection, giving waiting drivers a clear view of ecoMOD4. The bungalow was in a state of disrepair, and had been acquired by the city of Charlottesville after a drug and prostitution raid on the place. The city was trying to figure out what they were going to do with the house, and felt the backyard, with an existing curb cut, was large enough for a small home. (See the next section for information about the development of the bungalow into the ecoREMOD1 project.) The city has been trying to encourage more urban-infill affordable housing, so this is how the lot came into the hands of Habitat.

The site is a classic affordable housing lot. In a city like Charlottesville, if there is an empty lot somewhere that hasn't been built on yet, there is probably a good reason. Either the owner is holding on to it as an

investment, or it will be very difficult to build on. Sharing characteristics with the ecoMOD1 and 3 lots, the site revealed on our first visit that the latter was probably the case. Trash and construction debris were clearly visible at and just below the surface. In addition, the lot was filled with scrub trees—volunteer species that had taken over the lot, but with little value in restoring the local ecosystem. Most of these trees were not healthy specimens, and they made solar access challenging. In addition, the property setbacks constrained the design choices, and the location on a busy street (on a steep hill) meant the required off-street parking space had to allow for a driver to back around and return to the street front-end first—without going over the strict square footage limit for a parking area in front of a home. To make matters worse, the house needed to be aligned with Elliott Avenue, due to its location in the historic district, but Elliott Avenue is almost exactly 45 degrees off of the north-south axis—the most unfortunate orientation possible when you want to get good solar incidence on a PV panel. (Paxton and I had begun the project with the assumption of using renewable energy technologies for this home.)

Throughout the semester the architecture students developed a lot of design ideas, and ultimately settled on the simple volume of two 13'6" × 34' modules stacked on top of each other, with two smaller stair modules stacked off to one side. The team endeavored to make visual connections that aligned through the house into the landscape—hence the THRU house name—and to make the small home feel as large as possible. A slightly higher

ceiling and attention to clear zoning of storage and wet areas helped reinforce this spatial idea. The graduate architecture, landscape architecture, and planning seminar students researched affordable housing issues, developed prototypical structural framing strategies, researched materials and sustainability issues, and developed the landscape guiding principles, while the studio began the design process. At the same time, the engineering students researched HVAC and renewable energy systems; continued to develop the ecoMOD wireless monitoring system; participated in the structural, stormwater management, and landscape design; and worked with the architecture students to reduce the building's energy loads so that we could get as close as possible to achieving our goal of a net-zero energy home—one that uses less energy over the course of a year than the renewable energy systems can generate for it.

An ongoing collaborative relationship with a local subcontractor, Albemarle Heating and Air (AHA), was the basis for our eventual strategy of combining PV panels with a geothermal system to help us come close to what we think may be a net-zero energy home. The PVs wouldn't do it alone, but would help handle the peak energy loads during the hot summer. A relatively shallow slope for the roof allowed us to get excellent sun when it is high in the sky—during the summer, and at midday during the other seasons—despite the unfortunate solar orientation. The geothermal system takes advantage of the temperature of the earth to both cool and heat the home—and is a strategy that is not impacted by solar access. AHA had been involved in some aspects of

the Trojan Goat, as well as heating and cooling systems for ecoMOD1 and 3. Their advice and interest in supporting affordable housing with high-level aspirations for sustainability has helped the project a great deal. An anonymous donor and the local utility, Dominion Virginia Power, contributed funding for the PV and geothermal systems.

During the spring semester, when the undergraduate and graduate students were combined into one studio and the engineering students continued into another class with Paxton, the team developed the design further and began to prepare construction drawings. On the very first day of the semester, the newly configured team—with more new participants than original ones—decided to mirror-image the house on the site. Yet they also respected and reinforced the core ideas of the design. As the semester progressed, the team also developed the design at the scale of townhomes and duplexes for use by

other affordable housing organizations. The modules the team designed are flexible enough to be deployed in a wide variety of ways.

A combined group of architecture and engineering students worked with Eric Field, the architecture school's computer teaching resource coordinator and an expert in advanced modeling and simulation. During previous ecoMOD projects, we were largely dependent upon the simulation expertise of a single graduate engineering student who worked closely with a few undergraduate engineering students and one or two architecture students to study building orientation, glazing, insulation, daylighting, and solar incidence questions. She was a terrific team member but had moved on to other activities. Eric's interest in passive design, and background in both architecture and engineering, made him the perfect addition to our team. We coordinated the simulation process with a handful of

architecture and engineering students, using a variety of software including EnergyPlus. Nancy Takahashi continued to advise the landscape architecture team—striking the right balance between a concern for design rigor and a practical response to limited resources.

The Board of Architectural Review was supportive of the THRU house, and accepted the contemporary nature of the design—in part because the building form was modest and attuned to both passive design and the scale of the neighborhood. They also recognized that the lot was not situated in the middle of the houses facing Ridge Street—but instead behind and down the hill from one of them. We probably would have had much tougher questioning from the BAR if it was right on the historic street.

Construction Begins

Towards the end of the spring semester we began framing the modules at the Milton

hangar, and then moved into full-time construction mode during the summer. To better mimic the typical construction strategies of modular builders—and of Habitat—we elected to build the home of conventional wood studs, using lumber certified by the Forest Stewardship Council. However, to help us achieve the high performance building envelope we would need to create a net-zero energy building, we used foam insulation between the studs and rigid insulation on the outside of the sheathing to help eliminate thermal bridging—effectively matching the performance of the SIPs and ThermaSteel panel systems from the previous ecoMOD housing units. It is a very similar strategy to the one we used for the Trojan Goat. The modules were framed up quickly, and we also elected to build them from the inside out—meaning we installed the gypsum wall board on the inside before the sheathing and siding on the outside, so we could simultaneously mud and finish the wall board as we installed the electrical, plumbing, and insulation. This is a common modular housing strategy, and something only possible with off-site construction.

The original soil borings indicated probable construction waste or other inappropriate fill on the site, but the results where a little unclear about the extent of it. To be safe, we estimated excavation costs to be twice what you might expect for a house of this size. However, as we began to excavate the site for the foundation, it became immediately clear that the construction debris—in the form of unusually large and thick chunks of concrete—were going to make the team's intended placement of the home on the site

on the western part of the site—the higher part of the lot, with less debris—the additional excavation costs made it difficult for Habitat to afford the project. Fortunately, the city administration and city councilors recognized that they had some responsibility for the situation. They had given the lot to Habitat, and it was also clear to them that their predecessors at the city had been responsible for improperly dumping the construction debris on the lot during the construction of Elliott Avenue several decades before, and so they contributed to the cost of the excavation.

The modules were well under construction out at Milton, so the building design could not change that much when the position and orientation on the site had to change. The primary concern with the new orientation was the need to adjust the solar shading of windows. With the new location, different windows were going to be exposed to southern light. In addition, the landscape design had to be entirely reworked—turning the area on top of the primary debris field into a very generous yard space—especially large for such a small home and lot. The end result is generally believed by the team to be a better solution than the original. It was a strategy that was not previously considered because of the very close proximity to the original bungalow—ecoREMOD.

Another major concern was the lack of utilities on the site—due to the fact that it had not been used as a house site before. Tapping off the existing utilities of ecoREMOD was not a legitimate option, and the full scope of the financial problem was not immediately clear. We had to connect to water supply and

prohibitively expensive. These huge pieces of concrete were found quite deep in some parts of the lot—as deep as twenty-five feet—and a good foundation depends upon consistent and stable soil. We initially thought we could remove the concrete and other debris and then bring in new fill, but we couldn't even get deep enough to find original soil along the eastern part of the site. Each bucket from the excavator found a new chuck of concrete.

It was quickly decided to move the house to the western part of the lot and rotate the design 90 degrees off the original orientation. This was necessary to help us to reduce the cost overrun. The entire budget of the project, less the grant-supported geothermal and photovoltaic systems, was only $120,000. Even

sewer lines a significant distance from the lot. The delay over how financially to handle this impacted much of the site work for several months—pushing the team into the fall of 2009 to finish construction. The modules arrived before the utility connection, and the team worked on finishing off as much as we could without water and sewer. The utilities were finally connected in the spring of 2010, and the homeowners moved in soon afterward.

The engineering team completed their next-generation monitoring system with the intent of monitoring the performance of the home, including the PV and geothermal systems. The first couple of months of

monitoring revealed a highly energy efficient home—likely the most efficient of any eco-MOD design. The homeowners will be given a post-occupancy evaluation questionnaire after they have been in the home for one year.

The engineering and landscape architecture team is assessing the stormwater at the site and monitoring the performance of the rain garden. As of this writing, the LEED for Homes certification is pending.

ecoMOD4 DESIGN FEATURES

ENERGY SIMULATIONS The ecoMOD4 team worked closely with faculty in architecture and engineering to develop accurate energy simulations that could influence the design process. The house was modeled using Google Sketchup and Energy Plus, two free, publically available software packages from Google and

the U.S. Department of Energy respectively. The software allowed us to predict seasonal energy usage and comfort levels from a variety of inputs such as wall construction, window size and placement, occupant activity, and passive ventilation strategies. In addition, the ecoMOD team used these energy modeling tools to determine the correct size and orientation of our rooftop PV array. We were able to simulate power output based on weather data collected in Charlottesville and compare that with predicted hourly electric loads in the house to effectively design the system for our specific needs.

DESUPERHEATER The waste heat from the geothermal heat pump is typically released into the ground. During the summer, eco-MOD4 employs a desuperheater to transfer that waste heat to the hot water—effectively reducing the water-heating energy load during that season. Although the savings is not that significant in the mid-Atlantic climate zone, the upfront cost is minimal.

PHOTOVOLTAICS Some of the electricity used in the house is produced by a rooftop PV array, consisting of four-kilowatt PV polycrystalline silicon panels installed by Solar Con-

nexion of Blacksburg, Virginia. The system is connected to the utility grid, and the team is monitoring the energy production.

GEOTHERMAL HEATING AND COOLING After insulating the house, orienting the home to take advantage of the positive aspects of a climate zone, and using the most efficient windows you can afford, the next step to reducing your energy load is an efficient HVAC system. By far the most efficient is a ground source heat pump—often referred to as a geothermal system. Unlike a standard heat pump that exchanges heat with the air outside of the window—so that efficiency varies with the outside temperature—a ground source heat pump exchanges heat with the much more constant and predictable ground temperature. The expected combined heating and cooling costs for ecoMOD4 are expected to be under $500 a year.

INSULATION The first step in designing a highly efficient housing unit is to insulate the house as well as possible. In the case of ecoMOD4, and previous projects, we targeted several aspects of the Passive House standard, a high performance building system. Although we cannot afford the triple-glazed windows typically required for Passive House, we consistently invest in the recommended high level of insulation. While some forms of insulation have unintended environmental impacts, over the life of the building the environmental savings will more than make up for the damage. We used a combination of open and closed cell foam. Closed cell foam has double the resistance to heat flow, but also double the cost. We used closed cell in the roof, getting an R-value of over 60 (code requires R-20 in new construction), and open cell in the walls, with an R-value of 30. Creative Conservation installed the insulation. It is worth noting that a more thorough report about the environmental impact of closed cell and rigid foam insulation was published during the summer of 2010, calling into question their use. It is likely that future ecoMOD teams will use open cell foam and other forms of insulation.

DOMESTIC GREYWATER SYSTEM It makes little sense that the water used to flush the toilet should be just as clean as the water we drink from the tap. With that in mind, ecoMOD4 has a small, inexpensive greywater system that takes the wastewater from the bathroom sink and reuses it in the nearby toilet. It is estimated to save nearly 5,000 gallons of fresh water per year, and requires little maintenance.

We decided against a full house greywater system because of the significant upfront cost. The system in ecoMOD4 fits under the bathroom sink, and costs less than $250.

MANIFOLD The standard plumbing in a house runs a single line from the hot water tank to the farthest fixture, branching off from the main line at any intervening fixtures. To save energy, we used a manifold system. A manifold is a short length of pipe with one entrance and multiple exits. The manifold is located a few feet from the hot water heater. By running smaller pipes from the manifold to the fixtures, it is possible to save a significant amount of energy. The volume of water in a ½" pipe is half of that in a ¾" pipe. In ecoMOD4, this system saves over 5,000 gallons of hot water per year, and the energy required to heat that water.

LANDSCAPE DESIGN The ecoMOD4 house was built upon a previously developed brownfield—a parking area, doghouse, and shed with a lot of concrete and other construction debris underneath—which required large-scale site remediation to restore the land as a buildable location. Responding to the natural topography of the site, the landscape design focused on three main strategies: collecting and managing stormwater runoff, using native vegetation to define exterior spaces, and framing the relationship between interior and exterior rooms. Material and plant choices closely followed the sustainable site guidelines set out by LEED for Homes, which focus on linking natural and built systems to achieve balanced environmental and social outcomes that improve quality of life and the environment. The hardscape materials (in part, porous concrete) were chosen to be permeable and light in color and are shaded in order to reduce the heat island effect on the site. A variety of native grasses and plants serve as natural and layered screening elements to ensure privacy along the site's busy street.

STORMWATER MANAGEMENT As a new home, ecoMOD's roof and hard surfaces decrease the area available to absorb stormwater before it runs into neighboring yards and the local watershed. This increase in stormwater runoff can disrupt ecosystems, overwhelm streams and rivers, and contribute to pollution. The ecoMOD landscape design minimizes and stops water from running off of the site. Using permeable surfaces on the drive and walkways and directing yard runoff through a swale toward a rain garden, the stormwater design

minimizes environmental impact in a manner that is affordable.

INTERIORS The interior of the home is designed to emphasize the relationship between the inside and outside. Affordable and durable IKEA cabinetry is mixed with custom cabinetry to provide sufficient storage space and reinforce the design ideas. Low-VOC paints are used throughout, and the team found inexpensive, discontinued bamboo flooring—recognizing that despite the rapidly renewable aspect of bamboo groves, there is a large carbon debt produced by shipping the flooring from China.

INSULATED CONCRETE FORMWORK The ecoMOD4 team selected insulated concrete formwork (ICF) for the foundation because it could be assembled by the team, and contributed to the high performance building envelope. The ICF system was contributed by Allied Concrete and AMVIC.

**STUDENT ESSAY BY
JAMES PERAKIS**

James Perakis, BSArch '09,
was one of the project
managers for ecoMOD4.

The ecoMOD4 project presented an incredible opportunity to see a project through from the earliest stages of conceptual design to post-occupancy evaluation and beyond. This is an opportunity that is rarely given to undergraduate or even graduate architecture students today.

Some of the best features of the ecoMOD4 house are the result of ideas brought to us by local businesses, politicians, and community development agencies, as well as our team of architects and engineers. To me, the ecoMOD project is as much about fostering a stronger sense of community as it is about finding affordable, sustainable, and replicable solutions for the built environment. For example, Dominion Virginia and Albermarle Heating and Air worked with our engineers to develop the photovoltaic array and geothermal system used on the ecoMOD4 house. The companies wanted to demonstrate the viability of these technologies for single-family homes and challenge conventionally held beliefs about their cost-effectiveness. It is this kind of community involvement that makes ecoMOD a success. And while working with multiple organizations can be frustrating and exhausting at times, it is an experience that has shown me that great ideas are only as good as the support they have in the community.

I feel that I have come away from ecoMOD with a stronger sense of what sustainability means and how to build a sustainable future. It is a concept that is much more complex than I was originally led to believe and one that requires a keen understanding of grassroots development and community action in addition to knowledge of environmental and technological issues. I learned that in order to achieve a truly sustainable future, we need to simultaneously address social inequity and growing environmental concerns through community action and technological innovation. These are lessons that are all too often withheld from standard college curricula, but because of my experiences with ecoMOD, I am much better prepared to negotiate the intricacies of the design process in order to bring about positive changes in our communities.

**STUDENT ESSAY BY
WHITNEY NEWTON**

Whitney Newton, BSEngr
'09, MUEP '11, and MArch
'13, served as one of the
engineering project
managers for ecoMOD4.

The ecoMOD4 project speaks directly to my interests as a student of both civil and environmental engineering and urban and environmental planning. I appreciate the way the project so easily stretches beyond the academic world and aligns with my interests as a member of a community. The ecoMOD4 house was designed to reduce waste and reuse materials and resources, to be built efficiently, and to consider context and community as the way to build a livable house. This project addresses the house as the fundamental element of a community. It recognizes that planning a healthy community is a collaboration of many different parts that must work together. It incorporates efficient-energy technologies like solar panels and a geothermal heat pump with a practical, and impressive, architectural design that optimizes natural solar access and shading by addressing its surroundings. While these details are unique to the ecoMOD house, the project communicates to the community that affordable and practical should mean (and easily can mean) the same as environmentally responsible. It seems to challenge the traditional boundaries that connect innovative design to the affluent population and allows such solutions to penetrate the mainstream home and commercial building sector. This connection should be commonplace. Working on ecoMOD showed me that by challenging the ordinary, we can surpass communities that lack collaboration, environmental respect, and beauty and instead create communities that are truly livable.

STUDENT ESSAY BY ALISON SINGER

Alison Singer, MArch '10, was one of the project managers for ecoMOD4.

I first became involved with Habitat for Humanity in 2003, after joining my undergraduate college's local chapter in New York. I thought the practical experience of learning to build a house through Habitat's volunteer program was an excellent way to test my interest level in building design and also to learn how exactly things went together.

At some point during the overwhelming process of applying to graduate schools, I came across UVA's ecoMOD project and was instantly drawn to both the school and the scope of work offered by ecoMOD's design/build program. My involvement began in the Fall '08 ecoMOD research seminar where I was involved with research on material selection, life cycle analysis, indoor air quality, and design work for ecoMOD4. Knowing full well that ecoMOD was partnering with Habitat for their next project, I began to consider how this project could become a great testing ground for Habitat and could help drive the organization into the regular practice of building more sustainably and being more selective with their choice of building materials.

As one of the project managers for the ecoMOD4 THRU house I was granted new responsibilities as well as new opportunities to reconnect and engage with Habitat for Humanity; this time more directly and more effectively. Since the ecoMOD4 project is an applicant for LEED for Homes certification, I charged myself with the role of advocate for sustainable building practices that fit the LEED for Homes guidelines, the ecoMOD4 project teams' design principles, *and* the intentions and limited financial means of the Habitat organization. I knew full well that this would not be an easy role but that it would be crucial and a defining element of this project.

Working with Habitat as the client for ecoMOD4 proved to be an eye-opening experience. In the context of affordable housing, issues of sustainability, durability, and budget became increasingly more critical and more complex and seemed to pervade most of our meeting agendas and conversations. I can say that this project was not without its challenges—financial, aesthetic, and site-related, just to name a few. When our project almost hit a standstill during site excavation it became clearer than ever to me that: 1) you cannot build anywhere you like, 2) faced with such a challenge, a group of strong minds working together toward a solution has never been so important, and 3) there is truly a design *opportunity* in every difficult challenge.

CURRENT WORK

Next Steps

The project teams continue to both broaden the scope of our efforts and to deepen the commitment to sustainability and affordability. Emerging from the integration of historic preservation into ecoMOD3, we have established a parallel project called ecoREMOD that creates rigorously energy-efficient retrofits of existing housing units, some of them historic. At the same time, in 2011, the project received a multi-million-dollar grant to bring highly energy-efficient ecoMOD modular designs to the marketplace. The grant is in partnership with Virginia -based affordable housing organizations and housing manufacturers.

ecoREMOD: Adapting the ecoMOD Idea to Existing Homes

In 2009 the city of Charlottesville approached Paxton Marshall and me about using our expertise to help with energy-efficiency education programs in the city, and participating in grant-funded activities to facilitate green buildings. It was in one of those conversations that they mentioned an interest in doing a sustainable home renovation dem-onstration project in the city and using the completed house as a temporary exhibit and office space for one of these programs. They were planning to buy a home for the effort, and I immediately suggested they consider a house they already owned—the bungalow on Ridge Street next to ecoMOD4. The left hand checked with the right hand within the city administration, and within a few days they committed to the idea. The project was quickly dubbed ecoREMOD1, the Energy House, and, during the summer of 2009, a small team consisting of a graduate architecture student, an undergraduate engineering student, and a graduate architectural history student began designing the renovation of and researching the background on the home. I reenlisted architectural history professor Louis Nelson to advise on historic preservation issues, in a role similar to the one he played on ecoMOD3. The spirit of creativity in material reuse and the focus on revealing the narrative of the building continued into this project. The team, which included city employees and a local architecture/construction firm, Alloy Workshop, struggled with the need to retain as much of the original building materials as possible, while trying to ensure it achieved our goals for energy efficiency. We learned a lot about these issues, and as with the ecoMOD3 project, found the two are not in conflict. However, finding effective and affordable solutions requires considerable research. The project was completed in the spring of 2011, and serves as the home for the Local Energy Alliance Program (LEAP). LEAP hosts educational programs for homeowners, contractors, and school children to learn about the design

strategies and technologies used in the home. Paxton's engineering students created the educational displays for LEAP.

In 2011, an interdisciplinary team began the design for our first international project, ecoREMOD2, the ADAPT house, sited in the British colonial town of Falmouth, Jamaica. Falmouth is beginning to face development pressures due to the recent construction of a major international cruise ship terminal. The community has suffered from a lack investment for decades, with tourism development emerging in other cities on the north coast. For several years, the UVA School of Architecture has run a historic preservation

field school in Falmouth to document historic structures and work with the nonprofit Falmouth Heritage Renewal to restore them. Louis Nelson runs the program, and we had been discussing the possibility of mashing up our projects for several years. We decided to restore a tiny board (wood frame) house, and add a new kitchen and bathroom using contemporary, climate responsive design. The team also developed the design as a kit of parts that can be applied to board houses around Falmouth, in order to provide amenities for homes that lack them and are therefore undervalued in the community. Without modern plumbing, some of these homes are

being torn down and replaced with concrete structures.

A house was selected, and the usual interdisciplinary team was convened in a studio and seminar. Many on the team participated in a spring break visit to Falmouth, to meet the client and get to know our local partner, Falmouth Heritage Renewal. However, after working all semester on a tiny home for a single mother, problems arose related to the ownership of the property, and we had to move the project to another site. This happened after the final review for the semester, but before the team reconvened in Falmouth for the summer field school. The team quickly

and effectively responded to the situation and designed an entirely new project, including details, in about a week. As of this writing, the project is nearing completion.

Taking the Designs to Market

During the fall of 2010, a team of architecture and engineering students created the ecoMOD XS designs—"extra small" housing units to be used as urban infill accessory dwelling units (ADUs). Similar to the ADU at ecoMOD3, the designs are optimized for aging in place, with advice from our local partner, the Jefferson Area Board for Aging. Five small units were designed, but the team was not tasked with building them. Instead, the designs are being submitted for preliminary planning approval for future use in backyards of homes

in Charlottesville and elsewhere. Individuals and organizations will have the opportunity to license the designs or have a modular manufacturer build a unit for them.

The initial aspiration of bringing the ecoMOD homes and the unbuilt ecoMOD XS prototype designs to other affordable housing organizations has taken a big step forward with a grant from the Virginia Tobacco Indemnification and Community Revitalization Commission. The commission, established to distribute funding from the multistate tobacco industry settlement in the late 1990s, is focused on generating economic development in Southside and Southwestern Virginia, the region most directly impacted by the reduction in tobacco production. We are creating townhome and duplex versions of previous designs for two affordable housing organiza-

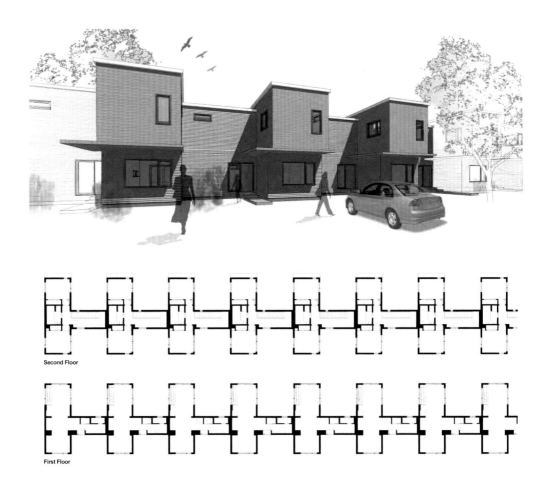

Second Floor

First Floor

tions, Southside Outreach Group, from South Boston, and People Incorporated of Abingdon, in Southwest Virginia. The industry partners include Cardinal Homes and SIPs of America, both in Southside. The first phase involves creating four housing units: two as a side-by-side duplex for a site in South Boston and another similar duplex in Abingdon. The duplex designs will be identical, and one of the two houses on each site will be constructed of SIPs, with the other built from a high performance version of standard wood framing. The four housing units will be occupied, and the energy performance of each will be monitored to assess the differences between the sites, the construction methods, and the energy habits of the occupants. We are structuring the process to ensure we have the most useful and rigorous evaluation process yet, with the aim of using the information to help create truly net-zero energy housing units that housing organizations and individuals can order from our modular housing partner. Quality design that blends aesthetics and performance remains the primary agenda.

RESOURCES

ecoMOD Project

ecoMOD project website: www.ecomod.virginia.edu

"The Case for Real Buildings with Real Budgets,"
John D. Quale, in *The Oxford Conference: A Re-Evaluation of Education in Architecture,* edited by
Sue Roaf and Andrew Bairstow (WIT Press, 2008),
pages 149–52

"Ecological, Modular and Affordable Housing," John D.
Quale, in *Eco-Architecture: Harmonisation between
Architecture and Nature,* edited by G. Broadbent and
C. A. Brebbia (WIT Press, 2006), pages 53–62

"ecoMOD2: the preHAB house," John D. Quale, in *Re-building after Katrina: Visions for the Gulf Coast,* edited by Betsy Roettger, volume 2 in the UVA School
of Architecture's Urgent Matters book series (distributed by University of Virginia Press, 2007)

"ecoMOD3—the SEAM House: Historic Preservation
as Social and Environmental Justice" and "Revising
the American Dream: Making Sustainable Housing
Affordable for All," John D. Quale, in *The Value of
Design,* proceedings of 2009 ACSA annual meeting
(March 2009)

Expanding Architecture: Design as Activism, John D.
Quale, essay on ecoMOD in collected volume, ed-
ited by Bryan Bell and Katie Wakeford (Metropolis
Books, 2008)

"Finding the Potential in Prefab," John D. Quale, in *Sus-
tain Magazine: Offsite Construction (OSC) Magazine
Supplement,* Summer 2006

"Hands On Learning: The ecoMOD Project," John D.
Quale, in *Eco-Architecture II: Harmonisation between Architecture and Nature,* edited by G. Broadbent and C. A. Brebbia (WIT Press, 2008), pages
171–80

Integrated Design in Contemporary Architecture, Kiel
Moe, section on ecoMOD1 house (Princeton
Architectural Press, 2008)

"John D. Quale/ecoMOD/Interview 06.20.2007," in
Summer Institute of Architecture Journal, "Assuming Responsibility: Investigating the Architecture of
Stewardship," special issue, volume 4 (Catholic University of America, 2007), pages 6–15

Lunch, Volume 1: Trespass, graduate student journal of
the School of Architecture, May 2006

Lunch, Volume 4: Margin, graduate student journal of
the School of Architecture, May 2009

"Prefab Housing Goes Green Gracefully," John D. Quale,
in *Next American City,* issue 11 (Summer 2006)

"The Rise of the Citizen Architect: Public Interest
Architecture," interview with John D. Quale, in
Metropolis Magazine, October 2008, pages 121–27

"A Sustainable Housing Response to Hurricane Katrina,"
John D. Quale and Kristina Iverson, in *Cityscape: A
Journal of Policy Development and Research,* special
issue on hurricane response (U.S. Department of
Housing and Urban Development, Fall 2008)

"Sustainable Opportunities in Prefabricated Construction," John D. Quale, in *The International Journal of
Environmental, Cultural, Economic and Social Sustainability,* volume 3 (2007)

Technology, Nature, and Sustainable Design: Behind the

Curtain of ecoMOD3, the students of STS 200-2 with B. R. Cohen (University of Virginia School of Engineering and Applied Science, 2008)

Trojan Goat: UVA Solar Decathlon Team

UVA Solar Decathlon team website: solarhome.lib.virginia.edu

Sustainable Homes USA, John D. Quale, essay on UVA Solar Decathlon house, edited by Jacobo Krauel, (Links International, 2009)

"Trojan Goat," John D. Quale, *306090, A Journal of Emergent Architecture + Design,* issue 4 (Princeton Architectural Press, Spring 2003), pages 86–91

Trojan Goat: A Self-Sufficient House, John D. Quale, preface by Kenneth Frampton, volume 1 in the UVA School of Architecture's Urgent Matters book series (distributed by the University of Virginia Press, 2005)

Other Resources

American Solar Energy Society, focused on active and passive solar strategies and technologies: www.ases.org

Athena Institute, life-cycle analysis information and software: www.athenasmi.ca/

The Builder's Guide to Mixed Climates: Details for Design and Construction, Joseph W. Lstiburek (Taunton Press, 2000)

Cepheus: Living Comfort without Heating, Helmut Krapmeier (Springer, 2001)

Climate Considerations in Building and Urban Design, Baruch Givoni (Van Nostrand Reinhold, 1998)

Climate Responsive Design: A Study of Buildings in Moderate and Hot Humid Climates, Richard Hyde (E&FN Spon, 2000)

Daylighting: Natural Light In Architecture, Derek Phillips (Architectural Press, 2004)

Daylight Performance of Buildings, Marc Fontoynont (James & James, 1999)

Ecohouse 3: A Design Guide, Sue Roaf (Architectural Press, 2007)

Green Building Handbook, Tom Woolley, Sam Kimmins, Rob Harrison, and Paul Harrison, 2 volumes (E & FN Spon, 1997)

Green Building Materials: A Guide to Product Selection, Ross Speigel (Wiley, 1999)

Green Building Products: The GreenSpec Guide to Residential Building Materials, Alex Wilson and Mark Piepkorn, 3rd edition (New Society Publishers, 2008)

Green Buildings Pay, edited by Brian Edwards (E & FN Spon, London, 1998)

Greenguard Environmental Institute, sustainable materials with particular focus on indoor air quality: www.greenguard.org

The Green House: New Directions in Sustainable Architecture, Alanna Stang and Christopher Hawthorne (Princeton Architectural Press, 2005)

The Green Studio Handbook: Environmental Strategies for Schematic Design, Alison G. Kwok and Walter T. Grondzik (Architectural Press/Elsevier, 2007)

Healthy House Building for the New Millennium, John Bower (The Healthy House Institute, 2000)

Home Truths: A Low-Carbon Strategy to Reduce UK Housing Emissions by 80% by 2050, Brenda Boardman (Environmental Change Institute, 2007)

Moisture Control Handbook: Principles and Practices for Residential and Small Commercial Buildings, Joseph W. Lstiburek (John Wiley & Sons, 1994)

The New Ecological Home: The Complete Guide to Green Building Options, Daniel D. Chiras (Chelsea Green Publishing Co., 2004)

Planting Green Roofs and Living Walls, Nigel Dunnett (Timber Press, 2004)

The Selective Environment, Dean Hawkes, Jane McDonald, and Koen Steemers (Spon Press, 2002)

The Small House Society: http://www.resourcesforlife.com/small-house-society

Sun, Wind, and Light: Architectural Design Strategies, G. Z. Brown and Mark DeKay, 2nd edition (John Wiley & Sons, 2001)

Sustainable Landscape Construction: A Guide to Green Building Outdoors, J. William Thompson and Kim Sorvig (Island Press, 2000)

Thermal Delight in Architecture, Lisa Heschong (MIT Press, 1979)

U.S. Green Building Council: www.usgbc.org

Usable Building Trust, useful information about post-occupancy evaluations: www.usablebuildings.co.uk/

The ZED Book, Bill Dunster, Craig Simmons, and Bobby Gilbert (Taylor & Francis, 2008)

RECOGNITION

ACSA / AIA Housing Design Education Award /
Curriculum Category, ecoMOD Project, (2011)
From American Institute of Architects and Association
of Collegiate Schools of Architecture

ACSA Creative Achievement Award, ecoMOD Project,
(2011)
From Association of Collegiate Schools of Architecture

Outstanding Sustainable Development Award,
ecoMOD4 and ecoREMOD (2010)
Presented by the City of Charlottesville Planning
Commission

VSBN Green Innovation Award for Best Green
Residential Project, ecoMOD4 (2010)
From Virginia Sustainable Building Network

UN World Habitat Award, finalist, ecoMOD Project
(2009)
From Building and Social Housing Foundation, U.K.;
one of nine finalists selected among sustainable, affordable housing programs from around the world; the only
finalist from the United States in 2009, and one of sixteen U.S. finalists since founding of awards in 1985

Award of Merit, Inform Design Award, ecoMOD3
(2009)
From the Virginia Society of the American Institute
of Architects

National Idea-to-Product Competition, second place,
ecoMOD Monitoring System (2009)
From the Social Entrepreneurship Initiative at Purdue
University

Spotlight Award, ecoMOD Project (2009)
From the Charlottesville Business Innovation Council

Excellence in Green Building Curriculum Award, eco-
MOD Project (2008)
From U.S. Green Building Council; interdisciplinary
sustainable design curriculum award for K–12, Community College and Higher Education Programs; inau-
gural year of the awards

Green Innovation Award for Best Green Residential
Project, ecoMOD3 (2008)
From Virginia Sustainable Building Network

National Collegiate Inventors and Innovators Alliance
(NCIIA) Advanced E-Team Grant Award (2008)
Grant of $15,000 awarded to support ecoMOD Moni-
toring System designed by ecoMOD engineering team

NCARB Grand Prize; ecoMOD Project (2007)
From National Council of Architectural Registration
Boards for "Creative Integration of Practice and Education in the Academy"; $25,000 Grand Prize given to
the ecoMOD Project in recognition of "efforts to creatively link education and practice"; jury consists of six
architecture school deans or directors and six practicing
architects; the jury emphasized their appreciation of the
project's integration of research, design, education, and
sustainability

AIA Education Honor Award, ecoMOD Project (2007)
From American Institute of Architects, to honor "ex-
ceptional and innovative courses, initiatives, or programs that deal with broad issues, particularly in cross-

disciplinary collaboration and/or within the broader community; contribute to the advancement of architecture education; have the potential to benefit and/or change practice; and/or promote models of excellence that can be appropriated by other educators"

Collaborative Practice Award, ecoMOD Project (2007)
From Association of Collegiate Schools of Architecture, to honor "the best practices in school-based community outreach programs"

Go Green Honor Award, ecoMOD3 (2007)
From James River Green Building Council, the top design award in the built project category

Go Green Grant Award, ecoMOD3 (2007)
From James River Green Building Council, to support green upgrades for ecoMOD3 project

Special Recognition, Ecological Literacy in Architecture Education, ecoMOD Project (2006)
From American Institute of Architects Committee on the Environment; funded by the Tides Foundation's Kendeda Sustainability Fund

Green Innovation Award for Best Green Residential Project, ecoMOD1 (2006)
From Virginia Sustainable Building Network

President's Higher Education Award for Excellence in General, Community Service, finalist, ecoMOD Project (2006)
Included as one of five initiatives at the University of Virginia that were recognized in this national award

program sponsored by the Federal Corporation for National and Community Service, the U.S. Departments of Education and Housing and Urban Development, USA Freedom Corps, and the President's Council on Service and Civic Participation

P3 Award Grant recipient and honorable mention, ecoMOD1 evaluation process (2005–6)
From U.S. Environmental Protection Agency

Honor Award—Website Design, UVA Solar Decathlon website (2003)
From Entablature Website Design Awards; website designed by Visiting Assistant Professor Jason Johnson

Solar Decathlon, Trojan Goat (2002)
Sponsored by U.S. Deparment of Energy; architecture jurors Steve Badanes, J. Douglas Balcomb, Ed Jackson Jr., Edward Mazria, Glenn Murcutt, and Stephanie Vierra
- First Place—Design And Livability (Architecture)
- First Place (Tie)—Energy Balance
- Second Place—Overall
- Special Citation from the American Institute of Architects
- BP Solar Progressive Award, for most forward-thinking team

PARTNERS AND SPONSORS

ecoMOD1

CLIENT PARTNER
Piedmont Housing Alliance

MAJOR SPONSOR
Anonymous

SPONSORS
Albemarle Heating and Air
Allied Concrete
Artisan Construction
James Hardie Siding Products
KBS Construction Inc.
National Instruments
Nature Neutral
Pella Windows and Doors
Simpson Strong Tie
U.S. Environmental Protection
  Agency
UVA School of Architecture Foundation

W.A. Lynch Roofing
Fred and Mary Wolf

SUPPORTERS
Adelphia
Appalachian Sustainable Development
Automation Components Inc.
Bremo Trees
Deborah Caudle, NCMT, Body
  Restoration
Joe Celentano
Charlottesville Community Design
  Center
Commonwealth Solar Services
Continental Control Systems
Dupont Tyvek
Gray Ibbeken

Toshi Karato
Susan Ketron and Michael McKee
Judith Kinnard and Kenneth
  Schwartz
Elizabeth Meyer and William
  Bergen
Linn and Susan Moedinger
Rainwater Management Solutions
R-Control/Team IBS
Rhoads Electric & Communication
  Services
Rothwell Development Corporation
Robert Rubin
Sally Ann's Plumbing
Lonny and Amanda Sturgeon
UVA Corporate and Foundation
  Relations
Karen Van Lengen and Jim Welty

ecoMOD2

CLIENT PARTNERS
Habitat for Humanity International
Habitat for Humanity of Greater
  Charlottesville
Habitat for Humanity of the Mississippi Gulf Coast

MAJOR SPONSORS
Anonymous
John and Renee Grisham
Solar Light for Africa

SPONSORS
Forbo Flooring
Habitat for Humanity ReStore of
  Charlottesville

RWE Schott
USP Structural Connectors
Wiremold

SUPPORTERS
Cogswell Stone Fabrication
Concorde Battery Corporation

ecoMOD3

CLIENT PARTNER
Piedmont Housing Alliance

PARTNERSHIPS
Charlottesville Albemarle Technical
Education Center (CATEC)
Jefferson Area Board for Aging
(JABA)
Preservation Piedmont

MAJOR SPONSORS
Anonymous
James River Green Building Council, 2007 Grant Award
Russell Katz, Director, Sheldon &
Audrey Katz Foundation
National Council of Architec-
tural Registration Boards, 2007
NCARB Grand Prize
UVA Teaching + Technology Initiative

SPONSORS
Albemarle Heating and Air
Artisan Construction
KBS Construction Inc
Pella Windows and Doors
Simpson Strong Tie
Jill Tietjen, SEAS '76
U.S. Environmental Protection
Agency
UVA Community Engagement
Course Development Grant
UVA Institute on Aging, Community Based Research Initiative

SUPPORTERS
Altenergy Inc.
Atlantic Plywood
The Conservation Fund's Go Zero
program
GE Fanuc
Nature Neutral
The Roof Center
Wainwright Tile & Stone

FRIENDS
Charlottesville Festival of the Photograph 2007
Integral Yoga
Zazu's

ecoMOD4

CLIENT PARTNER
Habitat for Humanity of Greater
Charlottesville

PARTNERSHIPS
City of Charlottesville
Charlottesville Albemarle Technical
Education Center (CATEC)

MAJOR SPONSORS
Albemarle Heating and Air/Airflow
Diagnostics Institute
Anonymous (two)
Dominion Foundation, Dominion
Virginia Power
Jefferson Trust, UVA Alumni Association
Russell Katz, Director, Sheldon &
Audrey Katz Foundation
National Collegiate Inventors and
Innovators Alliance Advanced E-Team Grant
William Holt Plank
Solar Connexion

SPONSORS
Abrahamse & Company Builders
Allied Concrete
Amvic Insulated Concrete Forms
EcoTimber
Jay Hugo/3North/Grace Street
Latitude 38 LLC
Northland Forest Products
Pella Windows and Doors
John and Cary Schaperkotter
UVA Academic Community Engagement Program
UVA Inter-Greek Habitat for Humanity
UVA Jefferson Public Citizens Program
UVA School of Architecture Design
Council
UVA School of Architecture Foundation
Virginia Energy Services
WaterFurnace International
Willow Tree Construction

SUPPORTERS
Bella U.
Margaret Marshall Bly
Bremo Trees
C&O Restaurant
Contract Crushing
Crutchfield
Diamond Pier Pin Foundations
Edible Landscaping
Diana Ferrell, Jewelry Designer
Larry Galante/Habitat for Humanity Bike and Build
Paul Godfrin
Grelen Nursery
Hoffman Nursery, Inc.
Inn at Court Square
Emily Micklitsch/Habitat for Humanity Bike and Build
Noland Bath and Idea Center
Qdoda
Ragged Mountain Running Shop
Raising Cane's
Saunders Brothers, Inc.
Simpson Strong Tie

Smoothie King
John and Regina Stranix
UVA Beach Volleyball Club
UVA Habitat for Humanity Campus Chapter
UVA Landscaping
UVA Vice President for Student Affairs Office
Wainwright Tile & Stone

FRIENDS
Bang!
Belmont BBQ
Blue Moon Diner
Blue Ridge Building Supply
Blue Ridge Graphics
Blue Ridge Mountain Sports

Boylan Heights
Calvino
Downtown Grill
Brielle Gallinelli
Harris Teeter
Integral Yoga
Kroger
La Taza
Littlejohn's Deli
Market Street Wineshop
Jess Martin, Massage Therapist
Martin Hardware
Massage Envy
Maya
Milan
Orzo's
Otto's Burgers

Panera Bread
Pat-E-Cakes
Pet Food Discounters
Pita Pit
Cleta and Robert Schmitt
Seasonal Cook
Take It Away
Tavola
12th Street Tap House
University of Virginia Bookstore
UVA Green Grounds
Virginia National Bank
Vocelli Pizza
Judith and Frederick Wall
The White Spot
Whole Foods

ecoREMOD1

CLIENT PARTNER
City of Charlottesville

MAJOR SPONSORS
ADOBE
Alloy Workshop
Barton Malow Company
City of Charlottesville
Dominion Power
Local Energy Alliance Program (LEAP)
University of Virginia

SPONSORS
Albemarle Heating & Air
General Electric
Pella Windows & Doors

SUPPORTERS
AltEnergy
Anchor Insulation
Blue Ridge Builders Supply
Cavanaugh Cabinets
Cree Lighting

Ferguson
Lowe's
Night & Day Cleaning Services
Noland
Rainwater Management Solutions
Sheffield Metals International
Therma-Stor

FRIENDS
Southern Development

ecoREMOD2

CLIENT PARTNER
Falmouth Heritage Renewal

MAJOR SPONSOR
Russell Katz, Director, Sheldon & Audrey Katz Foundation
Royal Caribbean Cruises Ltd.
UVA Jefferson Public Citizens Program

UVA School of Architecture Deepening Global Engagement Grant
UVA School of Architecture Regenerate Center

SPONSORS
Mark Churchill, Churchill Ceramics
UVA Beach Volleyball Club
UVA School of Architecture Design Council

FRIENDS
Crutchfield Corporation
Kroger
Mudhouse Coffee and Espresso Bars
Para Coffee
The Pigeon Hole
Ragged Mountain Running Shop
Revolutionary Soup
Wings Over Charlottesville

TEAM MEMBERS

ecoMOD1

CLIENT

Piedmont Housing Alliance (PHA)
Stu Armstrong, Executive Director
Mark Watson, Project Development
  Manager
Peter Loach, Deputy Director of
  Operations

CONTRACTOR FOR PHA

Roger Rothwell and Roger Rothwell
  Jr. of Rothwell Development
  Corporation

ADMINISTRATION

John Quale, Project Director, Assistant Professor, School of Architecture (SARC)
Paxton Marshall, Engineering
  Director, Professor, School of Engineering and Applied Science
  (SEAS)
Carolina Cordera, Research Assistant, SARC
Michael Wenrich, Research Assistant, SARC

ADVISORS

School of Architecture Advisors
Ted Marrs, Abrahamse & Company
  Builders, Construction Advisor
Greg Sloditskie, Modular Building
  Advisor

Dr. S. Müjdem Vural, visiting schol-
  ar from Yildiz Technical Uni-
  versity, Istanbul, Turkey, Indoor
  Air Quality Advisor
Nisha Botchwey, Assistant Profes-
  sor, Community Planning Advi-
  sor, SARC
Chris Fannin, Lecturer, Landscape
  Architecture Advisor, SARC
Julie Bargmann, Associate Profes-
  sor, Landscape Architecture
  Advisor, SARC
Kirk Martini, Structural Engineer-
  ing Advisor, SARC
Robert Crowell, Lecturer, Mechani-
  cal Engineering Advisor

School of Engineering and Applied
Science Advisors
Harry Powell, Computer Systems
  Engineer, Engineering Advisor,
  SEAS
Julie Zimmerman, Engineering
  Advisor, Life Cycle Assessment
  Advisor, SEAS

McIntire School of Commerce
Advisor
Mark White, Associate Professor
  of Commerce, Business Plan
  Advisor

DESIGN TEAM

Arch 401/Arch 801/Lar 801,
Architectural Design Studio, Fall
2004
Christopher Brooks
Steven Cornell
Barrett Eastwood
Greg Harris
David Hill
Thomas Holloman
Susan Hughes
Marilyn Moedinger
Yvi Nyugen
Ben Petrick
Christina Robinette
Robert Schmidt

Arch 402/Arch 802/Lar 802,
Architectural Design Studio, Spring
2005
Christopher Brooks, Construction
  Manager
Carolina Cordero, Research
  Assistant
Page Durant
Barrett Eastwood, Construction
  Manager
Meredith Epley
Lauren Hackney
Greg Harris, Construction Manager
David Hill

Thomas Holloman, Project Manager

George Kincaid

Gus Lynch

Marilyn Moedinger, Project Manager

Ben Petrick

Christina Robinette

Garett Rouzer

Casey Servis

Kyle Sturgeon

Lacey Wolf

Engr 499, Building Energy Systems Design and Evaluation, Spring 2005

Alex Arsenovic

Godwin Nestor

Jeff Rominger

Kyle Yetter

BUILD TEAM

Students and Fellowship Recipients

Galin Boyd

Christopher Brooks, Construction Manager

Carolina Cordero, Research Assistant and Project Manager

Page Durant

Barrett Eastwood, Construction Manager, KBS Inc. ecoMOD Fellow

Meredith Epley

Lauren Hackney

Thomas Holloman, Project Manager, Allied Concrete ecoMOD Fellow

George Kincaid

Gus Lynch

Marilyn Moedinger, Project Manager, Artisan Construction ecoMOD Fellow

Garett Rouzer

Casey Servis

Kyle Sturgeon

Full-time Volunteers

Matthew Clay

Trevor Taub

Part-time Volunteers

Julie Bargmann, Heidi Baker, Laura Bandara, Corey Barnes, Anne Bohlen, Neil Budzinski, Mark Buenavista, Nathan Cunningham, Doug Daley, Brian Duffy, Stephen Dunstan, Ken Eastwood, Bonnye Eastwood, Carmen Fanzone, Whit Faulconer, Sarah Foster, Lauren Francescone, David Gardner, Mike Goldin, Brittany Gjormand, Mark Holmquist, Amy Lewandowski, Matthew Machaj, Catherine Manza, Kathleen Mark, JP Mays, Linn Moedinger, Susan Moedinger, David Mullen, Daniel Norman, Sarah Oehl, Jordan Phemister, James Pressley, Sarah Scruggs, Elizabeth Shoffner, Catherine Manza, Courtney Spearman, Amanda Taylor, Elaine Uang, Justin Walton, Michael Wenrich, Bret Wilhite

EVALUATION TEAM

Arch 530, Evaluating ecoMOD, Fall 2005

Christina Calabrese

Leyland del Re

Chris Dunn

Whit Faulconer

Mark Holmquist

Anand Kanoria

Andy Klepac

Amelia McKeithen

Greta Modesitt

Melinda Sathre

Lauren Shirley

Betul Tuncer

Elaine Uang

Arch 536, Evaluating ecoMOD, Spring 2006

Christina Calabrese

Patricia Vaz De Carvalho

Adam Donovan

Sally Foster

Mark Holmquist

Beth Kahley

Chad Logan

JP Mays

Molly O'Donnell

Rosalyn Schmitt

Carol Shiflett

Lauren Shirley

Matthew Young

Toby Zhang

Engr 495, Building Energy Systems Design and Evaluation, Fall 2005

Tristan Becker

Sarah Foster

Scottie Gambill

Benjamin Kidd

Alex McCarthy

Joshua Palmer

Alison Tramba

Debora Wesner

Brooke Yamakoshi

Caroline Zennie

Engr 499, Building Energy Systems Design and Evaluation, Spring 2006

Tristan Becker

Sarah Foster

Scottie Gambill

Ping Guan

Benjamin Kidd, Teaching Assistant

Michael Lewis

Alex McCarthy

Joshua Palmer

Alison Tramba

Debora Wesner

Brooke Yamakoshi

Caroline Zennie

SPECIAL THANKS

Karen Van Lengen, Dean, SARC

William Sherman, Chair, Department of Architecture and Landscape Architecture

Julie Bargmann, Director, Landscape Architecture, SARC

Charlie Menefee, Director, Architecture, SARC

Elizabeth Fortune, Associate Dean

for Finance and Administration, SARC

Susan Ketron, Director, SARC Foundation

Leslie Nelson, Former Associate Director, SARC Foundation

Nancy Scogna, Associate Director, SARC Foundation

Derry Wade, Director of Publications, SARC

Dale Abrahamse, Abrahamse & Company Builders, Inc.

Bryan Bell, Executive Director, Design Corp

Cris Benton, Professor, University of California Berkeley

Julie Eizenberg, Konig Eizenberg Architects

Jane Ford, UVA News Services

Charlottesville Community Design Center

Eric Gilchrist, Appalachian Sustainable Development

Tom Kavounas and Jeff Saul, Albemarle Heating and Air, Inc.

Carlos Martin, U.S. Department of Housing and Urban Development

John Meggs, Nature Neutral

Sara Osborne, Q&O Design and Nelson Byrd Woltz Landscape Architects

Roger Rothwell and Roger Rothwell, Jr. of Rothwell Development Corporation

Robert Rubin, Ph.D. candidate, Columbia University

Alyson Sappington, Thomas Jefferson Soil & Water Conservation District

Mark Schuyler, Mark Schuyler Lighting Design

Rob Smith and Anna Van Clief of UVA TV News Office

The staff of the School of Architecture, especially: Michelle Allen, Lisa Benton, Jennifer Hitchcock, Michele Monger, Dick Smith, Jake Thackston, John Vigour, and David Williams

The faculty of the School of Architecture, especially: Michael Bednar, Anselmo Canfora, W. G. Clark, Rich Collins, Robin Dripps, Eric Field, Ed Ford, Cecilia Hernandez, Judith Kinnard, Jenny Lovell, Bill Lucy, Earl Mark, Kirk Martini, Beth Meyer, William Morrish, Lucia Phinney, Lisa Reilly, Theo van Groll, Peter Waldman, and William Williams

ecoMOD2

CLIENT

Habitat for Humanity of Greater Charlottesville

Kelly Eplee, Director of Development

Jeff Erkelens, Construction Manager

Habitat for Humanity International

Victor Alfsen, Construction Manager

Erik Cullen, Construction Director

ADMINISTRATION

John Quale, Project Director, Assistant Professor, SARC

Paxton Marshall, Engineering Director, Professor, SEAS

Michael Wenrich, Research Assistant, SARC

ADVISORS

School of Architecture Advisors

Ronald Peron, Structural Engineering Advisor, Dunbar, Milby, Williams, Pittman & Vaughan

Kirk Martini, Structural Engineering Advisor, SARC

Greg Sloditskie, Modular Building Advisor

Robert Crowell, Lecturer, Mechanical Engineering Advisor

School of Engineering and Applied Science Advisors

Harry Powell, Engineering Advisor, SEAS

DESIGN/BUILD TEAM

Arch 402/Arch 802, Architectural Design Studio, Spring 2006

Sara Anderson

Maria Arellano

Kelly Barlow

Rasheda Bowman, Construction Manager

Adrienne Hicks

Nakita Johnson

Ginger Koon

Amy Lewandowski, Project Manager

Jamie Norwood

Carol Shiflett, Project Manager

Jessica Soffer

Tommy Solomon, Project Manager

Ginny Wambaugh

Joy Wang

Engr 499, Building Energy Systems Design and Evaluation, Spring 2006

Brian Hickey

Benjamin Kidd, Project Manager

Michael Pilat

Gregory Redmann

Part-time Volunteers

Kevin Bell, Barrett Eastwood, Zoe Edgecomb, Chris Fano, Kristin Hennings, Toshi Karato, Joshua King, Christine Lewandowski, Payam Ostovar, Luka Radakovic,

Andrew Stronge, Elaine Uang, Justin Walton

EVALUATION TEAM

Engr 495, Building Energy Systems Design and Evaluation, Fall 2006
Brian Hickey
Benjamin Kidd
Michael Pilat

Arch 531, Evaluating ecoMOD, Fall 2007
Laura Hammett
Michael Plehn

SPECIAL THANKS

Karen Van Lengen, Dean, SARC
William Sherman, Chair, Department of Architecture and Landscape Architecture
Elizabeth Fortune, Associate Dean for Finance and Administration, SARC
Derry Wade, Director of Publications, SARC
Bryan Bell, Executive Director, Design Corp
Jane Ford, UVA News Services
Sara Osborne, Q&O Design and Nelson Byrd Woltz Landscape Architects
Andrew Stronge, Fat Rabbit Designs
The F.O.G.'s of the Habitat midweek crew—thanks guys!
The staff of the School of Architecture, especially: Michelle Allen, Lisa Benton, Jennifer Hitchcock, Dick Smith, Jake Thackston, John Vigour, and David Williams
The faculty of the School of Architecture, especially: Dean Abernathy, W. G. Clark, Phoebe Crisman, Eric Field, Nataly Gattegno, Cecilia Hernandez, Judith Kinnard, Jenny Lovell, Kirk Martini, Beth Meyer, William Morrish, Lucia Phinney, Betsy Roettger, and Peter Waldman

ecoMOD3

CLIENT

Piedmont Housing Alliance
Stu Armstrong, Executive Director
Mark Watson, Project Development Manager
Peter Loach, Deputy Director of Operations

CONTRACTOR FOR PHA

Bruce Guss, Housewright Inc.

ADMINISTRATION

John Quale, Project Director, Assistant Professor, SARC
Paxton Marshall, Engineering Director, Professor, SEAS
Barrett Eastwood, Construction Director, SARC
Nathan Foley, Research Assistant, SARC
Kristina Iverson, Research/Teaching Assistant, SARC
Jeff Ponitz, Research/Teaching Assistant, SARC
Ernest Bowden, Graduate Teaching Assistant, SEAS
Ping Guan, Graduate Teaching Assistant, SEAS
Benjamin Kidd, Graduate Teaching Assistant, SEAS
Brooke Yamakoshi, Graduate Teaching Assistant, SEAS
Maria Bninski, Research Assistant, Liaison with PHA

ADVISORS

School of Architecture Advisors
Nancy Takahashi, Distinguished Lecturer, Landscape Architecture Advisor, SARC
Louis Nelson, Associate Professor, Historic Preservation Advisor, SARC
Daniel Bluestone, Associate Professor, Historic Preservation Advisor, SARC
Greg Sloditskie, Modular Building Advisor, Modular Building Solutions
Nisha Botchwey, Assistant Professor, Community Planning Advisor, SARC
Veronica Warnock, Assistant Professor Planning/Aging Advisor, SARC
Theo Van Groll, Professor Emeritus, Architecture Advisor, SARC

School of Engineering and Applied Science Advisors
Harry Powell, Engineering Advisor, SEAS
Jose Gomez, Structural Engineering Advisor, SEAS
Mike Curry, Structural Engineering Advisor

DESIGN TEAM

Arch 401, Architectural Design Studio, Fall 2006
Tina Cheng
Christopher Fano
Angie Ferrero
Brielle Gallinelli
Jordan Gravely
Taryn Harunah
Carolyn Hiller
Lindsay Hochman
Deborah Ku
Sheena Mayfield
JP Mays
Mario Moore

Melinda Sathre

Lauren Shirley

Arch 530, ecoMOD Seminar, Fall 2006

Emily Anderson

Lorenzo Battistelli

Eryn Brennan

Rachel Cohen-Stevens

Adam Donovan

Kristin Hennings

Tom Hogge

Andrea Hubbell

Beth Kahley

Mary Catherine McLamb

Marta Skupinska

Tran Ngoc

Arch 402/Arch 702/Arch 802/Lar 702, Architectural Design Studio, Spring 2007

Lorenzo Battistelli, Historic Preservation Manager

Eryn Brennan, Historic Preservation Research

Christina Calabrese

Rachel Cohen-Stevens

Christopher Fano, Project Manager

Brielle Gallinelli, Construction Manager

Jordan Gravely

Taryn Harunah

Kristin Hennings, Construction Manager

Tom Hogge

Mark Holmquist

Andrea Hubbell

Beth Kahley, Project Manager

Christa Kolb

Deborah Ku

Sheena Mayfield, Construction Document Coordinator

JP Mays

Engr 495, Building Energy Systems Design and Evaluation, Fall 2006

Kyle Adams

Anna Badyoczek

Bridgette Baugher

Ernest Bowden

Michael Britt-Crane

Christopher Donnelly

Sarah Foster

Ginger Friar

Ezekiel Fugate

Brian Hickey

Kyle Jones

Jae Hyung Lee

Farhad Omar

Cody Pennetti

Michael Pilat

Navid Rahimi

Greg Redmann

Jeff Rominger

Kum Sackey

Emily Shiflett

Alison Tramba

Jonathan Zimmerman

Engr 499, Building Energy Systems Design and Evaluation, Spring 2007

Kyle Adams

Anna Badyoczek

Bridgette Baugher

Ernest Bowden

Christopher Donnelly, Project Manager

Sarah Foster

Ginger Friar

Ezekiel Fugate

Brian Hickey, Project/Construction Manager

Kyle Jones

Jae Hyung Lee

Lindsay MacDonald

Meghan Magennis

Farhad Omar

Cody Pennetti

Michael Pilat, Project Manager

Greg Redmann

Jeff Rominger

Kum Sackey

Emily Shiflett

Alison Tramba

Jonathan Zimmerman

BUILD TEAM

School of Architecture

Lorenzo Battistelli, Historic Preservation Manager

Eryn Brennan, Historic Preservation Research

Christina Calabrese

Rachel Cohen-Stevens

Adam Donovan

Christopher Fano, Project Manager

Angie Ferrero

Nathan Foley

Brielle Gallinelli, Construction Manager

Jordan Gravely

Taryn Harunah, Historic Preservation Manager

Kristin Hennings, Construction Manager

Tom Hogge, Historic Preservation Manager

Mark Holmquist

Beth Kahley, Project Manager

Christa Kolb

Deborah Ku

Sheena Mayfield, Construction Document Coordinator

JP Mays

Ngoc Tran

Melinda Sathre

Lauren Shirley

School of Engineering and Applied Science

Bridgette Baugher

Ernest Bowden

Ayman El-Barasi

Tim Freeman

Ezekiel Fugate

Ping Guan, Graduate Teaching Fellow

Brian Hickey, Project/Construction Manager

Benjamin Kidd, Graduate Teaching Fellow

Farhad Omar

Michael Pilat, Project Manager
 (part-time)
Colin Powell
Jonathan Zimmerman

Regular Volunteers and Independent Study Students
Pete Chimicles
Stephanie Harvin
Suzanne Mathews
Leslie McDonald
Whitney Odell
Brian Williams

Charlottesville Albemarle Technical Education Center Student Volunteers
Andy Bastian
Frank Busofsky
Aaron Hackett
Ryan Hammer
Nick Kevey
Eimile McIlnay
John McKeon
Beth Russell
Lauren Shaver
Kelly Short
Josh Smith
Kathryn Wesson

EVALUATION TEAM

Arch 531, Evaluating ecoMOD, Fall 2007
Sarah Brummett
Peter Chimicles
Jonathan Coble
Sarah Collins
Jaime de la Re
Nima Govind
Laura Hammett
Stephanie Harvin
Amanda Hubal
Leslie McDonald
Sunmi Moon
Michael Plehn
Elaine Quick
Elana Ruff

Ryan Wall
Torrence Warren

Engr 495, Building Energy Systems Design and Evaluation, Fall 2007
Christine Devlin
Timothy Freeman
Jason Guy
Christopher Huang
Maggie Kirkpatrick
Claudia Leahy
Suchit Ligade
Alexander Hy Martin
Harrison McGehee
Farhad Omar
Colin Powell
Kevin Richards
Angad Sachdeva
Emily Shiflett
Christine Stawitz
Vanessa Trahan
Tessa Wheeler

Engr 499, Building Energy Systems Design and Evaluation, Spring 2008
Ernie Bowden
Kacy Burnsed
Adam Burton
Matthew Cleveland
Christine Devline
Paul Emery
Greg Erickson
Tim Freeman
Dan Gavarkavich
Ping Guan
Hamid Hashime
Kate Howling
Claudia Leahy
Suchit Ligade
Hy Martin
Harris McGehee
Michelle Morris
Whitney Newton
Farhad Omar
Colin Powell
Emily Shiflett
Christine Stawitz
Francis Tan

Tessa Wheeler
Susanna Wong

SPECIAL THANKS
Karen Van Lengen, Dean, SARC
James Aylor, Dean, SEAS
William Sherman, Chair, Department of Architecture and Landscape Architecture
Kristina Hill, Director, Landscape Architecture, SARC
Craig Barton and Charlie Menefee, Director, Architecture, SARC
Elizabeth Fortune, Associate Dean for Finance and Administration, SARC
Susan Ketron, Director, SARC Foundation
Angie Fellers, Associate Director, SARC Foundation
Nancy Scogna, Associate Director, SARC Foundation
Derry Wade, Director of Publications, SARC
Ingrid Townsend, STS Thesis Advisor, SEAS
Benjamin Cohen, STS Thesis Advisor, SEAS
Jane Ford, UVA News Services
Yitna Firdyiwek, Instructional Technology Advisor, UVA ITC
Sara Osborne, Q&O Design and Nelson Byrd Woltz Landscape Architects
Matthew Brennan and Benjamin Fey, for assistance with 3-D scanning of the historic house
Joel Loveland, Professor, University of Washington
Steve Badanes, Professor, University of Washington
Sergio Palleroni, Visiting Associate Professor, University of Texas at Austin
Darah Bonham, Jason Ritter, Deborah Gannon and Charlie

McRaven, Charlottesville Albemarle Technical Education Center

Karen Beiber, Jefferson Area Board on Aging and Institute on Aging

Robin Felder, Medical Automation Research Center

Jason Pearson, Whit Faulconer and Alec Gosse, GreenBlue

Bruce Odell

Carol Rogers

April Coughlin

Dave Davidson, Wainwright Tile and Stone

John Hall, Shenandoah Valley Reclaimed Lumber

Jeff Saul and Tony Casey, Albemarle Heating and Air

Mike Perry, Building Logics

Paul Risberg, AltEnergy

Bruce Fuller and Sonny Biel, UVA Recycling

The staff of the School of Architecture, especially: Michelle Allen,

Lisa Benton, Selene Mak, Lisa Shifflett, Dick Smith, Jake Thackston, John Vigour, Derry Wade, and David Williams

The faculty of the School of Architecture, especially: Dean Abernathy, Julie Bargmann, Craig Barton, W.G. Clark, Anselmo Canfora, Phoebe Crisman, Robin Dripps, Eric Field, Judith Kinnard, Jenny Lovell, Earl Mark, Kirk Martini, Beth Meyer, and Peter Waldman

ecoMOD4

CLIENT

Habitat for Humanity of Greater Charlottesville

Dan Rosensweig, Executive Director

Ken Hankins, Chief Operating Office (through early 2009)

Audrey Storm, Senior Construction Supervisor

Robin Francis, Volunteer Coordinator

Bruce Hogshead, Site Development Manager (through summer 2009)

ADMINISTRATION

John Quale, Project Director, Assistant Professor, SARC

Paxton Marshall, Engineering Director, Professor, SEAS

Jeff Erkelens, Construction Director, SARC

Ernest Bowden, Graduate Teaching Assistant, SEAS

Benjamin Kidd, Graduate Teaching Assistant, SEAS

Farhad Omar, Graduate Teaching Assistant, SEAS

Jeff Herlitz, Research Assistant, SARC

Sarita Herman, Research Assistant, SARC

ADVISORS

School of Architecture Advisors

Nancy Takahashi, Distinguished Lecturer, Landscape Architecture Advisor, SARC

Eric Field, Teaching Resources Coordinator, Digital Simulation and Computing Advisor, SARC

Greg Sloditskie, Modular Building Advisor, Modular Building Solutions

Nisha Botchwey, Associate Professor, Community Planning Advisor, SARC

School of Engineering and Applied Science Advisors

Harry Powell, Engineering Advisor, SEAS

Ronald Williams, Engineering Advisor, SEAS

Joanna Curran, Civil Engineering Advisor, SEAS

Mike Curry, Structural Engineering Advisor

DESIGN TEAM

Arch 401, Architectural Design Studio, Fall 2008

Bernie Doherty

Del Hepler

Joe Medwid

Chris Oesterling

James Perakis

Tommy Schaperkotter

Katie Stranix

Clare van Montfrans

Juliana Villabona

Ryan Wall

Arch 530, ecoMOD Seminar, Fall 2008

Allegra Churchill

Katie Clinton

Regine Kennedy

John Kupstas

Rachel Lau

Patrick Nedley

Alison Quade

J. Quarles

Alison Singer

Engr 495, Building Energy Systems Design and Evaluation, Fall 2008

Edric Barnes

Rebekah Berlin

Cory Caldwell

Matthew Cleveland

Gregory Ericksen

Hamid Hashime

Kaitlyn Howling

Winnie Lai

Yuxun Lei
Suchit Ligade
Courtney Mallow
Whitney Newton
Cassandra Pagels
Melissa Pancurak
Zachary Pruckowski
Kevin Rouse
Ben Stephens
Francis Tan
Justin Urquhart
Tessa Wheeler
Andrew Zacharias

Arch 402/ALAR 702/ALAR 802,
Architectural Design Studio, Spring
2009
Emily Anderson
Katie Clinton
Lauren DiBianca
Larry Galante
Alex Garrison
Andrew Hamm
Steven Johnson
Leslie McDonald, Construction
   Manager
Patrick Nedley
James Perakis, Project Manager
Graham Peterson
Rachel Robinson
Heidi Shoemaker
Alison Singer, Project Manager
Brian Williams, Construction Man-
   ager

SARC Independent Study
Matt Bowyer
Sarah Collins

Engr 495, Building Energy Systems
Design and Evaluation, Spring 2009
Edric Barnes, Project Manager
Rebekah Berlin
Cory Caldwell
Matthew Cleveland
Kevin Eady
Gregory Ericksen
Hamid Hashime

Ethan Heil
Kaitlyn Howling
Winnie Lai
Yuxun Lei
Suchit Ligade
Courtney Mallow
Whitney Newton, Project Manager
Cassandra Pagels
Melissa Pancurak
Zachary Pruckowski
Kevin Rouse
Ben Stephens
Francis Tan
Justin Urquhart
Tessa Wheeler
Logan Whitehouse
Andrew Zacharias

BUILD TEAM

School of Architecture
Emily Anderson
Katie Clinton
Sarah Collins
Alex Garrison
Andrew Hamm
Steven Johnson
Jennifer Jones
John Kupstas
Rachel Lau
Leslie McDonald, Construction
   Manager
Joe Medwid
Chris Oesterling
James Perakis, Project Manager
Graham Peterson
Alison Quade
J. Quarles
Rachel Robinson
Tommy Schaperkotter
Shelley Schwartz
Alison Singer, Project Manager
Clare van Montfrans
Juliana Villabona
Ryan Wall
Brian Williams, Construction
   Manager

School of Engineering and Applied
Science
Edric Barnes, Project Manager
Matthew Cleveland
Ethan Heil
Whitney Newton, Project Manager
Farhad Omar
Melissa Pancurak
Adrian Sitler

Other Volunteers
Matt Bowyer
Cory Caldwell
Zach Lucy

CATEC Student Volunteers
Alex Bragg
Meg Carpenter
Daniele Diner
Steven Jackson
Megan Mina
Richard Rabbett
Cole Smith
Malcolm Strickland
Samantha Tognetti
Michael Willson

EVALUATION TEAM

Arch 5300, Evaluating ecoMOD,
Fall 2009
Benjamin Chrisinger
Alex Garrison
Lauren Nelson
Whitney Newton
Michael Perry
Leah Stockstrom
Valeria Teran
Laura Voisin George
Michael Zoghby

Engr 4595, Sustainable Housing
Design and Evaluation, Fall 2009
Andrew Ashworth
Sheila Attipoe
Jaleesa Boykin
Matthew Cleveland
Kevin Eady
Elizabeth Engel

Rowshaun Epps
Chris Greenwood
Joi Hayes
Ethan Heil
Kate Howling
Karen Joseph
Matt Jungclaus
Mo Kienle
Christine Lan
Brock Lascara
Sara Mathias
Ashley McCormack
Farhad Omar
Philip Patnude
Matthew Rippe
Michael Schuh
Molly Tyeryar
Quinn Weber
George White
Veronica Yeh

SPECIAL THANKS
Kim Tanzer, Dean, SARC
Karen Van Lengen, Former Dean, SARC
James Aylor, Dean, SEAS
Craig Barton, Chair, Department of Architecture, SARC
Lloyd Harriott, Chair, Department of Electrical and Computer Engineering

Kristina Hill, Chair, Department of Landscape Architecture, SARC
Charlie Menefee, Former Director, Architecture, SARC
Elizabeth Fortune, Associate Dean for Finance and Administration, SARC
Gloria Walker, Department of Electrical and Computer Engineering Fiscal Adminstrator
Warren Buford, Director, SARC Foundation
Angie Fellers, Former Associate Director, SARC Foundation
Kim Wong, Assistant Director, SARC Foundation
Zachary Richards, Senior Writer and Production Manager, SEAS Foundation
Derry Wade, Director of Publications, SARC
Milton Adams, UVA Vice Provost for Academic Programs
Megan Raymond, UVA Office of University Community Partnerships
Phil Parrish, UVA Assistant Vice President for Research
Pace Lochte, Director of the UVA Office of Economic Development
Jane Ford, UVA News Services

Darren Young, Willow Tree Construction
Ted Marrs, Abrahamse and Company
Mac Vanderploeg, President, Digs Inc.
Jeff Christian, Oak Ridge National Laboratory
Tom Kavounas, Jeff Saul and Tony Casey, Albemarle Heating and Air
Bryan Walsh, Solar Connexions
Darah Bonham, Deborah Gannon and Randy Scott, Charlottesville Albemarle Technical Education Center
Sara Osborne, Q&O Design and Nelson Byrd Woltz Landscape Architects

The staff of the School of Architecture, especially: Dav Banks, Lisa Benton, Leslie Fitzgerald, Dick Smith, Jake Thackston, John Vigour, and David Williams
The faculty of the School of Architecture, especially: Anselmo Canfora, W. G. Clark, Kirk Martini, Beth Meyer, Bill Sherman, Peter Waldman, and William Williams

ecoMOD XS

CLIENT
Jefferson Area Board for Aging
Chris Murray, Business Development Director
Julie Ulrich, Community Planner

ADMINISTRATION
John Quale, Project Director, Associate Professor, SARC
Paxton Marshall, Engineering Director, Professor, SEAS

ADVISOR
Eric Field, Teaching Resources Coordinator, Digital Simulation and Computing Advisor, SARC

DESIGN TEAM
Arch 4010, ecoMOD XS Studio, Fall 2010
Stephanie Arbieto
Shehzeen Cassum
Peggy Chang
Ben Dance
Erik de los Reyes

Elizabeth Farrell
Nathan Glassman
D.J. Hickman
Britteny Madine
Lauren Nelson
Elizabeth Rivard
Lynn Teng

Engr 4595, Sustainable Housing Design and Evaluation, Fall 2010
Ethan Heil
Lauren Kaufmann
Richard Passarelli
Logan Whitehouse

ecoREMOD1

CLIENT

Neighborhood Development Services, City of Charlottesville
Jim Tolbert, Director
Kathy McHugh, Housing Development Specialist
Kristel Riddervold, Environmental Manager, City of Charlottesville

CONTRACTOR

Dan Zimmerman and Zach Snider, Alloy Workshop

ADMINISTRATION

John Quale, Project Director, Associate Professor, SARC
Paxton Marshall, Engineering Director, Professor, SEAS

ADVISORS

Louis Nelson, Historic Preservation Advisor, Associate Professor, SARC
Eric Field, Teaching Resources Co-ordinator, Digital Simulation and Computing Advisor, SARC

DESIGN TEAM

Marilyn Moedinger, project manager, SARC
Rob Couch, project manager, SARC
Emily Gigerich, architectural history research, SAR

ecoREMOD2

CLIENT

Falmouth Heritage Renewal
Clinton McPherson, Project Manager
Leonord Wilson, carpenter/joiner
Peter Maxwell, carpenter/steelwork
Calvin Hall, carpenter
Ke-Vaughn Harding, intern architect

ADMINISTRATION

John Quale, Project Director, Associate Professor, SARC
Paxton Marshall, Engineering Director, Professor, SEAS
Louis Nelson, Falmouth Field School Director, Historic Preservation Advisor, Associate Professor, SARC

ADVISORS

Nancy Takahashi, Distinguished Lecturer, Landscape Architecture Advisor, SARC
Eric Field, Teaching Resources Co-ordinator, Digital Simulation and Computing Advisor, SARC
Nisha Botchwey, Associate Professor, Community Planning Advisor, SARC

Matthew Webster, Historic Architectural Resources Director, Colonial Williamsburg Foundation
Edward Chappell, Director of Architectural Research, Colonial Williamsburg Foundation
Emilie Johnson, Ph. D Candidate Art and Architectural History, SARC

DESIGN TEAM

ALAR 4020/ 7020/ 8020, Architectural Design Studio, Spring 2011
Stephanie Arbieto
Shiguang Cheng
Jonathan Coble, project manager
Laura Devine
Doug Dickerson
Michael Goddard
Brandon Moul
John O'Hara
Jessica Underhill
Leah Wener

SARC 5500, ecoMOD Seminar, Spring 2011
Brian Duffy
Libby Engel, project manager
Ethan Heil
Matthew Jungclaus

Lauren Kaufmann
Alexandra Lauzon
Bich Tran Le
Effie Nicholaou
Richard Passarelli
Jason Shapiro
Logan Whitehouse

BUILD TEAM

Falmouth Field School

University of Virginia
Stephanie Arbieto
Jonathan Coble, project manager
Libby Engel, project manager
Marina Freckmann
Michael Goddard
Ethan Heil
Matt Jungclaus
Alexandra Lauzon
Bich Tran Le
Effie Nicholaou
John O'Hara
Elizabeth Rivard
Kirsten Sparenborg
Jessica Underhill
Leah Wener

University of Technology, Jamaica
Latoya Campbell
Shardae Hoilett

University of Mary Washington
Hannah Beckman
David Casteel
Erika deBroekert
Chris Young

Lake Forest College
Laura Frye
Jerrold Rosema

ecoMOD WEB DESIGN

Ashley Joost, Pierre Gibert

Additional Assistance
Dav Banks, Eric Field, Yitna Firdywek

Student Web Design Team
Christina Calabrese, Chris Fano, Taryn Harunah,
Mark Holmquist, Steven Johnson, Brock Lascara,
Ashley McCormack, Rachel Robinson

IMAGE CREDITS All drawings and photographs are courtesy of the ecoMOD, ecoREMOD, and Trojan Goat teams, with the exception of the following:
Dan Addison, 100 (*left*), 111
Courtesy of Future Cities Lab (Johnson/Gattegno), 20
Sarah Oehl, 184, 190–91, 193 (*bottom*), 196, 197, 198, 199

Prakash Patel, 62, 70–71, 72, 75
John Quale, 21, 31, 50, 54, 81, 82, 83, 84, 95, 100 (*upper right*), 102, 103, 116, 122, 131, 150, 195, 206
Scott Smith Photography, 88, 93, 94, 96, 97, 100 (*lower right*), 104, 105, 108, 110, 142, 147 (*bottom*), 154–55, 158 (*right*), 160, 161, 163, 164, 169, 170, 171, 187